acting in the 18th century; the style of Edwin Forrest, America's first star performer, who initiated the strenuous realism of the heroic school of acting; the classic school of tragedians; the school of emotionalism; the personality school; and the school of psychological realism. Wilson presents each style in nearly first-hand detail and clarity. He writes, for example, of Edwin Forrest's realism, "When Forrest was playing Iago to Kean's Othello, a husky canalboatman was seated in the front row of the pit, so close to the stage that he leaned his elbows on it. He was absorbed in the machinations of Iago, and became so convinced of Forrest's villainy that when the actor passed close to him he glared savagely and hissed: 'You damned lying scoundrel, I would like to get hold of you after this show is over and wring your infernal neck'." Nearly all forms of acting are discussed, including the techniques of the motion picture; thus scope as well as depth is given to this study of acting in America. Concluding sections consider the 20th century outlook in the commercial theatre and the phenomenon of the rapidly growing campus and regional repertory theatres.

GARFF B. WILSON, Professor of Speech and Dramatic Art at the University of California, Berkeley, and Associate Editor of the *Educational Theatre Journal*, has taught almost every subject in the field of speech and drama and has contributed articles to *Quarterly Journal of Speech*, *Educational Theatre Journal*, *Speech Monographs*, *Western Speech*, *Journal of Higher Education*, and *Readers Digest*. He is also known for his play direction, acting, and play readings.

16 pages of illustrations

A HISTORY OF AMERICAN ACTING

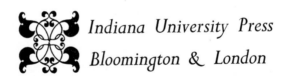 Indiana University Press
Bloomington & London

A HISTORY
OF AMERICAN
ACTING

by Garff B. Wilson

for
ANN V. CRAIG
Selfless Citizen, Faithful Friend

CONTENTS

ILLUSTRATIONS

following page 86

Interior of the Park Theatre, New York
Exterior of the Park Theatre, New York
Edwin Forrest at the age of twenty
Edwin Forrest in his later years
John McCullough
Mary Ann Duff
Fanny Janauschek
Mary Anderson
Charlotte Cushman
Charlotte Cushman in her later years
Edwin Booth as Richelieu
Edwin Booth by John Singer Sargent
Lawrence Barrett as Count Lanciotto
James E. Murdoch in *The Stranger*
Anna Cora Mowatt in *As You Like It*
Mrs. Leslie Carter
Fanny Davenport
Clara Morris, "Queen of Spasms"

following page 214

Viola Allen in *The Eternal City*
Julia Marlowe
Maude Adams in 1904
Ada Rehan in *Much Ado about Nothing*
Henry Placide

GENERAL INTRODUCTION

WRITING A BOOK ON THE HISTORY OF AMERICAN ACTING IS A HAZARD-
ous project. It involves an imaginative re-creation of the personality
and performances of long dead actors. It also involves an evaluation
of their techniques and achievements on the basis of evidence which is
sometimes sketchy, usually subjective, and always second-hand. As the
late A. M. Drummond once said to me, "In evaluating a performer of
the past, you can study every critic, scan every photograph, read every
memoir, sift every shred of evidence, and still reach a conclusion which
is one hundred per cent wrong." True. But it is also true that there is
no living person who can prove that you are one hundred per cent
wrong. Moreover, anyone who challenges your judgment must base his
opinions on the same evidence that you have used.

Despite the hazards involved in analyzing the great performers of
the past, and despite the subjective nature of much of the evidence on
which a judgment is based, it is surprising how often one feels that he
has reached a reliable estimate. There are voluminous reviews of most
of the notable players of the nineteenth century. Critics may differ,
reports may vary, the taste of audiences may change, and yet a firm
outline and a clear image usually emerges from what may seem to be
confused or conflicting testimony. Over and over again I have been surprised and gratified to discover how frequently this happens. In the
pages which follow, I hope I have been able to convey this impression
of clear image and firm outline.

This book is not intended to be a general history of the American
theatre covering the development of playwriting, stagecraft, playhouses, finances, the influences of social, political, and economic
change, and all the other elements which contribute to the over-all history of the theatre. I am, instead, presenting a history of American
acting as recorded in the lives and achievements of the notable players

of the American stage. It will be necessary, of course, to sketch a background against which to view the performers. These "notes on the setting" will introduce elements of theatrical history other than acting, but the "notes" will be relatively brief and throughout the book the emphasis will be on acting and on the influences which shaped the styles of performance.

SCHOOLS OF ACTING

Previous records of American acting have been, for the most part, a series of unrelated critical reviews. Few attempts have been made to discern the similar methods and ideals of various performers or to group their styles into distinct schools. But an over-all survey of the history of American acting reveals a series of important relationships and discloses a significant pattern in the dramatic styles of American performers. Players can be grouped, at least loosely, into schools of acting to which their art belongs. Each of these schools has identifying characteristics: similar ideals and methods, similar approaches and practices, similar aims and results. The factors which determine the style of an individual performer often apply with equal strength to several performers and thus produce a group or school with a similar style. Often the group is shaped and influenced by the force of a dominating personality, like that of Edwin Forrest. Often the members of a school are contemporary, developed in response to the taste of a particular period. However, it must be noted that the various schools of acting which are discernible in an over-all view of the American theatre are not chronologically separate. In general, the schools do not succeed each other like links in a chain; that is, a school does not develop, flourish, decline, and then give way to a succeeding school— although sometimes this does happen. The various schools overlap and intermingle like the closely woven strands of a rope. During all of the nineteenth century and well into our own time, the cast of any single play represented several different types or styles of acting. Members of widely differing schools performed and competed with each other on the same stage. For example, Edwin Forrest, born in 1806 and chief representative of the heroic, muscular school, acted in the same production with a child named David Belasco, who became high priest of a sentimental, realistic style of acting which he taught until 1931. The lives and careers of most of the notable performers in the American theatre are closely interrelated. Thus, in reading the following chapters one should bear in mind that although the players are discussed separately, and although they seem to move in separate worlds, they are, in fact, very close to each other—often exactly contemporary. Their styles of acting do not form a series of isolated, individual pictures; rather, they are the closely woven colors of a single rich tapestry.

It should be remembered that the grouping of performers into various "schools" of acting is not intended to be definitive or final. The grouping is done to reveal similarities and trends in the practice of acting, to show the relationship between individual players and groups of players, and to suggest a pattern for a large body of critical material which has hitherto been largely unorganized. There will be, of course, many admirers of the theatre who will resent my grouping of actors into schools and who will deplore my choice of labels to identify these schools. Some will feel that any attempts to classify or categorize the actors of the past is unnecessary and pedantic. Others will disagree with the categories or schools I have suggested and with the players I have assigned to them. Such disagreements are inevitable. How can it be otherwise in a subject which involves so many value judgments? But such disagreements can be useful, too, if they lead to a closer examination of the similarities and differences in the theory and practice of acting throughout the history of the American stage, and if they awaken an interest in an area of theatre which needs far more attention than it presently can claim.

EMPHASIS ON THE NINETEENTH CENTURY

Another aspect of this history which may raise a question is the emphasis on the nineteenth century and its now-legendary performers. There are a number of reasons for this emphasis, some objective and some purely sentimental.

The past exerts the fascination of legend and romance. At the same time, it can be viewed in perspective. The record is complete and can be studied more objectively than is possible in the case of contemporary acting. More than this, American acting was born in the nineteenth century; it developed, matured, and gained world attention during that period. It evolved styles and techniques which were studied then and can be re-studied profitably today. It laid the foundations for theatre practice in the twentieth century and thus has the interest of originality.

In the nineteenth century the figure of the actor towered over all other theatrical artists and artisans. During most of the century, the playwright, the company manager, the stage manager, the scene painter, the carpenter, and the stage hand were subordinate figures. There were no designers or directors as we know them today. Often the leading actor served as the company manager, the stage manager, the playwright, and even as the scene painter. The entire world of the theatre revolved around the actor, and so he was far more conspicuous than is his counterpart today.

In the nineteenth century the living stage was supported and enjoyed in American communities all over the nation. There were playhouses everywhere and, without the competition of movies, radio, and television, and without the ready availability of fast travel, thousands of citizens patronized the legitimate theatre. They knew the standard repertory of plays, and they knew all the traveling stars as well as the resident players of their own town. Their support and interest helped to stimulate fine acting by a host of talented players. Even discounting the glamor which history has given to actors of the "palmy" days, the record of their versatility and achievement is impressive. The greatest of them inspired admiration, emulation, and worship, and the impression remains that the nineteenth century might truthfully be called the golden age of American acting.

The performers of the past attract scrutiny for another reason. Surviving them are, very often, lengthy and careful analyses of their art by critics and observers who took the time to think about the craft of acting and to write about it with knowledge and affection. Today's review of a play is apt to be brief and succinct, composed under severe restrictions of time and space. The star of the performance may earn three or four lines of comment; supporting players are often dismissed with a phrase. There is no analysis of style or discussion of aesthetic principles or comparison with other performers of similar style or similar roles. Contrast such a modern review with one written by a leading critic of the nineteenth century, say William Winter or J. Ranken Towse or Henry Austin Clapp. Their reviews are detailed and thorough. Leading players are carefully evaluated aesthetically, theatrically, and often morally. The role under discussion is compared to the same actor's performance of last week or last year and to the performances of the other stars who played the same parts. Whether one agrees or disagrees with the aesthetic principles or the moral judgments, one has a quantity of material to study and vivid descriptions to evaluate. Analyses of this kind are hard to find in the recent or contemporary theatre and so, again, one is tempted to linger in the nineteenth century.

In my descriptions of the notable players of the past century, I have drawn heavily upon the comments of the leading critics of the time. These men, of course, were products of their own age. They represent the principles and the prejudices of the nineteenth century. Their aesthetic, social, and moral ideals differ markedly from our own. In particular, they mix moral judgments with aesthetic criteria, which is usually repugnant to the critic of today. Although we often disagree with them, we must remember that they reflect the taste and standards of their time. They react as other intelligent playgoers of the nineteenth century must have reacted. Their evaluation of a player or of a performance reveals the effectiveness of that player or performance for the audiences of the period. When tastes and aesthetic principles change, style in acting changes too. But the critic of a later period cannot properly evaluate the art of an earlier actor by applying contemporary criteria to a past performance, just as it is unfair to denounce the costumes, makeup, and hairdo of a nineteenth century actor as ridiculous just because our tastes in these things have changed since then.

USE OF THE TERM "POPULAR THEATRE"

Although the actors of the legitimate theatre claim the lion's share of attention in this book, I have not ignored the influence of what I term "popular theatre": vaudeville, minstrelsy, burlesque, the circus, etc., in the nineteenth century; the movies, radio, and television in the twentieth century. My use of the term "popular theatre" will, no doubt, cause perplexity. The term is somewhat ambiguous because it suggests that the living stage was or is *un*popular compared to vaudeville, minstrelsy, or television. I do not intend such an interpretation. The term "popular theatre"—the least ambiguous one I can find—is intended to suggest that there are many forms of theatrical entertainment different from the legitimate stage and that these forms have usually commanded greater attention from the masses of ordinary people than have the standard plays of the legitimate stage.

The popular theatre in its many sprightly forms has a fascinating history. Perhaps it deserves more attention and analysis than I have given it. Yet in the chapters I devote to it I hope it is clear that I recognize the importance of popular theatre, that I am aware of its continuing appeal to spectators in every period of our history, and that I do not underestimate its considerable contributions to acting in the American theatre.

STYLE AND ITS DETERMINANTS IN ACTING

Before the styles of acting evolved by the notable players of the American stage can be understood and before their careers and achievements can be evaluated, it is necessary to consider two basic questions: What is style in acting? and, What are the factors or influences which determine an actor's style? The history of American acting was written by the colorful personalities who dominated our stage and evolved unique manners of performance which made them stars. The basis for an appreciation of the ever-changing panorama of American acting is an understanding of the meaning and origins of style.

Style in acting, a term which is often misunderstood and misused, means the individual characteristics of appearance, voice, movement, and temperament which distinguish one actor from another; it is the distinctive mode of presentation used by an actor in the performance of a role. This distinctive mode or style is the result of at least seven determining factors, all of which must be recognized in evaluating style.

The first of these factors is the player's physical endowments. Nature gives to a performer a certain face, figure, and voice, and on these endowments he must build his art. For example, Edwin Forrest had a massive, muscular physique which gave him the strength and appearance of the Farnese Hercules. He chose roles which suited his physique—like Damon, Metamora, Jack Cade, and Coriolanus—and performed them with intensity and power. Edwin Booth, on the other hand, was graceful, slender, and of average height. He was not physically capable of the strenuous emotional displays of Forrest, so he rejected them for an intellectual, spiritual quality which earned him praise as "the foremost poet of his profession." [1] That Booth was fully aware of the influence of his physical endowments on his style is revealed when he said, "It is rather safe to assume that actors establish their school upon their physique—for one must cover up what one cannot physically do." [2]

Like the male performers, the actresses of the American stage have also adapted their style to their physical endowments. The slight, boyish figure of Maude Adams impelled her to such boyish, whimsical roles as Peter Pan and L'Aiglon, while the strong, masculine physique of Charlotte Cushman made her an ideal Queen Katherine and (to her contemporaries) an acceptable performer in the roles of Romeo, Hamlet, and Cardinal Wolsey.

Facial characteristics and vocal endowments also influence style. Actors with droll or homely faces often become eccentric comedians so that they can capitalize on their facial peculiarities. Actresses with beautiful faces often rely on external charm alone and thus their style may remain cold and listless. Charlotte Cushman, who was *not* endowed with a beautiful face, developed an intense, restless manner of moving about the stage and, when asked to explain it, replied that if she were beautiful like Mrs. Siddons she could afford to stand still and be gazed at, but without beauty she had to occupy the eye of the spectator with action and movement or half her influence would be lost. [3]

The influence of Cushman's voice on her style is a further illustration of the effect of physical endowment on an actor's manner of performance. As will be related in a later section, Miss Cushman originally aspired to be a singer but after a successful debut in grand opera she ruined her singing voice by overstraining it in a large theatre. Her speaking voice was left with a husky, hollow quality, "a woody or veiled tone," as James Murdoch described it. This unique quality, plus wide range and unusual power, made Cushman's voice capable of expressing intense, sustained grief without loudness or sudden variations. These vocal characteristics became a noticeable feature of the actress's style, just as the thunderous tones of Forrest or the rich contralto of Mary Anderson identified and influenced their manner of performing.

The mental and spiritual attributes of an actor are also important determinants of style. The player with vivid imagination will tend to act with intensity and insight. The actor with a nervous, high-strung temperament may develop a tense, explosive style of performing. The player with a scholarly mind may intellectualize his roles. Edwin Booth, who possessed a penetrating, poetical mind, endowed his roles with a spiritual quality which was unique. William Winter said of Booth that "the distinctive quality that illuminated his acting was the personal one of poetic individuality." [4] It is said that Henry Irving, the English actor, could neither walk nor talk but achieved success on the stage through "the character and quality of his intellect." [5] Likewise, Mrs. Fiske's keen mind and analytical approach gave her acting a subtle, intellectual quality which was praised by most critics.

The manners and customs of the period in which a player lives present a third and exceedingly influential factor in determining style. Just as styles of dress change with the years, so do fashions in etiquette and behavior fluctuate. A player automatically and unconsciously absorbs and incorporates these changing fashions in behavior. Where the Restoration gallant would bow and kiss a lady's hand with (to us) an exaggerated flourish, the modern gentleman will merely smile and give a barely perceptible nod of the head. Where the nineteenth-century heroine would blush and hide her face with a fan, the twentieth-century lady will raise an eyebrow and light a cigarette. In Mrs. Siddon's day a lady cultivated an erect carriage, a graceful walk, and elegance in all her movements. It was very natural, then, for Mrs. Siddons to stand, walk, and move in a stately fashion when she took the stage. Today the fashion in behavior dictates that a lady be casual, nonchalant, athletic—and so an audience shows no surprise when, in a modern play, Katharine Cornell slouches across the stage with hands in pockets, or when Katharine Hepburn, dressed in tennis shorts, lolls in a chair with one bare leg draped over the arm of the chair.

A fourth factor in determining style is the aesthetic ideals of a period. The formative effect of an aesthetic milieu is striking and pervasive not only in acting but in all the arts. For example, the eighteenth-century belief in balance, discipline, and good form—based on the ideals of classicism—produced the neat couplets of Alexander Pope, the precise, symmetrical paintings of David, and the restrained formal music of Handel and Thomas Arne. In the theatre, these ideals produced acting characterized by conventionalized tones and gestures and by the acceptance of tradition in the interpretation of a role. When the aesthetic ideals of a period fluctuate, all the arts are affected— including the art of acting.

An additional factor is the force of training, example, and experience. The instructors who guide an apprentice actor, and the examples set by fellow players, inevitably exert an influence in developing an actor's style. When native Americans first began appearing on the stage, there were no schools of dramatic art to train them but there were the inspiring examples of many English players. A novice actor could study performances which illustrated any one of four distinct styles of acting, each of which had flourished in Great Britain in the eighteenth or early nineteenth century. A brief description of these styles will be useful in illustrating the influence of one actor upon another in the formulation of style, and it will also serve as a guide to those particular English styles which set an example for many early American players.

The first of the styles which dominated English acting in the early years of the eighteenth century can be called the neo-classical style. It was characterized by the following of certain traditions in acting a character, and by the acceptance of conventionalized tone and gesture in delivery. The author of a play taught the first actor of a part what characterization to use. "It was assumed that the author of plays knew how they should be acted, and that his interpretation of his own characters was not only the most accurate, but also the most effective interpretation." [6] This interpretation became fixed and was passed down from player to player. Critical judgment assumed that "the closer the imitation of the older actor by the younger, the better was the presentation of the play." [7]

In 1741 Charles Macklin appeared on the stage as Shylock, and David Garrick made his debut as Richard III. A second period, characterized by "realistic romanticism" was inaugurated. This was a period of revolt against the accepted traditions. Both Macklin and Garrick reinterpreted their characters. Their break with the past earned public acclaim, and thus they established the right "to go to nature herself, and to re-interpret a play in the light of life itself." [8] The Macklin-Garrick school rejected the conventionalized tone and gesture with which tragedy had been rendered and substituted a more easy, colloquial manner of speaking. In developing a characterization they believed in a literal imitation of nature. Their creed was, "the closer the imitation of nature in art, the better the art."

A third style in English acting of the eighteenth century appeared in the late years of the century. During these years, Thomas Sheridan and John Walker stimulated a new interest in the propriety of pronunciation and in declamation as a separate art. Also, a new theory of art emerged, championed by Sir Joshua Reynolds. He said that the purpose of art, including the art of acting, was *not* to imitate the literal details of nature but to raise and elevate nature—to exclude the ugly and to exalt the ideal. John Philip Kemble and his sister, Sarah Kemble Siddons, the new leaders of the English stage, were deeply influenced by both the Sheridan-Walker theories of declamation and the Reynolds theory of art. Espousing both, they evolved a new style of acting in the practice of which there was no attempt to copy nature slavishly. Rather, nature was elevated and idealized. Grand declamation was substituted for the naturalistic diction of the Garrick school. Dignity and nobility took the place of true-to-life representations. So gifted were the Kembles that they made this style of performing acceptable and popular.

In 1814, Edmund Kean played Shylock at the Drury Lane Theatre, and his performance inaugurated a new period of tempestuous, passionate acting. The stateliness and elevation of the Kemble school gave way to fiery outbursts of emotion and dazzling displays of vocal pyrotechnics. Scenes in which the emotional intensity was low or the action was listlessly performed were alternated with tremendous, impassioned climaxes. Edmund Kean and Junius Brutus Booth both helped to popularize this style.

The period of great acting in America by native American players began shortly after the advent of Edmund Kean. It is not surprising that American performers were influenced by the several English styles which they observed around them. For example, Edwin Forrest modelled his early acting after the style of Thomas A. Cooper, a disciple of the Kemble school. Some time later, Edmund Kean visited the United States and Forrest was engaged to play second leads in Kean's troupe. Thereafter, Forrest altered his style to include the fiery, passionate displays which characterized Kean's performances.

Throughout the entire history of American acting, the factor of training and example has been influential in shaping an actor's style. Players in the early period studied their fellow performers—especially the visiting stars—and adopted those methods and manners which seemed most effective. Actors in the later periods have come under the influence of dominating teachers or directors and have learned a style from them. In the later nineteenth and early twentieth centuries, for example, David Belasco molded many performers to fit his concepts of acting. Augustin Daly did the same. In our own day, the effect of the Group Theatre's instruction and training, as carried on by the Actors' Studio, can be seen in the performances of many players, and certainly the students of a great university teacher, like the late A. M. Drummond of Cornell, can recognize in each other the influence of the unique instruction they received.

The repertory popular in the early nineteenth century was a powerful factor in shaping the style of the first American actors. With few exceptions, this repertory came entirely from English and other European dramatists. Shakespeare provided the bulk of the plays, to which were added the tragedies of Dryden, Otway, and Rowe, and the comedies of such dramatists as Farquhar, Goldsmith, and Sheridan. The remainder of the plays consisted of the new successes which came year by year from the pens of contemporary dramatists. Among the most popular of these playwrights, as the century advanced, were Sheridan Knowles with such dramas as *Virginius* and *The Hunchback;* Edward Bulwer-Lytton with *The Lady of Lyons* and *Richelieu;* Dion Boucicault with *London Assurance* and dozens of others; Tom Taylor with *Still Water Runs Deep* and *Our American Cousin;* the German dramatist, Kotzebue, with *The Stranger, Pizarro in Peru,* and *The Virgin of the Sun;* and French playwrights, such as Sardou, whose tearful domestic melodramas were introduced to his fellow countrymen by the American actor and dramatist, John Howard Payne. In general, American playwrights in the nineteenth century were neither very popular nor very prolific, and what plays they did produce were largely imitative of foreign models.

It is evident that such a repertory, consisting largely of heroic tragedies in blank verse and sensational melodramas in turgid prose, would powerfully influence the style of the actors who performed them.

A final factor which influences the manner of performance of a player is the physical environment in which he performs, that is, the playhouse and the setting in which the play is produced. This can be illustrated clearly if we contrast the environment which surrounded the early American actor with the settings and playhouses of today.

The first structures erected in the colonial period by Lewis Hallam and David Douglass were merely oblong wooden boxes filled with rough benches and embellished with a narrow stage at one end. In some of the larger buildings might be found a few stage boxes decorated and upholstered for the accommodation of distinguished patrons like George Washington. As American towns increased in population and wealth, more elaborate playhouses began to be constructed. All of them followed European models and featured a wide forestage, proscenium doors, pit or orchestra, boxes, and galleries. The lighting for both stage and auditorium was dim and crude. Until 1816, all illumination was furnished by candles or oil lamps. After 1816, gas lighting appeared but considerable time elapsed before its use became widespread. Electric lighting did not appear until the 1880's.

For many years, stage scenery was as crude as the lighting. Throughout the eighteenth and half of the nineteenth centuries it consisted of a series of wings and drops. The rear wall of the stage was hidden by a canvas curtain or drop and the sides were masked by canvas wings set parallel to the backdrop. The scenery—trees, waterfalls, rivers, meadows, and most of the furniture—were painted on the wings and drops. The floor was the bare wood of the stage.

The effect on acting of the dim lighting of the early playhouses is described by one historian of the drama as follows: "When the footlights consisted of half a dozen or more oil lamps, the point where their rays converged was properly known as the 'focus'. Here all important passages of the piece had to be delivered, since elsewhere a player was not clearly visible. It was not possible, of course, to develop naturalistic acting under the circumstances. . . ." [9]

On such a stage, so sparsely decorated and so dimly lighted, the player was the center of attention. If he expected to capture and hold the interest of his audience—most of them uncomfortably seated and often too hot or too cold—he had to project strong emotion and vivid action. The dimness of the lighting forced him to use broad, sweeping movements and exaggerated facial expressions. The size of the auditorium (in the nineteenth century many of them were huge) and the uncertainty of the acoustics forced him to use stentorian tones. His style of performance could not possibly duplicate the style of the modern player who appears, for example, in an arena theatre surrounded closely by spectators and illuminated by powerful, flexibly controlled electric lights. In the modern setting, the player can perform with subtle, delicate art, both physically and vocally.

One can summarize the seven factors that determine style in acting by saying that nature supplies an actor with certain basic endowments of body and voice, mind and spirit. These are the raw materials out of which he shapes his art. His training and experience, molding his natural endowments, occurring in a particular social and aesthetic milieu, and applied to a particular role in a particular play presented in a particular playhouse, will determine his style. All of these influences must be kept in mind if one is to appreciate the history of American acting as recorded in the careers and achievements of its notable players.

IMPORTANCE OF A STUDY OF THE PAST

Historians often tell us that those who ignore history will sooner or later find themselves repeating the mistakes of history. This observation, while not entirely applicable to a study of the actors of the past, does have a certain relevance. Those who love and serve the theatre of today can learn much from the records of American acting. There is inspiration here and excitement and instruction, too. The problems faced by a contemporary actor or director are not entirely new. A host of gifted artists in the past have confronted and solved most of them with varying success in a great number of ways. Perhaps the old solutions can still offer comfort and guidance.

But a study of the development of American acting and of the notable performers who have contributed to it offers more than guidance and instruction. It offers enjoyment and delight. The magic of theatre is never-failing, and the fascination of studying that rare variety of human personality, the actor, is inexhaustible. Beyond enjoyment and delight there is another emotion: pride. The history of our stage is rich and colorful; the achievement of our native performers is notable; the theories, discoveries, and wisdom of American artists of the theatre have enriched the storehouse of world theatre and have touched the minds and hearts of men everywhere. A study of the history of American acting can give us pride in our past as well as hope and guidance for the future.

[NOTES ON THE SETTING]

The Early Years

 THORNTON WILDER, IN ONE OF HIS FANCIFUL THREE-minute plays, introduces a background for the action which consists of an old-fashioned revolving cyclorama depicting Egypt and the Holy Land. A stage manager turns the scroll: the Tigris, the Euphrates, the Pyramids pass in swift review. In front of this moving background the characters of the play appear, speak their lines, act their roles, and then depart.

Such a device would be useful in presenting the history of American acting as it is reported in the careers of the notable players of the American stage. These players perform their roles, both as people and as actors, before a constantly shifting panorama: the social and political milieu changes from year to year; playhouses are built, they flourish, they decline, and new ones of altered form and machinery take their place; the scenery, lighting, and costuming change from decade to decade; dramatic literature varies in style and content; the public taste fluctuates and shifts; and the actor who appears before this moving background is shaped and molded in his manner of performance by the fluctuating influences around him. A glance at the ever-changing backdrop of the American actor is necessary for an understanding of his art and his achievement.

Theatrical activity in America, preceding 1752, was meagre. A few amateur dramatists had written plays; the newly founded colleges had presented dramatic dialogues; a couple of playhouses had been built;

a few amateur performances had been given. In 1752, a company of actors headed by Lewis Hallam arrived from England and produced a play in Williamsburg, Virginia. Three years before, a British troupe headed by the Messrs. Murray and Keane had performed in the colonies, and they continued to perform for some years. But it was the Hallam company, of 1752, consisting of twelve adults and three children, which introduced the first resident professional company in America. For several years this company, which was later reorganized and headed by David Douglass, traveled from town to town, giving plays wherever they could obtain permission. They built crude little theatres to house their productions or they performed in hotel dining rooms, warehouses, court houses, and even barns. Almost everywhere they fought the opposition of Puritans and Quakers and the legal bans against playacting. Often they resorted to amusing subterfuges in order to gain a hearing. When the Revolutionary War came, all forms of entertainment were forbidden in the colonies, so the Hallam company —which was now patriotically calling itself "The American Company" —retired to the West Indies. During the war the only playacting in the colonies was done by either British or American troops. But in 1784, the war being over, the American Company returned to the United States from Jamaica and professional theatre was re-established on American soil.

In the post-revolutionary era theatrical activity made progress. It was slow but steady. New companies were formed and more players arrived from England. New playhouses were constructed in such important towns as Charleston, Boston, Philadelphia, New York, and New Orleans. Most important, the anti-theatre laws were repealed in Philadelphia, Boston, and Rhode Island, and this established a pattern that was soon to be followed in other states and cities. In the post-war era the first comedy written by a native American was produced. Up until now, the repertory was made up almost exclusively of plays from Shakespeare, Restoration authors, and other English dramatists. In 1787, American audiences saw a play by a fellow countryman, Royall Tyler, entitled *The Contrast,* and in it the first stage Yankee made his appearance. About this time, America's first major playwright, William Dunlap, began writing and producing such dramas as *André,* and began introducing the works of the German dramatist, Kotzebue. The first of these adaptations from Kotzebue, entitled *The*

Stranger, was destined to become one of the most popular dramas of the nineteenth century.

The progress and development observable in the post-revolutionary period continued with increased momentum in the early years of the nineteenth century. By 1800, according to William Winter, there were one hundred and fifty professional actors in America, almost all of them British, of course, and their number was growing. More playhouses were built, more American plays were written. The towns and settlements along the Atlantic coast were organized into a regular theatrical circuit, and as the frontier was pushed westward, hardy pioneer actors followed. Amid astonishing hardships, they established theatrical activity in the wilderness.

In the early years of the nineteenth century, the leading theatrical cities were, of course, the centers of population on the Atlantic coast. Originally, Philadelphia was the most important town, but around the turn of the century New York began to surpass Philadelphia both in population and in importance as a seaport. Supremacy in theatrical affairs soon passed to New York, where it has remained ever since. But the theatre also flourished in other cities such as Boston, Charleston, Newport, Richmond, and New Orleans.

In 1810 occurred an event of major significance. George Frederick Cooke, a famous English tragedian, came to America and acted in the theatres of the leading towns. He was the first English star to deign to visit this country, and he set a precedent which was soon followed by most of the leading players of the English stage. In a few years, visiting stars—not only foreign but domestic—began to alter the character of the long-established resident stock companies. These companies were the only form of theatrical organization during the eighteenth century and during most of the nineteenth century. They consisted of a group of actors hired for the season to play a particular line of parts in one playhouse situated in one town. The company, which was supervised by a manager, presented a repertory of plays during the season and often the program was changed from night to night. The prosperity of the company depended, primarily, upon the strength of the group as a whole. The leading players remained unchanged throughout the season. When a visiting star like George Frederick Cooke appeared, he displaced the resident lead, and when the visitor departed the permanent company seemed to lose luster. As the century advanced, the resident companies came to depend more and more on visiting stars to stimulate business, and more and more visiting stars appeared to fill the need. However, in the early years of the nineteenth century the resident companies were still strong and independent.

It was in such a company, having such a background as I have described, that the first native born American star, Edwin Forrest, made his debut in 1820.

I

THE HEROIC SCHOOL

EDWIN FORREST OCCUPIES A UNIQUE POSITION IN THE HISTORY OF American acting. He was the first player born in the United States to achieve great fame both at home and abroad. He represented a type of acting so vigorous that it created a host of imitators, yet so individual that many of the imitations were caricatures. His personal life and his professional life were filled with controversy. During his lifetime, his style was praised and ridiculed; for more than five decades his plays attracted hosts of enthusiastic admirers and earned him a vast fortune. Today the player and his plays are practically forgotten.

Forrest made his professional debut in 1820, at the age of fourteen. At that time, as we have noted, the American theatre was dominated by English actors, English managers, and English dramaturgy. Political independence had been won some forty years before, but culturally the United States was largely dependent upon Great Britain. With the advent of Edwin Forrest this situation began to change. Born and reared in Philadelphia and passionately American in his loyalties, Forrest achieved a reputation in the United States as dazzling as the fame of the English stars. He played great roles for more than fifty years, during which his personality and his style of acting remained as typical of the vigorous young American democracy in which he grew up as were the rowdy young fans, the "Bowery B'hoys," who idolized him.

Forrest's formal education, both general and dramatic, was slight. He attended a public school in Philadelphia for a short time, but before he was thirteen he had been apprenticed successively to a printer, a cooper, and a ship-chandler. His instruction in elocution came, principally, from a year's study with Lemuel G. White, whom Lawrence Barrett calls "a distinguished professor in that branch of dramatic art." [1] Very little is known of the theory or methods of Mr. White. Barrett mentions that White was a disciple of the Garrick and Kean schools, that is, the so-called natural schools as opposed to the artificial, declamatory school of the Kembles, and that among his more noted pupils were David Ingersoll and James E. Murdoch. In *The Stage* Murdoch has left a note concerning White's influence on Forrest: "Mr. White, who first formed Forrest's manner out of the usual schoolboy style of reading, was a man of great intelligence and culture in his art, but eccentric, enthusiastic, and very egotistical. In his idea of delivery the principal thing was *emphasis,* and at this he labored and pounded with every kind and degree of pressure and force. But this quality did not adhere to Forrest's mode of reading after he had once tested the practical method of dramatic action. White's influence was, however, observable in his articulation, which was always distinct." [2]

Forrest's smattering of formal education was a minor influence in shaping his career. His style of acting was largely the result of his own study, observation, and experience on the stage. Fortunately, his early acting was done in the company of excellent players. For example, the cast which supported him when he made his debut at the Walnut Street Theatre in Philadelphia included Frederick Wheatley, Willam B. Wood, the elder William Warren, Mrs. H. A. Williams, and the elder Mrs. Joseph Jefferson. James Rees characterizes this cast as one "which could not have been equaled in the country then, nor has it been since. . . ." [3]

Such companies of players were thoroughly familiar with the dramatic repertory. Substantially the same program of plays was given year after year, and the player thus had ample opportunity to become matured and seasoned in his roles. Each play was cast with the full strength of the company, and each part was considered of real importance.

Besides the veterans, with whom Forrest had the privilege of observing and working, there was a group of talented younger men who provided the stimulus of keen competition. John R. Scott, David Ingersoll, Augustus Addams, Charles Eaton, Charles Webb, and James

Murdoch were men who, in the early years of Forrest's career, enjoyed a reputation equal and in some cases superior to his own. Barrett, writing in 1881, observed that "To the actors of today, educated in the modern sensational dramas, the splendor of this company of tragedians seems unreal." [4]

From association with these players the alert and ambitious young Forrest learned much. He studied the performances of his fellow actors carefully, experimenting with the styles and techniques which seemed to him particularly effective. He eventually adopted those techniques which best suited his ideas and temperament. In the formation of his mature style two men exerted special influence on him: Thomas A. Cooper and Edmund Kean.

Cooper, although born and trained in England, was considered an American actor. He had come to the United States at the age of twenty, after he had failed to achieve any great success in London. His success here was prodigious. He became the idol of the American stage and held the top rank in public favor for many years. He relinquished it only when age and the popularity of Forrest compelled him to take a subordinate place.

As a neophyte actor, Forrest studied Cooper's style with care. From him Forrest learned the dignified posture, the formal movements, the measured, declamatory reading, and the ideal of poetic elevation and repose which were characteristic of the Kemble school.

But Forrest was soon to be subjected to another more powerful influence. In 1825 Edmund Kean visited the United States for the second time, again taking the country by storm with the tempestuousness of his genius. For Kean's performances in Albany, Forrest was engaged to play second leads. He enacted Iago to Kean's Othello, Richmond to his Richard, and Titus to his Brutus. This was one of the great experiences of Forrest's life, and it left an indelible stamp on his acting.

There are many records of Kean's acting and descriptions of his style. I shall quote only one, an analysis of Kean's technique as it was at the time Forrest played with him. Written by W. R. Alger, Forrest's official biographer, it outlines those traits of Kean which probably most impressed the young American tragedian. Alger says:

The essential peculiarity of Kean's greatness in his greatest effects was that his acting then was no effort of the will, no trick or art of calculation, but nature itself uncovered and set free in its deepest intensity of power, just on the edge, sometimes quite over the edge of madness. He penetrated and incorporated himself with the characters he represented until he possessed them so completely that they possessed him, and their performance was no simulation, but revelation. He brought the truth and simplicity of nature to the stage, but nature in her most intensified degrees. His playing was the manifestation of inspired intuition, infallibly true and irresistibly sensational. It came not from the surface of his brain, but from the very centers of his nervous system, and suggested something portentous, preternatural, supernal, that blinded and stunned the beholders, appalled the imagination, and chilled their blood.[5]

Kean not only inspired Forrest by his example, but also encouraged him privately and complimented him publicly. He allowed Forrest to introduce new business and different readings into the part of Iago, and was so impressed with some of the innovations that he declared henceforth all Iagos would have to copy the young American. Later on, at a public banquet in Philadelphia, Kean said: "I have met one actor in this country, a young man named Edwin Forrest, who gave proofs of a decided genius for his profession, and will, I believe, rise to a great eminence." [6]

It is little wonder that after acting with Kean, Forrest's style underwent a great change. The natural, impulsive displays of passion, the fiery eloquence that "made the pit tremble," the realistic bursts of physical movement—all became incorporated in the young actor's technique.

The magnificent physique of Edwin Forrest is important to any analysis of his acting. Many critics believed that his physique was the greatest single factor in determining his style. Forrest was a handsome man. As a boy he had been frail, but through assiduous exercise he had developed an unusually powerful body. He was inordinately proud of it. The massiveness of his physique was doubly noticeable because he was not tall. His biceps bulged; his calves bulged. He never neglected an opportunity to demonstrate his strength on the stage.

Forrest believed intensely in the value of healthful food, fresh air, and, particularly, of physical exercise. He recommended physical culture to all his associates. As a young actor in New York, he took boxing and fencing lessons. Every morning he did strenuous exercises with dumbells and Indian clubs. He continued this until the very end of his life. It probably accounts for his excellent health; also, it may have been the reason for his death. On the fatal morning his servant found him lying on his bed suffering from a stroke of apoplexy. Possibly the stroke had been brought about by his taking exercise which was much too violent for a man of sixty-six.

Forrest possessed a voice that was as powerful as his physique. No orator or actor of his day could equal it. We are told that it was great enough to shake the rafters of the largest amphitheatre, and yet capable of the softest, tenderest tones. "He could range from piano to forte, from lowest bass to highest treble with ease, and his vocal chords could withstand the most severe strain . . . he could play through two trage-dies in one evening and still deliver his final dying words as clear as a bell. . . . In the delicate and tender passages he could sing in a soft tremulo that would move the hardest heart." [7] It is certain that For-rest's physical and vocal make-up had real influence on his style of acting and on the way he interpreted his roles.

From this glance at Forrest's background and at the influences af-fecting him, a fair outline of his general style of acting is apparent. The primary characteristic of this style was a strenuous realism. Under the influence of Kean's example, as Forrest interpreted it, the American tragedian sought to portray nature as it existed around him in actual life. He aimed for complete, detailed character portrayals, unchanged by any idealization. Alger says he attempted "a living resurrection of the crude truth of nature in place of that idealized softening and tem-pered reflex which is the genuine province of art." [8]

Forrest's method of studying his roles reveals the aim of his style. In preparing for the part of Lear he visited many asylums and old men's homes. He studied various manifestations of insanity—its approach, its full expression, its decline. He observed the walk, the gestures, the movements of old men. He read the best scientific books on old age and insanity, and discussed his ideas with eminent physicians. "He often insisted that he had never met a doctor who knew as much about insanity as he did." [9] As a result, the following criticism of Forrest's Lear is typical. Douglass Jerrold in London said: "We never saw mad-ness so perfectly portrayed. It is true to nature—painfully so." [10] One is reminded of Forrest's remark when a young admirer praised his act-ing in *King Lear*. Forrest exclaimed, "By God, sir, I am King Lear."

Forrest's role of the Indian Chief in the famous American play *Metamora* was prepared with equal care. At one time in his life Forrest had been a close friend of Chief Push-ma-ta-ha and had lived with the

Chief and his tribe for several weeks. "He adopted their habits, shared their food, slept in their huts, . . . smoked the pipe of peace . . . left the print of his own moccasins on the hunting ground . . . and the crack of his rifle echoed along the rocky sides of the hills and lakes." [11] In preparing the role of Metamora, Forrest drew exhaustively on this experience. Apparently he achieved great success in the realism of his portrayal. Harrison writes: "So accurate had been his observations that he caught the very manner of their breathing. . . . Everything that could be absorbed by one nature from another was absorbed and represented. In *Metamora* he achieved a piece of acting that seemed to transcend all criticism." [12]

One evening a large delegation of Western Indians witnessed Forrest's performance of *Metamora*. They followed the play with rapt attention. In the closing scene they were so excited by the performance and so convinced of its reality that they rose and chanted a dirge in honor of the great chief who was dying on the stage.

On another occasion, when Forrest was playing Iago to Kean's Othello, a husky canal-boatman was seated in the front row of the pit, so close to the stage that he leaned his elbows on it. He was absorbed in the machinations of Iago, and became so convinced of Forrest's villainy that when the actor passed close to him he glared savagely and hissed: "You damned lying scoundrel, I would like to get hold of you after this show is over and wring your infernal neck." [13] When Kean met Forrest in the dressing room afterwards he generously said, "Young man, if my acting tonight had received as high a compliment as that brawny fellow in the pit bestowed on yours, I should feel very proud. You made the mimic show real to him, and I will tell you your acting merited the criticism." [14]

Many other instances show how realistically Forrest conceived and acted his roles. Scenes of combat in which he participated were always a terror to the other actors. There was no shamming the battle. Forrest became so excited that he fought and hacked with terrifying gusto. His opponents were always in real danger and had to defend themselves as best they could. Many were the cuts and bruises they received in these encounters.

Forrest was no less hard on himself. Rees relates that one night, while acting Lear, the tragedian worked himself into such a passion he almost had apoplexy. He fainted away, and had to be carried off the

the stage in an unconscious state. T. H. Morrell relates another striking instance. He says:

One night while performing the role of King Lear, . . . in the last scene
of the second act, when depicting the frenzy of the old monarch, whose
brain was overwrought with passion, and maddened by the injuries of his
unnatural daughters, Goneril and Regan, in the excitement of the moment
Mr. Forrest tore the wig of whitened hair from his head and hurled it
twenty feet toward the footlights. The effect was a striking one, and the wig
thus removed, revealed to the audience a head of glossy raven locks, forming a strange contrast to the hoary beard still appended and fastened by a
white cord to the actor's chin.[15]

It might seem to a modern audience that such an incident would ruin
the scene. Evidently it did not. Morrell says: "Among that vast audience not a single titter could be heard and scarce a smile was discernible"—surely a striking tribute to the illusion Forrest had been able to
create.

The bulk of contemporary evidence seems to indicate that Forrest
appeared convincingly real in his acting. Opinion, however, is not
unanimous. Some critics felt that the tragedian enlarged his effects and
"muscularized" them beyond the point of credibility. Others asserted
that the "truth to nature" which the public professed to see in Forrest's
acting was merely truth to a crude *stage* convention of reality and far
removed from the realism of actual life. This is the opinion held by the
editor of the *Easy Chair* of Harper's Magazine for December, 1863.
After watching Forrest enact the role of Damon, the editor writes: "To
criticise it as acting is as useless as to criticise the stories of Miss Braddon and Mr. Ainsworth as literature. That human beings, under any
conceivable circumstance, should ever talk or act as they are represented in the Forrest drama and the Braddon novel, is beyond belief."

Forrest's brand of realism in acting included a great deal of detail.
He presented all the movements, gestures, attitudes, postures, and expressions which he felt revealed the character. He chose to supply the
details rather than leave them to the spectator's imagination. "The
suggestive school of art expression was not of Forrest's belief," says
Harrison. The great tragedian disliked the repressed type of acting introduced into "society plays." He felt it was suggestive only of the
"dead body without the breath, the eye without light, words spoken
without the detail of expression." Incidentally, Harrison—who was an

actor himself and had received some instruction and encouragement from Forrest—felt that Forrest's facial expressions were genuine and powerful. The tragedian modeled them "not on the Delsarte principle of facial expression, but on the soul's principle," says Harrison.

In his treatment of the details of stage business, Forrest seemed to change somewhat as he advanced in years. He eliminated many of the little naturalistic touches which at first had seemed effective to him. For example, in the part of Virginius, Forrest was for some years accustomed to using a knife with a hollow blade filled with red fluid. When he struck his daughter, the pressure of a spring released the fluid and it spurted out like blood from a wound. One evening a lady in the audience fainted at this spectacle. The incident made Forrest realize that such a device was a crude artifice and not art. He never afterwards repeated it.

In his readings, too, Forrest changed by omitting certain vocal tricks of imitation. We are told that in the famous lament of Othello, "Farewell the tranquil mind," he was accustomed to use a kind of musical recitative and to imitate the sounds mentioned in the passage. He uttered the words "neighing steed" in equine tones. He reproduced the shrillness of "the shrill trumpet." He gave a deep boom to the phrase "spirit stirring drum." And he swelled and rattled his throat to portray "the engines whose rude throats the immortal Jove's dread clamors counterfeit." Alger asserts that eventually "he learned to see that however effective this might be as elocution, it was neither nature nor art, but artificiality; and then he read the passage with consummate feeling and force, his voice broken with passionate emotion, but not moulded to any pedantic cadences or flourishes." [16]

Curiously enough, Forrest's desire for dramatic realism did not extend to the scenery of the play. He never cared a hang for the settings that surrounded him. They could be as tawdry and unconvincing as possible. He believed that *acting* should create the illusion of reality and not scene painting. In the latter part of Forrest's career, Edwin Booth appeared in a series of elaborately mounted Shakespearean revivals. Forrest witnessed some of these productions, but was not impressed by them. He called Booth's production of *Julius Caesar* the "scene painter's drama." He described the elaborate trappings as "gaudy kickshaws by which modern dramatic art is swaddled and smothered." [17]

Forrest had seen how Kean could electrify his audience with bursts of passion. He felt this was immensely effective and also true to nature. And so whenever the occasion arose, he used his voice and body with great freedom. He could rage and thunder magnificently. "Give him a hero fired with democratic passions who slashed out at a tyrant, and he could arouse an audience to shouting." [18] He could also produce tears with his pathos and tenderness.

The detailed action and bursts of passion which Forrest presented through the medium of his powerful voice and body led some critics to assert, first, that he was a melodramatic ranter; and, second, that he never used his mind but only his muscles. He was called everything from a "bovine bellower" to "a bewildered animal with a little grain of genius." Charles T. Congdon said he could play only such roles as were "specially written for his private legs and larynx." Montrose Moses, writing in 1929, has concluded that he was "never able to exercise restraint" and that he was "an ungovernable man in all respects, as regards his personal behavior and his artistic methods." [19]

It cannot be denied that there is some truth in these charges. Even Alger, his loyal and worshipful biographer, admits two faults in his acting: one, an "excess . . . of physical and spiritual force in the expression of passion," and, two, a lack of *"souplesse,* of physical and spiritual mobility." James E. Murdoch acknowledges that Forrest "was often charged with rudeness and violence in his impersonations and even ridiculed for muscularity of manner." But he points out that he had never yet seen any tragedian who did not use all his physical powers in portraying passionate scenes. The actors of the day who followed the lead of Kean all used the utmost intensity and feeling which they could command. Forrest stirred up comment, not because he followed a different method from his rivals, but principally because he was a much stronger man. When he became excited, says Murdoch, "his passions appeared more extreme than those of one more delicately organized." [20]

Gabriel Harrison claims that he had seen Forrest act more than four hundred times. He asserts that even in Forrest's younger days, when he was most romantic and unrestrained—in roles like Damon, Rolla, the Gladiator, and Jack Cade—he was never melodramatic. "He had no tricks," writes Harrison, "and whatever the character he always invested it with the qualities of naturalness." [21]

The charge that Forrest never used his mind but only his muscles was ill founded. Most critics agree that he was one of the most careful and analytic thinkers and analysers the stage has ever seen. He studied his author's text with scrupulous care. He investigated the background of the play, the customs and manners of the people represented. After research in all the pertinent fields, he built up a conception of his role, consistently and logically. No actor was more mental in his approach.

Forrest's analytical mind and careful habits of study were evidenced in the intelligibility of his reading. No actor could surpass him in the clearness with which he could convey the meaning of a line. This was admitted even by the newspaper which had always been most hostile to him—against which, in fact, he had once instituted proceedings for libel. The Philadelphia *Dispatch,* on December 17, 1872, said: ". . . Mr. Forrest had a strong analytical brain and habits of study which enabled him to grasp the meaning of a passage in Shakespeare more firmly than any actor we have ever heard. So far as interpretation of the sense was concerned, he was the greatest reader on the stage. . . . We despair of ever hearing such majestic delivery again." But, adds the *Dispatch,* "with unusual powers of comparison and analysis, he was deficient in imagination—a faculty essential to the actor of Shakespeare." [22]

The "deficiency in imagination" mentioned by the Philadelphia *Dispatch* names Forrest's greatest weakness as an actor: he lacked spiritual insight and the highest type of creative imagination. Whenever a character could be analyzed and grasped by *logic,* Forrest was able to achieve a convincing portrayal. He could understand figures like Damon, Metamora, Jack Cade, and Coriolanus, whose motives were uncomplicated and whose passions were strong and clear and physically demonstrable. King Lear, though one of the great and complicated characters of Shakespeare, was also within his grasp. In the actor's younger days, the strength of his mimic wrath and the realism of his mimic madness rendered his performance of Lear effective. In his later life, his sorrows—real or fancied—gave him a deep insight into the old king's character. However, in more subtle roles like Hamlet or Macbeth Forrest's deficiency was very clear. He could not logically understand these men. No amount of analyzing enabled him to feel the character of Hamlet. The prince's vivid imagination, the spiritual conflict which agonizes him and furnishes the key to much of his behavior, were quite beyond Forrest's comprehension. He read the lines with wonderful accuracy, says the Philadelphia *Dispatch,* but nothing could overcome his "want of appreciation" of the character. In *Macbeth* the same lack of imagination and spiritual insight was apparent. Forrest did not seem to grasp how a strong man could be terrorized by imaginary horrors. He seemed to have no comprehension of that terrible vision-creating faculty which tortures Macbeth. Forrest's performance of the part offered isolated passages of beautiful reading but, according to the critics of the times, "the witches he could not see, the ghost of Banquo did not appall him, and the horrors of Macbeth's remorse he could not depict."

Nevertheless, his style of acting was immensely appealing to the majority of playgoers. They idolized this handsome, powerful man who handled his body like an athlete. They enjoyed watching his naturalistic movements and gestures, and especially the explosions of physical action in his portrayals. Despite traces of the formal grace of the Kemble school, Forrest's physical actions were broad, powerful, and often startling—effects which especially pleased the Bowery B'hoys. And his voice, as we have mentioned, had tremendous range and matched his physical activity in versatility and power. At the same time, his delivery never lost the clarity and precision which he had learned in his youth. Other features of his acting, which must be remembered in any summary of his style, were the detailed realism of his characterizations and mimic passions based upon a careful, analytical study of his roles, and the passionate conviction with which he lost himself in his portrayals. The heroic, strenuous style of acting he created was unique and exciting. In summarizing Forrest's appeal, Richard Moody writes: ". . . no native-born, native-trained actor climbed so high, summoned American writers to the drama with such fervor, spread the enduring glories of the mighty Shakespeare so widely, and carried the raging democratic fever to the stage with such fierce passion. And no actor compelled so many Americans to pay so much for a tempestuous evening in the theatre." [23] Perhaps Lawrence Barrett was right when he said ". . . take him all for all, we shall not look upon his like again." [24]

During his long and dazzling career, Forrest exerted considerable influence upon the actors of his time. The popularity of his style attracted a host of imitators. Some of these were gifted players who gained considerable success; others were hacks who, as W. R. Alger says, reflected discredit on Forrest "by imitating his faultiness instead of reproducing his excellence." [25] By far the most successful follower of Forrest was John Edward McCullough.

JOHN E. McCULLOUGH, CHIEF DISCIPLE
OF EDWIN FORREST

Born in Ireland, John Edward McCullough emigrated to the United States at the age of fifteen, arriving in the country unknown, destitute, and illiterate; he could not even write his own name. Yet before his death at the age of fifty-three, he was known and loved from New York to California as "genial John," and he was considered by his friends and fans to be second only to Edwin Booth in his eminence as a tragic actor.

The early struggles and ultimate success of John McCullough make a heart-warming story. His eventual collapse and death were tragic, yet before misfortune overtook him he had fulfilled the classic American ideal of winning fame and fortune through hard work and sterling character.

McCullough was born November 14, 1832, in the tiny village of Blakes near the northeast coast of Ireland. He was reared in ignorance and poverty. In 1847, he left his native land and journeyed to Philadelphia, where he searched out a cousin who had established himself as a chair maker. McCullough began learning the trade of chair making, and he also began teaching himself to read and write. He had a husky build, a handsome face, and ambition tempered by humility. A workman in his cousin's shop introduced him to the plays of Shakespeare. McCullough's interest in dramatics was aroused—and this led to membership in an amateur dramatic association and to elocution lessons from Lemuel White, the teacher of Edwin Forrest. One evening, the manager of Philadelphia's Arch Street Theatre saw McCullough perform in an amateur play and, impressed with the young man's looks and sincerity, hired him to play minor roles at $4 per week. McCullough's ambition to become an actor, born in a chair shop, was now confirmed; henceforth he was to devote his entire life to the theatre.

McCullough's professional development was slow. He had much to learn not only about acting but about art and education in general. He studied assiduously and read omnivorously. His progress was aided by his deep sincerity, his capacity for hard work, and his phenomenal memory. Two stories illustrative of the latter are featured in the accounts of his early life. One story records that in a single month's time, during the period he was employed as a chair maker, he read and absorbed the whole of Chambers' *Encyclopedia of English Literature* digesting it so thoroughly that "he could quote from its data as reliably as if the volumes were open before him. . . ." [26] The other story records that when he was playing small parts for E. L. Davenport, in Boston in the season of 1860-61, the star was stricken with rheumatism and that McCullough, at eleven in the morning, had to be ready to read the star's role from a manuscript at the evening performance. The role was Robert Landry in Selby's play *The Dead Heart,* and was considered one of the longest parts in the whole range of romantic drama. McCullough determined to *act* the part that night without the manuscript. He spent the afternoon in intensive study memorizing both the lines and the business. When curtain time came, he astonished the company and the audience by a letter-perfect performance of the role.

After four years of apprenticeship, most of them spent in Philadelphia, McCullough's great opportunity came when Edwin Forrest hired him to play second leads to Forrest's starring roles. The choice of the younger actor by the older is easy to understand when the similarities between the two men are considered. Both were muscular, well built men; both had voices of great range and power; and both had physical strength and animal vitality which lent abundant force to their acting. According to one story, the first time McCullough acted with Forrest he engaged him in a vocal duel which enraged but also impressed the star. Forrest was playing an engagement in Philadelphia in the theatre where McCullough was employed, and one evening he had a scene with McCullough. The younger man determined to make an impression on Forrest and so, says McCullough, "I went after him in a vocal sense. He gave me one startled, savage look, and came right back at me with a volley of roars that rattled the big chandelier. We had it out then and all through the evening, and although Forrest was mad all over at the minute, he came around the next day." [27]

Although this story may be apocryphal, it is the kind of thing that could have happened, and it illustrates some of the qualities which Forrest found attractive in McCullough. The young actor, besides possessing ambition, physique, and vocal power, was intensely earnest, and hard working; he was a devoted student and planned his roles with meticulous care; he was vigorous, healthy, and handsome; and he had a genial warm-heartedness which lent charm to his acting and which won him the affection of all his associates. One critic describes him at this time as "a splendid type, beautiful in his modeling, handsome of face, free of movement, natural in grace with a rich, round, resonant voice . . . ," [28] and Susie Clark, his adulatory biographer, adds that "His fine, frank face and grand head, with its wealth of brown hair, was illuminated by kindly soulful, blue eyes and one of the sweetest smiles . . . ever seen on the lips of man. . . ." [29]

McCullough remained with Forrest for five years playing such roles as Laertes, Macduff, Iago, Edgar, Richmond, Pythias, and Icilius, while Forrest played the starring parts. At this time, and for several years thereafter, McCullough style of acting was very similar to Forrest's. Both had studied under Lemuel White, who stressed vocal force and emphasis in his instruction, and they had similar physical endowments. Joseph I. C. Clarke, a prominent New York journalist and one-time dramatic editor of the *New York Tribune,* aptly describes McCullough's early style in these words: "My first impression was that his art was noisy, scorned repose, laughed at subtlety but hammered its points with a force that meant sincerity at least. It was virile without virtuosity. . . . It was, I take it, the 'Forrest school' going to seed, bold, noisy, direct to the audience, careless about settings, almost random as to costumes. The old triumphant carelessness that aimed at 'the gods' with a thunderclap speech, and if a 'hit' was scored, let that suffice." [30]

In 1866, McCullough and Forrest traveled to California and acted together at Maguire's Opera House. McCullough's performances received only luke-warm notices, the critics using such descriptions as "a fair piece of acting," "a decided improvement," "only fair to middling," etc. At the end of this engagement, Forrest and his protégé parted company, with the old actor delivering this farewell advice to McCullough: "Stay here. Leave off imitating me. . . . A lot of infernal fools are doing that, all over the country. Build yourself up here, and you will do well." [31]

McCullough followed Forrest's advice; he remained in San Francisco and prospered both financially and artistically. His desire to improve himself and to develop in his art were as strong as ever, and he began to free himself from the influence of his old master. He had often been criticized for his imitation of Forrest; now the critics began to notice a change and they praised him for it. They noticed also that McCullough improved steadily and perceptibly from season to season; in fact, a constant note in the critical reviews received by McCullough during his lifetime is a recognition of his growth and development as an actor. Year by year, until almost his final season, McCullough was congratulated for the steady improvement of his dramatic powers. Such praise is tribute, not only to his acting, but to his basic sincerity, humility, and devotion of character.

McCullough was identified with the theatre of San Francisco for almost ten years. After his partnership with Forrest ended, he acted at various playhouses in the city and the surrounding area. In January of 1869, he began a partnership with Lawrence Barrett as co-manager of the beautiful new California Theatre, built by a group of San Francisco financiers to give the city a perfect theatre and a company superior to any in the nation. Barrett withdrew as co-manager in 1870, and for the next five years McCullough was sole manager and a leading actor of the company. As manager, he was energetic, resourceful, even-tempered, generous and helpful to all his company, and lavish in the care and money he spent on his productions. As an actor he continued to grow in polish and artistry and attracted a large group of admirers. When he retired as manager, after the theatre had encountered serious financial difficulties, his departure was universally regretted. Even his arch rival in management, Tom Maguire of Maguire's Opera House, said: "Mr. McCullough did a great deal for San Francisco. . . . A squarer man never lived. He was above doing anything mean, small or underhanded. . . ." [32]

Some years before relinquishing his position at the California Theatre, McCullough had begun a series of starring tours throughout the United States. After leaving San Francisco he continued these tours, and they constituted his major theatrical activity until his final illness and retirement.

After McCullough's return to the East, his consuming ambition for improvement led him to take dramatic lessons from Steele MacKaye, who was then spreading the gospel of François Delsarte on the American stage. MacKaye's instruction seems to have crystallized and harmonized the improvements which McCullough had been laboring to achieve since his separation from Forrest. Joseph I. C. Clarke, who had described McCullough's early style as one which was "noisy" and which "scorned repose" and "laughed at subtlety," now witnessed McCullough in his favorite role of Virginius and, looking back on the performance, said: ". . . this was a new McCullough indeed. Here was a chaste spirit, a sure, tempered emotion, utmost grace, restraint overlying power that only flashed out on the mountain tops." [33] A similar estimate of McCullough's improvement and change of style was made by A. C. Wheeler, the famous critic "Nym Crinkle," who wrote, in

1878, that when McCullough "played his last season at Booth's Theatre, everyone was amazed at the leap he had made in his art. His Othello and Richelieu astonished me by being entirely unlike his former impersonations of those characters. The native vigor, resonance, and fire were there, but they were disciplined and controlled. A nicer balance of faculty was apparent. The intelligibility of the subtler emotions had been made sharper and clearer. There were noble climaxes of passion, less waste of energy in making himself felt, a cleaner adaptation of tone and gesture to the exigent thought—more repose, more dignity, more grace." [34]

During the years from 1877 to 1883, McCullough's acting reached its highest level of achievement. The abilities which he had so earnestly cultivated through the years flowered and matured and won him a secure place in the estimation of both critics and the general public. However, it must be recognized that his reputation with the public was always higher than his standing with the critics. The warmth of his personality and his great sociability off the stage won him an unusual amount of personal popularity, and this popularity brought hundreds of customers to the theatres where he played. His multitude of admirers ignored such a critic as Alfred Ayres who said that McCullough was, at the best, "a tragedian of the third rate"; [35] so great was their esteem and affection for the man and so effectively did his acting appeal to them, that they hailed him uncritically as a "genius," a "great tragedian," and "second only to Booth." [36]

While McCullough's achievements in acting were impressive, it is doubtful if he belongs in the same class with Booth—or, indeed, with Forrest or Davenport or other eminent tragedians of the time. He lacked their versatility, their poetic fire, their power of imagination. William Winter, who was a devoted friend of McCullough's—but also an experienced critic—gives a fair judgement of McCullough when he says: "He was a tragic actor of fine natural talents, thoughtfully, carefully and thoroughly cultivated." [37]

McCullough had abilities and natural endowments which, utilized in the right roles, enabled him to achieve genuine excellence. His handsome build, his finely modeled head, and his rich, powerful voice have already been mentioned. These were real factors in his success for, it is said, no actor ever wore tights or a toga with more grace and authority and no actor was a more perfect embodiment of the ideal Roman of such plays as *Virginius, Brutus, Damon and Pythias,* and *Julius Caesar.*

McCullough's great-hearted generosity, his manly sweetness, his simple dignity, and his deep sincerity—all of them qualities which characterized the actor when off the stage—were other factors in his success on the stage. McCullough was able to incorporate these qualities into his characterizations and, furthermore, he was able to project them successfully to an audience. Thus it followed that he excelled in roles "emblematic of noble manhood and lofty and tender feeling; parts that implicate splendid deeds, fidelity to duty, self sacrifice for love or honor; parts that move in the realm of the affections." [38] To act such parts required the ability to project manliness, dignity, pathos, tenderness, nobility, etc. McCullough was eminently successful in embodying such feelings, but he could also startle an audience with outbursts of anger, scorn, and tumultuous grief. He had reserves of passion which would erupt in the manner made popular by Edmund Kean and duplicated by Edwin Forrest. As a result, his portrayals of *King Lear* and *Othello* were magnificent in the scenes of rage or pathos but fell short in those scenes requiring subtlety of imagination. His Hamlet, says William Winter, "was little more than laboriously correct," [39] although the portrayal was often praised for being "human" and a "man of flesh and blood." His Macbeth was, in general, tame and uneven, rising to power and conviction only in the final scenes of action. However, in plays like *Virginius, Damon and Pythias,* and *The Gladiator,* McCullough was entirely at home and entirely successful. He looked the parts; he understood the parts; he embodied them convincingly and appealingly. The leading character in each of these plays is a man of strength, dignity, and simple passion. Virginius, for example, is the heroic Roman father who loves virtue and manliness, who serves his country loyally and unswervingly, who defends innocence and fights tyranny, and who, in the climax of the play, slays his adored only child to save her from dishonor. In this type of role, McCullough reached the zenith of his achievement. His success as Virginius is described by William Winter as follows: "It was a high, serious, noble work. . . . The sustained poetic exaltation of that embodiment, its unity as a grand and sympathetic personage, and its exquisite simplicity, were the qualities that gave it vitality in popular interest, and through those it possesses permanence in theatrical history. . . . The perfect finish of the performance, indeed, was little less than marvelous, when viewed with reference to the ever-increasing volume of power and the evident reality of afflicting emotion with which the part was carried." [40]

McCullough's style of acting was never colloquial or realistic in the manner of the man-in-the-street. The traditions of his time and the plays in which he appeared demanded an elevation of manner which included graceful and dignified action and smooth, poetic elocution. Such a manner did not mean, however, that the actor appeared static, cold, or unreal. For example, in McCullough's performance of Virginius, according to Winter, "The intention to be real . . . was obvious, through its harmonious fulfillment; yet the realism was shorn of all triteness, all animal excess. . . . McCullough did not present *Virginius* brushing his hair or paying *Virginia's* school-bills; yet he suggested him clearly and beautifully. . . ." [41]

McCullough was able to portray the elemental passions of rage, grief, and despair with force and fire but without the effect of ranting. Explosive strength was a mark of the Forrest school and McCullough had it—and used it effectively—yet in his mature period he was generally praised for his freedom from extravagance. One critic, for example, in reviewing McCullough's performance of Lear said: "His appeal to the winds and the elements when he is wandering in the storm is all the more effective because its vehemence and terrible earnestness are unmarred by an extravagance in declamation or action," [42] and Henry A. Clapp, in the *Boston Advertiser* for February 26, 1878, said that McCullough's Virginius "has dignity without bombast, and immense force without violence."

In his portrayal of emotion, McCullough evidently shared the feelings he was projecting to his audience. There is evidence of this even though the actor has left no record of his theories of acting or of his methods of performing a part. For example, fellow players have reported that after the scene in *Virginius* when the Roman father kills his own daughter, McCullough would often be shaking with emotion, his face wet with tears; on these occasions his fellow actors were careful not to speak to him or intrude on his suffering. Furthermore, in an interview with a journalist of the period, McCullough was asked if he could easily put off his character with his costume. "Not at all," answered McCullough, "often when I play *Lear* I remain Lear half the night, and awake next morning weary and nervous and unrefreshed." The reporter then asked if this meant that McCullough really experienced the same emotions as those of the character he was acting, and

McCullough answered: "Exactly . . . sometimes when I act *Virginius* I feel at the moment I despatch *Virginia* as though I were killing my own child." [43]

The solid success McCullough achieved in the roles which especially suited him came to a tragic end in 1884. For more than a year preceding this date, his health had begun to fail and he had noticed a decline in his dramatic power. He took a vacation from the stage and tried to rebuild his strength but, though he refused to recognize it, his affliction was mortal. He returned to the stage in the fall of 1884, but on September 29, at McVicker's Theatre in Chicago, he suffered a mental and physical breakdown and had to be helped from the stage. Later, he revived somewhat, but his mental deterioration could not be arrested. In June of 1885 he was placed in the Bloomingdale Sanitarium in New York City, where he remained for four months. At the end of this time he was moved to his home in Philadelphia, and died two weeks later, on November 8, 1885. His family and friends tried to conceal the nature of his illness, but it is known that he died of paresis, the result of congenital syphillis.

Few actors have been mourned so deeply and universally as John McCullough, and few actors have received, both in life and in death, the demonstrations of affection received by this actor. During his active career he was the recipient of innumerable honors, banquets, and receptions; after his death, and after the impressive funeral services which attracted thousands of mourners, an ornate monument was erected to his memory in the Mount Moriah Cemetery in Philadelphia. He will be remembered as a personality who was sincerely loved and admired by many thousands throughout the country; he will also be remembered as an actor who, within his range and limitations, achieved a generous measure of success.

OTHER DISCIPLES OF THE HEROIC SCHOOL

Although John McCullough came closest to being the Elisha to Edwin Forrest's Elijah, there were other gifted players who can be considered disciples of the heroic school and who at one time provided keen competition for Forrest. Among the most notable of these were the following: Augustus A. Addams, David Ingersoll, John R. Scott, Charles H. Eaton, Joseph Proctor, and J. Hudson Kirby. All of these men acted the leading roles in tragedy and melodrama, performing them in a robust, strenuous style. All of them, at some point in their careers, knew or acted with Edwin Forrest and thus had first-hand opportunity to observe the master and to learn from his success.

Addams, Ingersoll, Eaton, and Kirby must have been an unusually gifted and promising quartet. They all died before reaching the age of thirty, yet each, during his brief career, achieved national popularity. Augustus Addams, for example, "had every element physical and intellectual to place him in the highest niche of theatric fame." [44] He possessed a handsome, expressive face, a fine physique which he used with grace and confidence, and a voice of "great sweetness and power." Alfred Ayres thought he was superior to Edwin Booth as a tragedian [45] and many critics felt that he excelled Forrest in such heroic parts as Damon, Virginius, and Pierre, and would have eclipsed the old master if he had lived long enough.

David Ingersoll, who had barely reached the age of twenty-five when he died, was deemed a prodigy, according to William Winter, and was repeatedly described as "the silver tongued" by Lawrence Barrett. When Ingersoll was twenty-three years old he created the role of Jack Cade in the drama which was later to become a favorite of Edwin Forrest, and he too might have challenged Forrest's position had he lived longer.

Charles Eaton was called a "notable member of the Forrestian school" [46] and was said to have "few superiors in the histrionic arts." [47] Equal praise was given to J. Hudson Kirby, whose career lasted only ten years. He, too, was of the robustious, strenuous school of acting, although he did not possess the physical size or strength of other followers of the style. But the intensity of his emotional projection and the power of his voice were enough to win him a devoted following.

Joseph Proctor and John R. Scott both lived longer than the youthful quartet of Addams, Ingersoll, Eaton, and Kirby. For several years, John R. Scott was considered a dangerous rival to Forrest, although Wemyss asserts that "his reputation rested more upon the support he rendered Forrest, than any real merit of his own as a tragedian." [48] However, he was greatly admired for his commanding bearing and robust vigor and was a favorite with audiences of his time. When he appeared upon the British stage he displayed such power that, according to Lawrence Barrett, *The Times* of London said, "no actor possessing so many beauties and so many faults had ever been seen before upon the English stage." [49]

Joseph Proctor, although closely identified for many years with the leading role in *Nick of the Woods,* acted all the leading parts in tragedy and melodrama and developed a following in all the theatrical towns of the United States. He was by far the longest lived of Forrest's disciples, for his acting career covered almost sixty years, but even at the end of his career when Otis Skinner observed his acting, Proctor still exhibited the traits and methods of the heroic school.

It is interesting to note that all the performers of this school of acting achieved their greatest successes before so-called "popular" audiences. Forrest was the idol of the Bowery B'hoys and so were Scott, Kirby, Addams, and Proctor. All of them appeared repeatedly at the Bowery Theatre or the Chatham or the Franklin and less frequently, or never, at the more fashionable Park Theatre. When they visited London, they acted at such theatres as the Surrey more often than at Drury Lane or Covent Garden. Evidently their heroic, muscular style appealed strongly to the less sophisticated members of the public just as the muscular exploits of television's Western cowboys and gunmen appeal to the mass audiences of today.

Forrest and the style of acting he practiced had other followers, like J. A. Neafie, McKean Buchanan, and Daniel H. Harkins; in fact, Forrest's popularity begot what Alger calls "a whole brood of disciples." [50] Many of them, unfortunately, produced strange imitations or crude caricatures of the style and thus discredited it in the eyes of the public. Also, while Forrest and his disciples were still in their prime, the versatile tragedians of the classic school were developing a style of acting which was to become far more popular and influential than the heroic school. Nevertheless, the type of acting represented by certain aspects of the Forrest school has never completely disappeared. In the years which have followed the death of Forrest, occasional actors have appeared whose primary appeal has been their muscular physiques, manly bearing, and powerful voices. They have succeeded in heroic, masculine roles in which they were able to exploit their physical endowments in a realistic way. One of the best examples of this kind of actor was the New Jersey born Melbourne MacDowell, who flourished in the last quarter of the nineteenth century. His earliest role was that of Charles, the wrestler, in *As You Like It,* and his greatest success was achieved as Marc Antony in Sardou's *Cleopatra.* With his superb physique and his sincere, forthright manner, MacDowell was considered the perfect embodiment of the Roman warrior—just as Forrest and McCullough had been before him. Other actors of the same mould have followed him, and in our own time the brawny heroes of Western melodrama all suggest the physical attributes of the Forrest school. In the stock characters they play, they are not called upon to read blank verse or to thunder the lines of a Metamora or a Spartacus, but they must excel in physical strength and agility and must exercise them realistically in defense of justice and virtue. As long as this type of hero holds the stage, we shall not lack a reminder of the heroic style of acting so successfully practiced by Edwin Forrest, the first great American star.

II

THE CLASSIC SCHOOL:
THE LADIES

WHILE EDWIN FORREST AND HIS DISCIPLES WERE EARNING THE plaudits of American and foreign audiences, "there was being nurtured," says Lewis Strang, ". . . a class of players destined in the end to outlive and to outact the school of heroic histrionism of which Forrest was the founder." [1] I shall call this school of acting the classic school, using the term "classic" to indicate a manner of performance "of the first rank, perfect in its way, a model of its kind."

These players, from whose ranks came some of our greatest performers, were close to the traditions of the European theatre. Like their predecessors, they benefited from rich and varied apprenticeships in stock or repertory companies in which they appeared in parts which ranged from low comedy to high tragedy. They prided themselves on their range and versatility, and in their maturity they played the great roles of the standard drama, usually specializing in Shakespearean drama. They revered the art of acting as a noble calling of great usefulness and benefit to society and, as a result of their long apprenticeships, they acquired a mastery of the techniques of their art. They learned to move with grace and dignity; they learned to execute their actions economically and effectively. They also trained their voices to be flexible, responsive, and varied, so that their elocution was characterized by correct pronunciation and skillful management of cadence and poetic rhythm. Like the members of the Heroic School, they valued the art of elocution and worked constantly to perfect the beauty and clarity of their speech.

The classic players aimed to be "natural," but their concept of naturalness was not the literal imitation-of-nature method practiced by Forrest; neither was it, of course, the suppressed, suggestive method of the modern school of psychological realism. They utilized a heightened, idealized treatment of speech and action which suited the greater elaborateness and elegance of the social manners of their time. They would have considered ludicrous, for example, the idea of giving Prince Hamlet or King Lear the speech and manners of a contemporary businessman or of reading the blank verse of Shakespeare or the rhetoric of Bulwer-Lytton in the tones and cadences used when gossiping at a tea party. Their type of idealized "naturalness" would undoubtedly appear artificial to a twentieth-century audience but it was both appropriate and convincing when it was used in the great roles of the standard drama of the nineteenth century.

These actors and actresses prepared their movements and delivery artfully and carefully with the result that their performances, at their best, appeared graceful and effortless; at their worst, they seemed studied and artificial. They studied the texts of their plays, analyzed the characters, and sought to create a consistent, unified delineation which fitted the design of the drama, and which was not a series of "points" but a portrayal of even texture and logical development. Edwin Forrest was a careful student who studied and analyzed his characters exhaustively, but the influence of Edmund Kean often led Forrest to play up the big scenes and to slight the other parts of the play.

The outstanding actresses of the classic school were Mary Ann Duff, Charlotte Cushman, Mary Anderson, Fanny Janauschek, and Helena Modjeska. The great male performers of the school were Edwin Booth, James Murdoch, Edwin L. Davenport, and Lawrence Barrett. In performance these players did not merely project their own personalities into their parts but sought to transform their personalities enough to project the illusion of separate dramatic characters. Like the players of the heroic school, they generally experienced a feeling of identity with the dramatic character and felt the emotions of the role—without, however, losing critical consciousness or control of body and voice. Unlike the players of the heroic school, they avoided tricks or mannerisms or exhibitionism of any kind in their effects. The art of these nine players, together with the achievements of their followers, exemplified the American stage during most of the nineteenth century, for Mary Ann Duff began her American career in 1810, and Helena Modjeska made her farewell appearances in 1907.

MARY ANN DUFF

Many students of the theatre believe that Charlotte Cushman was the first great actress of the American stage. While it is true that she was the first native-born American woman to achieve top rank both at home and abroad, for twenty-five years preceding Miss Cushman's debut the stage of the United States was graced by a woman, English by birth but American by adoption, whom Joseph Ireland has called "the legitimate and undisputed Queen of the American stage." [2] She is the neglected and almost unknown tragedienne, Mrs. Mary Ann Duff.

Mrs. Duff, often called "the American Siddons," was born in London in 1794, the eldest child of an Englishman who served with the East India Company. Her maiden name was Dyke. In 1809, under her mother's tutelage and in the company of her two sisters, she made her stage debut as a dancer in Dublin, Ireland. The following year she married the actor, John R. Duff, and in the same year accompanied him to the United States and settled here. With the exception of a brief visit to England in 1827, she spent the remainder of her life in America and died in this country. It was in the United States that she learned the art of acting, built her career, and achieved her reputation as the foremost tragedienne of her time. Despite her foreign birth, she must be recognized as the first great actress of the American stage.

The records of Mrs. Duff's career are scanty. She left no diary or reminiscences. Only one brief biography has been written. Her active career extended from 1810 to 1838, a time when magazines and newspapers featuring dramatic criticism were relatively few. Her name has been forgotten and her achievements neglected, yet few actresses have ever received the amazing acclaim accorded Mrs. Duff by critics, public, and her great contemporaries. Fortunately, from the brief records which have survived it is possible to form a general idea of the style and effectiveness of her acting.

Beauty of face, grace of figure, and richness of voice were among Mrs. Duff's natural gifts. Joseph N. Ireland, her biographer, describes her thus:

She possessed a person of more than medium height, and of the most perfect symmetry,—not so commanding, perhaps, as that of Mrs. Siddons, but far more available, in her maturer years, for the youthful heroines of the drama, and far more graceful and pleasing to the eye than Miss Cushman ever possessed. Her face, called beautiful in her girlhood, throughout life was irradiated by eyes of the darkest hue and most speaking intelligence. The varying expression of her features has never been surpassed; while her voice was as soft and musical, in its quiet tones, as (we are told) was that of Mrs. Clibber,—wild and plaintive in its ejaculations of distraction and despair, yet resonant and thrilling in its forceful utterances.[3]

When Mrs. Duff arrived in the United States with her actor-husband, her only formal training had been in ballet. Her knowledge of acting, such as it was, had been learned from observation and a limited amount of practical experience. Physical appeal and personal charm were her principal assets. In her early appearances in Boston, where she and her husband had settled upon their arrival in America, she was praised for beauty, tenderness, and "expressive simplicity." She was frequently cast as a boy or a page so that she could exhibit her shapely figure. She was admired for the "unusual lustre" of her eyes. When she first acted Juliet, in 1810, she was complimented for *looking* the part, but was criticized for weakness of spirit. Critics said her style was indifferent and that she lacked both "conception and power."

For seven or eight years, Mrs. Duff's acting continued to be charming but weak. She was content to let her husband win the plaudits. Presently, however, John Duff began to lose his popularity. The support of the growing family of children rested more and more on Mrs. Duff. Apparently she decided she must exert herself to develop the latent talent which few people suspected she possessed. By 1817 her improvement was marked and caused favorable comment. In 1818 she played Juliet to the Romeo of the great English tragedian, Thomas A. Cooper, and this time it was said that in addition to youth and loveliness she had "the fervor and force of passion, the ecstasy of joy, and the agony of grief, terror, and despair combined in her most harmonious and powerfully developed personation." [4]

The Boston critics were astonished at her unexpected emergence as a powerful dramatic actress. W. W. Clapp said that suddenly, as if she were "touched by a magic wand" she discarded "the languor of indifference" and displayed "in vivid intensity the true fire of genius." [5]

Mrs. Duff's growing ambition received a powerful stimulus in 1821 when Edmund Kean visited Boston and she was assigned to act Ophelia to his Hamlet, Cordelia to his Lear, and Hermione to his Orestes. By this time Mrs. Duff had achieved a reputation for "passion and fire," but in her performances with Kean she outdid herself. In rehearsal Kean is said to have requested her to act with less force and intensity "as he merely desired his efforts seconded, not rivalled." [6] In performance, Mrs. Duff won applause equal to Kean's and so impressed the great tragedian that he declared she was superior to any actress on the British stage. It is said that he often repeated this opinion.

Mrs. Duff continued to demonstrate her newly developed powers and to win increased popularity and praise. The elder Booth, after acting with her in *Lear* and *Hamlet,* described her as the greatest actress in the world. Edwin Forrest, Thomas A. Cooper, and William Conway all spoke of her as the finest leading lady of their experience.

Mrs. Duff continued to act, chiefly in Boston and Philadelphia, until 1835. She also appeared in New York and won a host of admirers. However, her career in New York is peculiar. She played chiefly at the smaller theatres, like the Franklin and the Richmond Hill, and never filled an extended engagement at the larger, more fashionable playhouses. Her following among the press and the public was devoted and worshipful, but it did not include the "dilettanti" of the city, who seem to have ignored her because of her "provincial" background. This did not prevent the New York *Mirror* in 1826 from declaring: "The opinion lately expressed . . . that this lady is superior to any actress on the American or British stage, we think has every probability of being correct, and we are more and more inclined to believe in it every time we witness her performance." [7] Furthermore, it did not prevent the eminent Horace Greeley from visiting the Richmond Hill theatre, in 1832, and recording in his *Recollections of a Busy Life* that, ". . . I saw Mrs. Duff personate Lady Macbeth better than it has since been done in this city. . . . I doubt that any woman has since played in our city—and I am thinking of Fanny Kemble—who was the superior to Mrs. Duff in a wide range of tragic characters." [8]

In 1836, Mrs. Duff, who had been a widow for some years, married J. G. Seaver, an attorney. She accompanied him to New Orleans and became a permanent resident of that city. In 1837 and 1838 she played brief engagements in New Orleans and then, becoming deeply religious, she retired from the stage. She lived in self-imposed obscurity until her death, which occurred in New York in 1857.

The acting of Mrs. Duff in her maturity was very different from her early style. As she matured, she retained great personal magnetism and in addition she learned to project strong emotion and to stir her audiences by the controlled intensity of her feelings. She did not imitate the tempestuous outbursts of Kean, but developed a quiet, sustained force which was powerfully suggestive rather than openly exhibitionistic. The noted manager, N. M. Ludlow, described Mrs. Duff as "refined, quiet, yet powerful; not boisterous, yet forcible; graceful in all her motions, and dignified without stiffness." [9] Incidentally, he adds that she was "undoubtedly the best tragic actress of the United States."

Mrs. Duff was praised for her freedom from mannerisms and for her avoidance of tricks. She did not rely upon making "points," that is, she did not alternate startling dramatic flourishes with dull and careless scenes. She treated each line and each scene with thoughtful care and thus achieved a uniform excellence in her acting which created admiring comment. The New York *Mirror* of May 5, 1827, says:

Mrs. Duff has *one* great characteristic—one peculiarity that strikes all who see her, and this is uniformity of excellence. . . . From beginning to end you see before you only the character she is personating. The unity of her conception, the *oneness,* is remarkable. No temptation can induce her to break it. If a scene offers ever so much opportunity for display, and it is not authorized by the whole design and tenor of the part, she suffers it to pass unembraced. . . . Kean startled us with electric flashes—Mrs. Barnes occasionally shines with great vividness—but Mrs. Duff pours out one unceasing blaze during the whole time she occupies the stage. . . .

In her maturity, Mrs. Duff learned to identify herself with her characters and to lose herself in her parts. During the performance of great roles she became completely absorbed and seemed to forget both herself and her audience. One critic said: "She seems to have a separate existence during the continuance of the play, and to have lost all knowledge, and even all power of seeing the realities around her." [10] Despite such absorption there is no evidence that her control and self-discipline were ever relaxed.

In achieving her effects, Mrs. Duff had the assistance of an unusually affecting voice. It was variously described by critics as "full and mellow," "powerful and harmonious," "plaintively tender," and "thrillingly expressive." But the phrase most frequently applied to it was "soul subduing." Though this phrase was not explained, it evidently meant that Mrs. Duff's voice had a quality which stirred the emotions of pity and tenderness very powerfully. Over and over the critics mention the "melting hearts" and the "streaming eyes" of Mrs. Duff's listeners.

The roles which Mrs. Duff acted most successfully and with the greatest popular appeal were those portraying grief, sacrifice, and noble suffering. She excelled in *The Distrest Mother* and *The Stranger,* in which she varied pathetic appeal with "lightening flashes of scorn and indignation." As Madame Clermont in *Adrian and Orilla* she achieved "the best sustained delineation of maternal affectation" which Edmund Kean had ever witnessed.[11] As Ophelia and Cordelia she was said to have no peer. Lewis Strang reports that: "Bathed in tears she was absolutely irresistible." [12]

Mrs. Duff's success as a generator of tears relates her to a long line of actresses who have excelled in this ability. But many of these belong to a school which can be described as "emotionalistic" because they confined themselves exclusively to tear-producing roles and to the limited techniques associated with these roles. Mrs. Duff played many other parts with eminent success. Ireland lists a minimum of 220 characters she acted during the twenty-eight years of her stage career. These parts included everything from farce to high tragedy and indicate a considerable degree of versatility. It was in the grand roles of Lady Macbeth and Queen Katherine that Mrs. Duff was supreme. In pathetic roles such as Hermione and Mrs. Haller she won a tremendous popular following. A fair percentage of comedy roles appear in the repertory, but in these roles, though Mrs. Duff acted with competence, she did not excel. Katherine, in *The Taming of the Shrew,* was her most successful comic character because, Ireland conjectures, little gaiety or joyousness is required in the portrayal. Her contributions to American acting, although now forgotten and ignored, were so impressive that they prompted the great comedian, John Gilbert, to declare more than twenty years after her death: "Mrs. Duff was the most exquisite tragic actress I ever saw, and I make no exceptions." [13]

CHARLOTTE CUSHMAN

In the same year (1835) that Mary Ann Duff was playing her farewell engagement in New York City, nineteen-year-old Charlotte Cushman, descendent of one of the Pilgrim Fathers, was making her debut in Boston. Miss Cushman's first appearance was not as an actress; it was as a singer in Mozart's *Marriage of Figaro*. She had been prepared for her debut by the coaching of James G. Maeder and the assistance of the celebrated vocalist, Mrs. Mary Ann Wood. She was successful enough to win favorable attention, and shortly after her Boston appearance she accepted an engagement in New Orleans, where she promptly ruined her singing voice by overstraining it in a large theatre. Since she was poor and burdened with the support of her mother, brothers, and sister, she desperately looked for some other employment, and was advised to try her luck as an actress. Without any professional dramatic training she launched a career which was eventually to win her great wealth and the topmost rank among American actresses.

After Miss Cushman's dramatic debut in New Orleans, she returned to the North and played in stock for eight years. Slowly and earnestly she learned the secrets of her profession. She had no formal instruction, but relied upon experience and observation to teach her. She was able to watch the work of many excellent players. The first of these to influence her were Thomas A. Cooper and Mrs. Powell. Both players were English by birth and training and they maintained the tradition of the stately Kembles. It is believed that the dignity and majesty of Cushman's manner were due, in part, to her admiration of the grand style of Cooper and Powell. Perhaps she received additional impetus toward this style from her early stage managers—Mr. Barton, of New Orleans, who was familiar with the acting of Sarah Siddons, and Peter Richings of New York, an English actor of the old school who was influential at the Park Theatre when Miss Cushman first acted there.

In 1843, the eminent tragedian William Macready played an engagement at the Park Theatre and Cushman supported him in several important roles. Macready was impressed by her ambition and undisciplined power, and took a sympathetic interest in her development. Cushman, in turn, was amazed at the polish and artistry of Macready's acting. In comparison, her own style was crude and uncontrolled. She resolved to discover his method and apply his techniques. From him she learned to study patiently, to examine the text and analyze the characters, and to search for the subtler meanings which might lie beneath the surface of a role. She also learned that all her efforts should be controlled; that both words and actions should be disciplined to fulfill the overall design of the character and the play. "It must have been a curious fellowship," says Edward Robins, "with inspiration on the one side, and, on the other side, abundance of merit without one flash of inspiration." [14] But the association was most fruitful for Miss Cushman. She maintained she had "groped in the darkness until she met Mr. Macready and learned his method" and after learning it, her performances acquired "a harmony and completeness" which they had never before possessed.[15]

Macready urged the young actress to visit London and gain the experience of playing with an English company. Borrowing the necessary money for her passage, Miss Cushman made the trip and it proved to be a turning point in her career. Until this time her rise on the American stage had been steady but not spectacular. The box-office record of the plays in which she appeared shows receipts ranging from $100 to $250 per performance. Not until 1841, when she created the role of Lady Gay Spanker in *London Assurance,* did her appearances attract larger houses. *London Assurance* brought receipts which ranged from $418.50 to $848.00.[16] However, after her conspicuous success in England, where for almost five years her Bianca, her Rosalind, her Queen Katherine, and her Romeo were hailed as masterpieces, she returned in triumph to the United States. The actress had acquired the glamor of a foreign reputation, and her acting had gained authority and polish. Crowded houses and critical hosannas now greeted her appearances. She was judged to be the best American tragedienne, a reputation which she maintained until her final retirement in 1875.

Just as Edwin Forrest's physique and temperament exerted a powerful influence on his manner of acting, so did Cushman's appearance and personality affect her style. She was a tall woman, with square shoulders and a sturdy frame. Her forehead was high and broad, her nose retroussé, and her chin prominent. Her bluish-grey eyes, which were large and expressive, were by far her finest feature and "gave an air of refinement to an otherwise plain and unattractive face." [17] Though her movements were somewhat ungraceful and awkward, she gave the impression of strength and dignity. She was generally described as commanding, rather than handsome, and as masculine in appearance, rather than dainty or feminine.

There was a streak of masculinity in Miss Cushman's temperament, too. As a child she was a tomboy who smashed dolls, climbed trees, and tyrannized over her brothers and sister. As a woman she was hard-headed and practical and enjoyed acting the masculine roles of Romeo, Cardinal Wolsey, Hamlet, and Claude Melnotte. Sometimes in her portrayals she exercised the same tyranny she had once used on her small brothers and sister. For example, George Vandenhoff said that in her early performances as Lady Macbeth she positively bullied the Thane. She "gets him into a corner . . . ," says Vandenhoff, and "as one sees her large clenched hand and muscular arm threatening him, in alarming proximity, one feels that if other arguments fail with her husband, she will have recourse to blows." [18]

It is not surprising that with her particular physical and mental endowments Cushman should have avoided the tender feminine roles and excelled in those parts which, when not completely masculine, showed the strength and audacity of a Lady Macbeth, or the majesty of a Queen Katherine, or the bizarre physical power of a Meg Merrilies. "Her true forte," said one critic, "is the character of a woman where most of the softer traits of womanhood are wanting . . . or in characters where, roused by passion or incited by some earnest and long-cherished determination, the woman, for the time being, assumes all the power and energy of manhood." [19]

If Miss Cushman's endowments hindered her assumption of certain roles, they were nevertheless her principal assets, for they enabled her to act great roles greatly and to project a stage magnetism which few players have ever equaled. "She was incarnate power:" says William Winter, "she dominated by intrinsic authority: she was a woman born to command: and of such minds as comprehend authentic leadership she achieved immediate, complete, and permanent conquest. There was, in her personality, a massive excellence that made admiration natural and entirely justified it." [20] Alfred Ayres felt that she could have ruled an empire and doubted if either Catherine of Russia or Elizabeth of England possessed her all-around mental gifts. Kate Reignolds said she did not woo her audience, she "seized upon them." This unusual power caused Lewis Strang to write: "As regards the potent spell of her personality, there can be no dispute, for scarcely a critic writes of her in cold blood and with satisfactory analysis." [21]

The unique power of Cushman's personality was enhanced by an unusual voice. Overstraining on the opera stage had left her speaking voice with a husky, hollow quality. Pure, ringing, elastic tones had given way to what Murdoch terms "a quality of aspiration and a woody or veiled tone." This unique quality, plus wide range and unusual power, made Miss Cushman's voice capable of effects which few players could duplicate. She was able to express intense, sustained grief without loudness or sudden variations. She could also rise to great vocal heights in scenes of anger or denunciation. Lawrence Barrett recounts that in her death scene as Nancy Sykes, when she called for Bill Fagin and begged him to kiss her, she sounded as if she "spoke through blood." Henry Austin Clapp reports that in her final scenes as Queen Katherine her use of the "sick" tone of voice surpassed anything of its kind he had ever heard. Adam Badeau declares that her superb vocal control enabled her "to break it with age, to thicken it with the choking sensation of death, to loosen it in the cry of agony, to repress it in the hollow murmur of despair." [22]

Not only was she great in coloring her voice with whatever emotion the scene demanded, Miss Cushman was also a superb elocutionist. In her reading, every syllable and every word were distinct, yet the full beauty of the rhythm and the balance of the lines were preserved. Intellectual content was not neglected; full expression was given to the significance of every phrase and every line. Alfred Ayres, who prized elocution above all dramatic virtues, said that Cushman and Forrest were the only great elocutionists this country has produced, and he approved the statement that in Miss Cushman's reading the meaning of the author was "as clear, as transparent, as if the thoughts themselves . . . were transfused through the senses." [23] James O'Neill, who acted Macbeth and Wolsey with her, declared that "she got more out of the language than anyone I have ever listened to." [24]

Miss Cushman believed that to project strong emotion a player must himself feel the emotion—especially if he is an English or American actor. The person of Anglo-Saxon blood, she explained, has too much self-consciousness to impress an audience if he does not lose himself in his part.[25] She testified that she felt the passion she assumed in her roles, and her fellow actors agreed that she indeed seemed to live everything that she did on the stage.

She saw to it that the painstaking care which Macready taught her to use in the study of a role was also applied to staging the plays in which she appeared. At rehearsals she was particular in the utmost detail. She insisted that every movement and gesture and piece of business be carefully worked out before a performance. Catherine Reignolds-Winslow recounts how Cushman rehearsed her for hours in a scene which took only thirty seconds to play—but the scene, when perfected, earned "deafening applause" in performance. Clumsy or careless work was abhorred by Miss Cushman, and when she achieved stardom she desired only expert and experienced players around her. In 1851 she wrote to J. B. Wright, manager of the National Theatre, Boston, and begged him not to engage a certain aspiring but inexperienced young actress. "I really have not the courage to act with novices," she said.[26]

The high standards Miss Cushman demanded of herself and her associates grew out of the pride she took in her profession and the earnestness with which she pursued her career. She believed that acting was the greatest of the arts, and that a genuine actor was one of God's gifted creatures. In a letter to Miss Elizabeth Peabody of Boston, she wrote: "But no one knows better than myself after all my association with artists of sculpture or painting, how truly my art comprehends all the others and surpasses them, in so far as the study of mind is more than matter. Victor Hugo makes one of his heroines, an actress, say, 'My art endows me with a searching eye, a knowledge of the soul and the soul's workings. . . .' This is a truth more or less powerful as one is more or less truly gifted by the good God." [27]

The earnestness and sincerity of Miss Cushman's attitude toward the stage was evident in all her work, and it was the theme of her farewell address to the theatre-goers of New York. On the evening of November 7, 1874, after her final performance at Booth's Theatre, Miss Cushman told the huge assemblage which had gathered to honor her: "I found life sadly real and intensely earnest, and in my ignorance of other ways of study I resolved to take therefrom my test and my watchword—to be thoroughly in earnest, intensely in earnest, in all my thoughts and in all my actions, whether in my profession or out of it, became my one single idea. And I honestly believe that therein lies the secret of my success in life. I do not believe that any great success, in any art, can be achieved without it." [28]

With the aid of a strong body, a powerful personality, a keen intellect, an unusual voice, a lofty ambition, and a large measure of dramatic genius, Miss Cushman inevitably developed an impressive manner of acting. Her style, as it finally evolved, had sweep and power and majesty. She painted with bold strokes and unmixed colors. Her characters emerged in heroic outline. Subtlety of coloration and fineness of detail were sometimes added, but these, in general, were distinctly subordinate. Some observers felt the lack of poetic imagination in her portrayals. Others believed that the poetry was present but it was epic rather than lyric in nature. James Murdoch says that she was "intensely prosaic" and although her understanding was keen and penetrating, "that glow of feeling which springs from the center of emotional elements was not a prominent constituent of her organization." [29] On the other hand, William Winter declared that "though she insisted on the basis of fact in acting, she was not mindless of the essential spirit of poetry. In each of her supreme performances—that spirit suffused the impersonation and made it radiant with intrinsic light." [30]

Miss Cushman's playing was sometimes sublime, but in the bold free style of her acting there lurked the danger of melodrama. At times, it is said, she was overly expressive and extravagant. Her Meg Merrilies was too wild and sensational for some tastes. Her Lady Macbeth occasionally exhibited an excess of physical energy. Often she was praised for the expressive force of her looks, gait, and gestures, but on one occasion an unkind critic described her movements as "a galvanized distortion of nature" and said that her constant activity conveyed the impression that she was "suffering under a violent attack of the colic." [31]

Another characteristic of Miss Cushman's style, at least in her later years, was a certain degree of "staginess." Her artful pauses seemed planned; her bold strokes seemed deliberate and calculated. A perceptive observer was conscious of the design and mechanism of her creations. A certain exaggeration of manner must have become habitual with Miss Cushman even when she was off the stage. She often visited the families of her friends, and Dr. S. R. Elliott, who enjoyed many of these visits, says: ". . . we grew to disregard the somewhat overexpressiveness with which she seemed freighted, and to regard, as evidences of genius, her reference to the weather in a hollow tone of voice, or her asking the hour with the solemn severity of a sibyl!" [32]

During Miss Cushman's career on the stage she acted at least 188 different roles. These covered every kind of character from low comedy to high tragedy. Such a wide variety of experience was not unusual for an actress in the mid-nineteenth century. Utility players in the stock companies of the time were required to act almost any part in any play at any time. Specialization did not come until the novice had served a thorough apprenticeship in all manner of roles. Charlotte Cushman was trained in this school, and the comedy parts in her record date mostly from the early years. It is strange to imagine her acting Beatrice or Lady Teazle or Lady Gay Spanker, but she did perform these roles, often with genuine effectiveness. However, as she gained experience and prestige, she dropped the more uncongenial parts from her repertory and specialized in the characters of high tragedy. Within this field she demonstrated a remarkable degree of versatility. Her successful parts, in addition to Lady Macbeth, Queen Katherine, and Meg Merrilies, included such widely different characters as Mrs. Haller in *The Stranger,* Bianca in *Fazio* (the part in which she made her London debut), Rosalind in *As You Like It,* Pauline and the Widow Melnotte in *The Lady of Lyons,* Portia in *The Merchant of Venice,* Belvidera in *Venice Preserved,* and the male roles of Romeo, Cardinal Wolsey, Hamlet, and Claude Melnotte. Here is a range which must have been impressive even in an age of versatility!

It seems strange to playgoers of today that Charlotte Cushman could act masculine roles with considerable success. Her foremost achievement in this line was Romeo. She had acted the part with success in America, but it was in England that her portrayal of the role became a sensation. She staged it in London late in 1845 with her sister Susan as the Juliet. The play ran for eighty nights and received almost unanimous critical praise. The reviewers thought she looked the part very well, affirming that her voice, her walk, and her general deportment perfectly conveyed the illusion of a dashing young man.* Especially praised was her fresh interpretation which discarded the hackneyed conventions of the character and created a Romeo who was a living, breathing, ardent human being. An occasional critic was

---

* The following story, to illustrate Miss Cushman's nerve and manly temper as Romeo, is told by Clara E. Clement in her book *Charlotte Cushman* (Boston, 1882, pp. 67–68): "At the National Theatre, Boston, during the season of 1851–52, as she was playing Romeo to the Juliet of Miss Anderton, in the midst of one of the most romantic passages between the lovers, some person in the house sneezed in such a manner as to attract the attention of the whole audience, and everyone knew the sneeze was artificial and derisive. Miss Cushman immediately stopped the dialogue, and led Miss Anderton off the stage, as a cavalier might lead a lady from a place where an insult had been offered her. She then returned to the footlights and said in a clear, firm voice, 'Some man must put that person out, or I shall be obliged to do it myself.' The fellow was taken away; the audience rose *en masse* and gave three cheers for Miss Cushman, who recalled her companion and proceeded with the play as if nothing had happened. . . ."

shocked at the spectacle of a woman playing the part and at the "un-sexing of the mind and heart" which the actress underwent in assuming the role. The great majority, however, were lavish in their praise. The peak in enthusiasm was reached by the eminent dramatist and experienced man of the theatre, Sheridan Knowles, who exclaimed in a letter to a friend:

I witnessed on Wednesday night with astonishment the Romeo of Miss Cushman! Unanimous and lavish as were the encomiums of the London press, I was not prepared for such a triumph of pure genius. You recall, perhaps, Kean's third act of Othello? Did you ever expect to see anything like it again? I never did; and yet I saw as great a thing last Wednesday night in Romeo's scene with the Friar, after the sentence of banishment. . . . It was a scene of top-most passion!—not simulated passion—no such thing—real, palpably real! . . . I listened and gazed and held my breath, while my blood ran hot and cold. . . . I particularize this scene, because it is the most powerful; but every scene exhibited the same truthfulness. . . . My heart and mind are so full of this extraordinary—most extraordinary performance—that I declare I know not where to stop or how to go on! Throughout it was a triumph, equal to the proudest of those I used to witness years ago, and for a repetition of which I have looked in vain until now. There is no trick in Miss Cushman's performance. No thought, no interest, no feeling, seems to actuate her, except what might be looked for in Romeo himself, were Romeo reality.[33]

Upon Miss Cushman's return to the United States, she played Romeo many times for the American public. Her success in the part continued to be great in spite of the minority opinion which deprecated the unnatural spectacle of a woman, in male costume, making passionate love to another woman. A photograph of Miss Cushman as Romeo shows a large lady wearing a skirt-like costume of knee length, a fancy sword, white hose, black slippers, and a cap set rakishly on a rather thick head of hair. The figure is broad of hip and full of bosom and, to the modern eye, looks precisely like what it is: a large woman of middle age masquerading as a man. Such a photograph, lacking the living personality and genius of Charlotte Cushman, conveys an unhappy impression of the Romeo which so many people found stirring and convincing.

Little fault can be found with either the photographs or the records of Miss Cushman's acting in her three greatest roles: Lady Macbeth, Meg Merrilies, and Queen Katherine. In the first two characters Miss

Cushman was memorable, but to most observers Queen Katherine was her masterpiece.

Although many reviews of Miss Cushman's impersonation of Queen Katherine survive, no better description can be found, perhaps, than the one contained in Clapp's *Reminiscences*. He reports that Miss Cushman made Katherine "a document in human flesh, to show how a heavenly minded humility may be a wellspring of dignity. . . ." In the early scenes of the play, Miss Cushman emphasized the grandeur and simplicity of the Queen. In the second act, Katherine's appeal to the King was given with an "unstudied eloquence" which Clapp believed could not be surpassed by any player. In the fourth act, after Katherine is deposed, Miss Cushman's "genius and art found their loftiest and most exquisite expression." It was here that the homely, discarded wife used the "sick" tone of voice which was so unique and so profoundly moving. Miss Cushman "avoided excess with the nicest art, but quietly colored the whole scene with this natural factor of pathos." As the scene progressed, she portrayed nobility, pity, magnanimity, weariness, and unearthly sweetness. Clapp writes that after her vision of the "blessed troop, . . . Her cry, out of the depth of her great storm-beaten heart, of infinite longing for the rest of paradise . . . will be recalled today by thousands of men and women, and at this mere mention the lines will echo and reecho through the chambers of their memories." As the scene continues, Katherine is aroused to queenly anger for a moment, then she relaxes and in a broken voice delivers the final messages of meekness and affection which are to be given to her daughter and her false husband. In these words of farewell, says Clapp, "the supreme point of pathos was reached. The throb and thrill of her voice . . . deserve never to be forgotten. . . . Throughout the final fifty verses of the scene, Miss Cushman caused Katherine's voice to grow gradually thicker, as the night of death closed in upon sight and speech. But Katherine's last command, that she 'be used with honour' after her death . . . was superb and majestic." [34]

In the opinion of her admirers, the whole art of this unusual woman and consummate actress deserves this same description: superb and majestic.

HELENA MODJESKA AND FANNY JANAUSCHEK

The classic school of acting, brilliantly exemplified in the United States by the careers of such early tragediennes as Mary Ann Duff and Charlotte Cushman, was carried on by two foreign born actresses who adopted America as their native land and who enriched the American stage by the artistry of their acting. Fanny Janauschek (Franziska Magdalena Romance Janauschek) and Helena Modjeska (Helena Modjeska Chlapowski, Countess Bozenta) were both stars when they came to this country. Janauschek, born in Prague in 1830, had been educated for the stage in Germany where, at the age of eighteen, she became the leading actress in Frankfurt-am-Main. She remained in Germany for twenty years, winning adulation and renown as one of the greatest tragediennes of Europe. Decorations and honors were heaped upon her by the princes and rulers of many states, so when she made her American debut in 1867 it was as a star of the first magnitude. Helena Modjeska, although an actress of equal fame in Europe, came to the United States as an immigrant rather than as a star. She had been born in Cracow, Poland, in 1840, and had received her first theatrical training in a small provincial stock company organized and directed by her husband. At the age of twenty-five she returned to Cracow and made a successful debut. Three years later she was invited to appear at the Imperial Theatre in Warsaw where, it is said, her triumph was the greatest ever known in the annals of that theatre. She was engaged for life as the leading lady of the Imperial Theatre and for seven years was the reigning actress of the nation. In 1876, nine years after Janauschek made her debut, Modjeska traveled to California with a group of other Poles to establish an ideal colony where she could regain her health, which was failing, and where she could escape the oppressive Russian regime in Poland. It was only when the colony failed that Modjeska returned to the stage, making an unheralded debut at the California Theatre in San Francisco in the year 1877. Her genius was recognized instantly; she appeared in New York before the year was over, and was soon accepted as the great actress she was known to be in Europe.

Modjeska made her American debut in English, which she had learned in a period of six months after her resolve to become an American actress. She never lost her foreign accent but, although some of the critics felt that it marred the beauty of her delivery and the meaning of her lines, the public as a whole accepted her accent and considered it "a piquant sauce to her acting." Janauschek, on the other hand, made her first American appearances in German, sometimes performing with German speaking actors and sometimes with an English speaking company. Persuaded by Augustin Daly to learn English, she retired from the stage for a year, and reappeared in 1870 as an English speaking actress. Like Modjeska, she never lost her accent —it always remained "noticeably marked"—but, as was the case with Modjeska, the defect of an accent "in no wise hindered or even marred the dramatic effect of her acting." [35]

In the first years after her debut as an English speaking actress, Janauschek achieved such popularity and success on the American stage that, following a return to Germany, she decided to make her home in the United States. For some time her career prospered, but presently the public taste for her style of acting began to decline and she slowly sank in popularity and fortune. When she died in Brooklyn in 1904, she was both impoverished and forgotten. Modjeska, on the other hand, maintained her hold on the public to the end of her career. She played almost continuously from the time of her American debut in 1877 until her last tour in 1907, which she was forced to cut short because of ill health. She died in California two years later, on April 8, 1909.

Although there are many similarities in the careers of Fanny Janauschek and Helena Modjeska, and although they both acted in the classic tradition, their styles of performance were markedly different. Janauschek's acting was intense, powerful, heroic. She was the ideal Brunhilde or Medea. Modjeska's acting, in contrast, was graceful, symmetrical, poetic. She excelled in such roles as Viola, Rosalind, and Adrienne Lecouvreur. The contrasting styles of the two actresses might be compared to the differences between Charlotte Cushman and Mary Ann Duff.

The contrasting physical attributes of Janauschek and Modjeska were powerful factors in shaping their respective styles. Janauschek was short and thick of stature, her figure being described as "majestic," "stately," or "massive." Her voice, which had been trained for grand opera, was deep, vibrant, and flexible, capable of great range and power. Her face, like Charlotte Cushman's, was not beautiful, but it was strong and expressive. "Nature planned her for heroic parts," [36] says Philip Hale, who reviewed her acting for the Boston *Journal*. Modjeska, in contrast to Janauschek, was slender and graceful of figure; she had a finely moulded face with a well-shaped nose, a sensitive mouth, and large, dark, luminous eyes. Walter Prichard Eaton described her face as "interesting, expressive, and gracious rather than conventionally beautiful," [37] but the majority of critics seem to disagree with him because she is usually praised for possessing "a rich, sensuous beauty." [38] Modjeska's voice was well modulated, musical, and flexible —in many roles impressing the hearers with the qualities of sweetness and refinement. However, when the situation demanded it, Modjeska could produce deep, strong tones—an accomplishment which was the result of careful training. Early in her career, she tells us, she worked an hour or more a day on exercises designed to add deep tones and strength to her voice.[39] However, she never acquired the power and range which were Janauschek's by natural endowment.

Perhaps Janauschek's outstanding gift as an actress was her tragic intensity. She preferred the great roles where power and passion are required, and she had the requisite strength to embody these roles. Her playing always suggested reserves of power and emotion which she could unleash at the required times with startling effects. John R. Towse recalls that she endowed her Brunhilde "with a majestic dignity and thoroughly heroic passion" and that by means of her "imperious carriage, fiery declamation, noble gesture . . . she realized the grandeur of the mythical personage." [40] He described her Lady Macbeth as "murderous in her ambition and energetic in the prompting of her husband to murder, but she loved him passionately and in her own tigress fashion, tenderly." [41] Philip Hale, in reviewing her acting, characterized Janauschek as "An heroic woman, suggesting primeval emotions; titanic in outbursts of passion." [42]

Although Janauschek was great in the delineation of strong feeling, she was capable of a wide variety of subtler effects. Her Mary Stuart was praised for the "depths of pathos" which she sounded, and her dual role in *Chesney Wold*, an adaptation of Charles Dickens' *Bleak House*, was tremendously admired for the range of emotions exhibited by the actress: she played both the "coquettishly sensual, maliciously sly, vitriolically minded French maid" and the "cold, haughty, arrogant Lady Dedlock, who, in spite of her caste and pride, had known passion, and shame as the reward of passion." [43]

In all her portrayals, Janauschek was superb in her use of facial expression and meaningful gesture. Her face and eyes mirrored and reflected the emotions she was portraying, and her slightest movement added to the effect. Otis Skinner, who once acted Seyton to Janauschek's Lady Macbeth, recounts that when she turned on him in an early scene of the play and opened her eyes wide, "it was the unmasking of a battery" and it gave him "a distinct electric shock." [44] Towse recalls that one of the finest strokes of Janauschek's acting in the banquet scene of Macbeth was her shielding the face of her husband from his own terrible visions "while she turned upon the audience a face bloodless, drawn, and lined with despairing pity." [45] Otis Skinner also affirms that Janauschek "could be almost as eloquent with scarves and hangings as in her voice and gesture" [46] and he recalls that she could stop in the middle of a sentence to rearrange her draperies and make the action both eloquent and dramatic.

Janauschek conveyed the illusion of complete absorption in her roles. Spectators forgot that she was assuming a part and identified her with the dramatic character she was portraying. Janauschek sustained this illusion through technical mastery of her art; in actual fact, she did not allow herself to be swept away by the emotions she was projecting. She never forgot to exercise conscious, artistic control of her effects. Otis Skinner, recalling the days when he was a novice in her company, says: "I have seen old Madame Janauschek, after a tragic scene, turn up stage, carefully arranging her drapery, and speaking a flippant aside to a supporting player, while the audience sat spellbound." [47] It was from this example, and others like it, that Skinner learned the important lesson that an emotional debauch on the part of the player "is not an expression of feeling in acting"; the spectators are the ones "to supply the emotion," the actor "supplies the suggestion." [48] Janauschek, in her prime, could supply the suggestion so powerfully that audiences accepted her as the living embodiment of the emotions she portrayed, and her fellow artist, Helena Modjeska, was moved to exclaim of her, "what genius! I wish I possessed half her powers." [49]

The tragic intensity which Janauschek brought to her roles was sometimes achieved by Modjeska, but tenderness, pathos, and lyrical romance were more characteristic of her acting. Again and again, spectators and critics alike were impressed by her grace, her daintiness, her innocence and joy, her womanly sweetness, her delicate pathos, her tenderness, her dignity and refinement, and her irresistible personal charm. William Winter says that "to think of her now is . . . to remember a presence of tender, poetic beauty, winning refinement, and perfect grace." [50] Added to these traits was an illusive, haunting quality which was difficult for a spectator to define, but which was vividly perceived by all who watched Modjeska's acting. John Creahan called it "that minor-like chord which seems to be a part of her being, which we have never discovered in any other actress. . . ." [51] Walter Prichard Eaton characterized the same quality as "an indefinable atmosphere of poetic elevation." [52] Jeanette Gilder called it a "charm so subtle, that we can find nothing to criticize"; while Otis Skinner, after describing Modjeska as "a wraith of a woman with a voice whose every cadence contained a caress" said "I know no better way to describe her Camille than to say it had fragrance." [53] Skinner further states that Modjeska's personal magic made the immoral *Camille* so captivating that "mamas were apprehensive of its effect upon their sons."

In creating a part, Modjeska always used the intellectual approach. She had to have a clear mental picture of her characters and to understand the workings of their minds before she could embody them. "I never undertake a role unless I can see it before me," she declared.[54] Her careful analysis of her parts was, unquestionably, one reason for the symmetry and balance of her conceptions and for the even texture of her acting. Perceptive spectators were always aware of a logic and consistency in her portrayals. The early scenes in her plays presaged the final scenes, and in the course of the action her characters progressively fulfilled a design which showed that the actress had firm grasp of a fully developed concept of the character. As the critic of the Brooklyn *Eagle* said, it was "the exquisite harmony, and proportion of all her scenes to each other" which placed her "upon a higher plane than actors who have more power in single moments." [55]

Another probable reason for the symmetry and even texture of Modjeska's acting was her practice of learning the words and actions of her roles at the same time. She did not memorize lines and then create the action to accompany the words but, as Mrs. Otis Skinner records after rehearsing with her in a new comedy, Modjeska "never learns [her part] by rote, but always goes through it, 'suiting the action to the word, the word to the action.' Only at the very last did she run through the lines without the business." [56]

Modjeska, like Janauschek, had mastered the techniques of her art through careful study and long apprenticeship and, in general, her technical skill was greatly admired. However, she was sometimes criti-

cized for permitting the mechanics of her art to show and for performing in a cold and studied manner. On certain occasions the critics were
disturbed because they detected the careful planning behind every
physical movement and every vocal inflection of the actress. Such a
reaction seems to contradict Modjeska's own statement that ". . . I
really passed through all the emotions of my heroines. I suffered with
them, cried real tears . . . during my whole career I could not succeed
in giving a performance without feeling the agonies of my heroines." [57]
If Modjeska were able to identify herself so completely with her heroines that she always relived their agonies, how could she have appeared
cold and studied on certain occasions? The answer seems to be that
although she may have aimed at close identification with her characters
during each performance, she sometimes failed of inspiration—as
every actor does on occasion—and so had to rely on a studied technique for her effects. As William Winter remarked, ". . . Modjeska,
like all great artists, was not invariably able to liberate all her facilities
and rise to her loftiest height," [58] but these occasional lapses do not
negate the impression that Modjeska's acting usually exhibited a beautiful balance of technique and inspiration.

Although Modjeska and Janauschek differed in temperament and in
certain aspects of style, they both had undergone the rigorous training
and apprenticeship of the classic European theatre, and they both held
the same lofty concepts of the nature of dramatic art. Janauschek was
fiercely loyal to such great roles as Medea, Brunhilde, Lady Macbeth,
and Queen Katherine. She scorned the sentimental, tearful roles of
French melodrama, which grew so popular during her later life, and
she refused to play such roles or to change her style to fit them. Only
in her last years, when she had fallen on evil days, did she stoop to
play such a part as Mother Rosenbaum in *The Great Diamond Robbery,* but she was ashamed of it and said that she "hoped Booth wasn't
looking down on her." Modjeska, likewise, believed in producing on
the stage only the distinguished dramas of eminent dramatists. She was
a priestess who worshipped at the altar of Shakespeare and served him
faithfully during her entire career. If she occasionally played such
roles as Camille, it was the exception rather than the rule, and even
then she ennobled the part and made it almost acceptable to so stern
a Puritan as William Winter.

Modjeska and Janauschek, although foreign born and foreign
trained, adopted the American stage as their own and enriched the tra-

dition of classic acting in this country by their high ideals of dramatic art and by their superb performances of many celebrated roles.

MARY ANDERSON

Modjeska and Janauschek, Duff and Cushman, all clearly belong to the classic school of acting. They learned their art in the richly varied school of the stock or repertory company. They played with actors steeped in the tradition of the European theatre. They appeared in Old Comedy, in Shakespeare, and in all the plays of the classical repertory. Their most famous roles were the great characters of the standard drama.

Mary Anderson belongs to the classic tradition, but with her the old order weakens. Her training was different and her repertory was limited. She chose her roles from the standard drama, but they were roles that required womanly emotion rather than tragic power. Her appeal was based more on personal charm than on dramatic genius. She was not of the school of feminine emotionalism most notably illustrated by Clara Morris, but neither did she achieve the same high plane as Duff and Cushman or Modjeska and Janauschek.

In many respects the career of Mary Anderson is unique and puzzling. She began as a star, and never acted anything but leading roles. She was adored by the public, but condemned by most of the critics. She was almost entirely self-taught, and lamented her lack of training, but she did nothing to acquire the instruction she needed. She retired at the height of her popularity, after only thirteen and a half years on the stage, and never resumed her career although she was offered fabulous sums to do so. She is undoubtedly remembered as a far greater actress than she actually was.

Mary Anderson became stage struck very early in her life. At the age of twelve, she was given a volume of Shakespeare's dramas and immediately was entranced. Shortly thereafter, she witnessed her first play, *Richard III,* starring Edwin Adams, and her fascination with the drama increased. Some time later Edwin Booth played in Louisville, Kentucky, Miss Anderson's home town, and the young lady's future was decided. After seeing him as Richelieu, Mary was so transported that she sat up all night planning a stage career for herself. When Booth's engagement ended, the girl made her mother a proposition.

She promised that if she were allowed to leave school and study by herself, she would work harder than she had ever done before. Since Mary had always been an indifferent student, her mother agreed to give the new arrangement a trial. Arming herself with Shakespeare's plays, Murdoch on Elocution, Rush on the Voice, and several other volumes, Mary retired to an attic room and there began her training as an actress. She studied her regular school lessons, and in addition she memorized the leading parts in a number of plays, including several male roles. With the guidance of Murdoch and Rush, she conscientiously exercised her voice and claimed that at the end of six months it had become so much fuller and stronger it was hardly recognizable. The system of self-instruction was so successful that Mary's mother allowed her to continue. Presently, Mary had a chance to read for the leading actor of the Louisville theatre and impressed him so favorably that later on he arranged an interview for her with Charlotte Cushman. In 1873, Mary traveled to Cincinnati to read for Miss Cushman, and received the encouragement that confirmed her determination to become an actress. Miss Cushman told the young aspirant that she had all the attributes for success, although her force and power would have to be modified. She advised the girl to take lessons from the veteran George Vandenhoff, and she ended by offering the unusual recommendation that Mary begin *at the top* and avoid the drudgery of small parts in a stock company. Whether the latter advice was sound will always remain a matter of dispute.

Acting on Miss Cushman's suggestion, Mary went to New York and took ten lessons of an hour each from George Vandenhoff. These lessons were the only dramatic coaching she ever received. They gave her instruction in elocution and stage deportment and were thoroughly unpleasant and disheartening to the young actress. She confessed that she "chafed and champed under the curb," but when the experience was over she said that it "had tamed, clipped, and done me general good, and I shall always be grateful to that capital actor and teacher of declamation for showing me the folly of attempting male characters, and for suggesting Juliet, Julia, Pauline, and Evadne as better suited to my sex and youth." [59]

Returning to Louisville, Mary studied and trained herself intensively for several months. When John McCullough, the popular tragedian, came to town, he was rather unwillingly persuaded to listen to her reading, but he liked it so well he recommended the girl to Mr. Barney

Macauley, manager of the Louisville theatre. This led to Mary's debut as Juliet on the stage of Macauley's Theatre, November 27, 1875, when the young actress was sixteen years old. The playbill for the evening does not give her name but merely lists her as "a Louisville young lady." The young lady made a great hit. The indulgent home town audience was delighted, and showered her with praise and encouragement. Three months later she again acted at Macauley's Theatre, playing the leading roles of Bianca, Julia, Pauline, and Juliet. Then followed short engagements in St. Louis, New Orleans, and Owensboro, all of which were popular and successful. Later in the year, which was 1876, John McCullough invited her to appear at the California Theatre in San Francisco, and here she experienced what she termed "the most unhappy part of my professional life." The critics were violent in their dislike. They declared that she could not act and, furthermore, that she seemed devoid of the capability of learning. But Edwin Booth was in the city at the time and after witnessing two of her performances, he comforted her and encouraged her, predicting that she was sure to succeed if she continued to act. The young tragedienne was further encouraged by a highly successful starring tour of the South and of Canada. In 1877, she made her debut in Philadelphia, Boston, and New York, and in these cities she won tremendous popular acclaim. For the next twelve years, until her retirement in 1889, she acted throughout the United States and England, winning public adoration wherever she went.

In many places her appearance created an absolute furor. During her first tour of the South she drew larger houses than any previous player except Edwin Forrest. Seats which ordinarily were priced at 75 cents frequently sold for $25. In Boston she played to audiences numbering four thousand, and the receipts for one day's matinee and evening performance were as high as $7,000. When she played at the Fifth Avenue Theatre in New York, the average weekly receipts were $9,000. In the British Isles her popularity was equally great. Her London managers were forced to turn away hundreds nightly from the theatre in which she appeared. In Edinburgh, on one occasion, she played to a house of £450, the largest sum ever collected for a single performance at the Lyceum Theatre. In Manchester she broke all existing box office records.

America was intensely proud of its beautiful young actress and lovingly named her "Our Mary." Her hold over the public is indicated by the newspaper headlines which heralded her return to the United States in 1899. In that year, after living abroad in retirement for almost ten years, she decided to pay a visit to her homeland. Excitedly and adoringly, the newspapers proclaimed: "OUR MARY IS COMING." Then followed the headlines: "OUR MARY HAS ARRIVED"; "OUR MARY IS IN OUR MIDST"; "AMERICA GREETS ITS FAVORITE DAUGHTER."

The qualities which won public affection for Mary Anderson were the same qualities which made her acting acceptable. They were: an attractive personality, a beautiful face and figure, a rich, melodious voice, a fair measure of dramatic instinct, and an admirable intellectual earnestness. On these endowments her acting was built, and it developed only so far as the limitation of these resources permitted.

Miss Anderson's physical endowments were outstanding. Her maidenly charm was hard to resist. She brought a purity and refinement to the theatre that were greatly admired, while the youth, the earnestness, and the virginal appeal of her personality touched many hearts and attracted huge audiences everywhere. "Singularly charming," "a vestal virgin," "the ideal of youthful womanhood," were typical of the comments she evoked. Personal magnetism of this sort has always been an important factor in success on the stage. With Mary Anderson, it was a factor of paramount importance.

In appearance, Miss Anderson had a classic kind of beauty. She was tall, with a sensuously curved figure and beautiful white arms. Her features were regular, her forehead smooth and high, and her eyes expressive. Many observers compared the purity and symmetry of her beauty to the goddesses of Greek sculpture.

Miss Anderson's voice was magnificent. Towse says: "It was a rich contralto, thoroughly feminine, but uncommonly full, deep, supple, and melodious." William Winter points out that it was clear and penetrating and yet possessed a velvety richness which "delighted every ear." The critic of *The Spirit of the Times,* after watching Miss Anderson's debut as Pauline in *The Lady of Lyons,* expressed distaste for her looks—he thought she was somewhat large and awkward—but he was captivated by her voice. He wrote: ". . . when she spoke a little thrill went through the assemblage. It was one of those low, round, sympathetic voices that stir you, and its articulation was so perfect that every shade of vocal meaning reached your ear. . . . I can only find one word to characterize her voice, and that word is rich. . . . It was warm, sensuous, and loaded with vitality. . . ." [60]

Another asset which Miss Anderson brought to her acting was intellectual earnestness. She trained herself for the stage with a youthful zeal and sincerity which she never lost in later years. She always studied her roles as carefully as she knew how, and if she failed in profundity of conception it was not from lack of effort. The Edinburgh *Scotsman* for April 28, 1884, compliments her on her "unmistakable capacity for grasping the essential significance of a character" and says that her delineation of character leaves the impression of "a thoughtful conception wrought out with consistency." Incidentally, Miss Anderson must have appreciated this compliment, for in her *Memories* she says that the chief difficulty in creating a character is to make it "harmonious from beginning to end." [61] This is one of the very few comments on the art of acting Miss Anderson has recorded.

Another comment on Miss Anderson's intellectual capacity and earnestness—and apparently a very penetrating comment—is contained in the Liverpool *Daily Post* for November 24, 1884. In reviewing a performance of *Romeo and Juliet,* the paper says: "Though Miss Anderson's personal charms are great, her intelligence is not less remarkable. She has thought the character out thoroughly and ably. Nothing has been taken for granted. The very faults of her execution show how elaborate has been her conception of the part, line by line. And, on the whole, her judgment is fairly sound. She makes the great points surely—some of them finely; and even if she were not at all beautiful, her impersonation would be acknowledged a thoughtful and intellectual one."

It is undeniable that Miss Anderson had a fair measure of dramatic talent. Cushman, McCullough, and the leading actors of the Louisville theatre all recognized the power in her schoolgirl elocution. Audiences who watched her first efforts on the stage felt a force and a magnetism which her lack of technique could not conceal. The young actress had an ear for the rhythm and sonorities of the language; she sensed the conflict and emotions in the scenes she enacted; and she was able to project much of her own sensibility to an audience. In her early years on the stage she was universally acclaimed for the promise of dramatic power which was a tantalizing concomitant of her opulent physical endowments.

Youth and beauty, charm and earnestness, refinement and talent, can win great personal popularity but they cannot create great acting. Miss Anderson's achievements, though always praiseworthy and popular, were strictly limited. Her playing never overcame certain defects which were partly due to her temperament and partly due to her lack of professional training.

The fact that she taught herself, and never enjoyed the experience of an apprenticeship on the stage, left her deficient in many theatrical techniques. She was criticized for not knowing how to make effective entrances and exits. She was not sure of her movements and so she often appeared awkward and self-conscious. When a situation did not call for specific action, she had little knowledge of the supplementary business and byplay which might be used. Some of her best vocal efforts were spoiled by crude or faulty delivery. The results of her deficient training are summarized by William Winter as follows:

With a superb voice, here is a defective elocution; with a magnificent figure, here is a self-conscious manner in the attitudes; with a noble freedom and suppleness of physical machinery, here is a capricious gesticulation; with a full and fine sense of opportunity for strong and shining points, here is but an incipient perception of the relative values surrounding characters . . . ; with a brilliant faculty for stormy and vehement declamation, here, as yet, is an imperfect idea of the loveliness of quiet touches, verbal shading, and suggestive strokes; with a vigorous and often grand manner of address, here is a frequent lack of concentration in listening. . . .

In short, says Winter, the achievement of Mary Anderson is, as yet, "the triumph of an exceptional personality shrined in a beautiful person." [62]

It appears that Miss Anderson was fully conscious of the handicap of her deficient training. At one point in her *Memories* she says: ". . . it was painfully disheartening to find myself stranded for lack of technical knowledge. . . ." At another point she confesses: ". . . most of my work was, to me, sadly immature and inartistic, and I felt it would take years of practical experience to remedy my lack of early training." [63]

As Miss Anderson continued her acting she naturally acquired polish and a more mature technique. After she returned from her first tour of England, many American critics noted her increased smoothness and conviction. However, these virtues seem to be confined to a limited range of effects. Long familiarity with a few roles had given her a mastery of certain techniques and these she repeated in all her delineations. Her competence had a narrow range. *The New York Times* for September 7, 1878, described her situation in these terms: "Her art is a graceful club—covered, indeed, with velvet, but swung always in the same circles." John R. Towse, the eminent critic of the New York *Evening Post,* is more direct and devastating. He says: "She had certain formulas in which she was proficient, and she applied them to corresponding types of situation with a deadly and unmodified re-iteration. In the mechanism of her art she never advanced beyond a moderate proficiency. What she had learned to do, she did well, but her executive ability was rigidly limited. It ceased to expand." [64]

Another defect in Miss Anderson's acting was its artificiality. The actress was often criticized for lacking sincerity and warmth. She seemed cold and mechanical. Her movements appeared to many observers to be obviously statuesque and self-conscious.* Her delivery often sounded false and oratorical. Certain of the London critics, noting the studied effects of her playing, thought she had been influenced too much by the artificial grandeur of the Kemble school, and urged her to learn spontaneity and abandon. Others felt that she lacked sensibility and should learn to feel the words she spoke and the situations she depicted. Many American critics were less kind. One of them declared that her acting made the stage "a hawking wilderness" and that it was as "untrue to nature" as it was "inimical to art."

A clue to Miss Anderson's artificiality can be found in the authorities on which she based her self-training. She used the texts of Rush and Murdoch for her instruction in elocution, and these teachers, however sincere their intentions, were always criticized for the stilted and unnatural delivery which their methods produced. Another of Miss Anderson's authorities was François Delsarte. Early in her career she discovered his system of movement and gesture. In her *Memories* she declares: "Always on the alert for improvement, I determined to study

* Miss Anderson's overuse of arm movements is noted rather amusingly in the following comment from *The New York Times* for September 14, 1878: "I don't mind telling you, *sub rosa,* that I think a dress which covers Miss Anderson's arms hampers and muffles her. She acts more with her arms than any other actress I ever saw. She is almost oratorical. She manifests the slightest emotion by a curvilinear sweep. When she is sad, something long and white and round flashes in the air. Her action thus resolves itself into a sensuous telegraphic system.

"A whole essay might be written on arms in the air. We have had the leg drama, why may we not have the arm drama?"

it. As far as mechanical exercises were concerned, it seemed to me perfect, for it overlooks no muscle or tendon of the face or body, and gives strength, suppleness, and control over them all. The rest of the system I afterwards found it best to discard." [65] It is likely that the young actress' use of the Delsarte exercises contributed to the studied effects of her stage movements.

A final defect in the acting of Mary Anderson—and it would naturally follow from the others—was her failure at identification. She could not transform her own personality and create the illusion of character. She was always the charming and beautiful Mary Anderson. Thus, writes Towse, "she reached her artistic boundaries when she learned to express herself freely and fully . . . and was only fully successful when her part fitted her like a glove." [66]

Miss Anderson's repertory of parts, compared to those of Cushman and Duff, was very small. She acted no more than eighteen roles during her entire career. But neither this limitation, nor any other, seemed to matter to her adoring public. They ignored the carping of the critics and flocked to see her. Even her severest judges, who would never rank her as a great or finished artist, recognized that she was wholly delightful in certain roles. Galatea in Gilbert's *Pygmalion and Galatea,* Parthenia in Holm's *Ingomar,* and Perdita in Shakespeare's *Winter's Tale* were accounted her most successful parts. All of them suited her temperament and personality. In all of them she could exploit her youthful beauty and her feminine charm. In these and other roles she gave delight to thousands of playgoers, and when she retired, before the age of thirty and at the height of her popularity, she was loudly lamented by audiences in both the United States and Great Britain.[67] Towse justly estimates her place in the history of the American stage when he writes: "Her beauty, her spotless character, her graciousness, her intelligence, her refined manner, and her unquestionable dramatic instinct and ability contributed greatly to the honor and glory of the American stage while she adorned it; but for all that she was never a great actress or a great artist." [68]

III

THE CLASSIC SCHOOL: THE GENTLEMEN

THE YEAR OF 1835, WHICH SAW THE DEBUT OF CHARLOTTE CUSHman, also marked the professional debut of Edward Loomis Davenport, one of the most gifted actors in a notable company of four versatile tragedians. The oldest member of this group, James Murdoch, was already established as a rising young player in 1835; the youngest of the company, Lawrence Barrett, was not yet born; and the greatest of the company, Edwin Booth, was a mere infant two years old. Yet despite the differences in their ages, these four distinguished performers became intimately acquainted; their careers and lives overlapped, and their combined brilliance illuminated the American stage for many years.

All four tragedians can be grouped with the classic school of Mary Ann Duff and Charlotte Cushman. They underwent the same arduous apprenticeship; they held the same splendid ideals of the art of acting; and they followed similar methods and practices with similar outstanding results. Of all their talents, perhaps their versatility was the most impressive. They became principally renowned for their acting in serious drama, but they also excelled in comedy, melodrama, and romance. In fact, says Lewis Strang, "whether they were best in tragedy, in comedy, or in romance, no man had the hardihood to declare." [1]

Edwin Booth, the most eminent, will be considered first.

EDWIN BOOTH

Booth was once asked why he always looked "insulted" when taking his curtain calls at the end of a play. He replied: "I have given my life to these great roles. I do not consider myself an entertainer! I am an interpreter. I reveal the soul of masterpieces. . . . They (the spectators) should bow their heads reverently before these poems I reveal to them." [2] The loftiness of purpose which Booth reveals in this statement is characteristic of his attitude toward the drama he loved and the high art of acting he served. He believed that only the best plays in the language should be given, and these in the noblest style of acting which could be achieved.

Edwin Booth was born in Belair, Maryland, on November 13, 1833, the fourth son of a famous actor father, Junius Brutus Booth, who was considered to be an arch rival of Edmund Kean. As a boy, Edwin had little formal education. For several years he travelled throughout the country with his gifted but eccentric father, serving him as a friend, guardian, and valet. Naturally Edwin's first conceptions of acting were gathered from his illustrious parent. The elder Booth was a fiery, impulsive actor who dazzled his audiences with mighty outbursts of emotion and thrilling vocal displays. Like the acting of Edmund Kean, the playing of the elder Booth was "a manifestation of the inspired intuitions, infallibly true and irresistibly sensational." [3] Inevitably, Edwin was influenced by this style, but the influence did not persist for long. The elder Booth died when Edwin was nineteen, and thereafter the young actor began the cultivation of an individual style which was to win him world-wide acclaim.

Edwin's debut on the stage was almost accidental. In 1849, while his father was performing in Boston, Edwin assumed the bit part of Tressel in *Richard III* in order to relieve the burden of an overworked prompter. Thereafter, Edwin occasionally played minor roles in his father's company. His serious apprenticeship began in San Francisco, where he had gone with his father in 1852. The elder Booth died later in the same year, but Edwin remained in the west until 1856, playing a great variety of roles in both tragedy and comedy. On one occasion during this period, he acted Richard III at a benefit, and so great was his success that the managers brought him out in other leading parts: Othello, Shylock, Sir Edward Mortimer, and Hamlet. However, he did not continue long in these roles. When the first excitement over his achievement died down, his elder brother Junius, who was in the management of the theatre, San Francisco Hall, again cast him for parts in comedy, farce, and burlesque. "You have had a wonderful success for a young man," said Junius, "but you have much to learn." [4] Three times, it is said, the young actor went from star parts back to utility roles without making a protest. One of his hits as a utility man was scored as "Dandy Cox" in a Negro farce produced by the Chapman family. Another was his impersonation of Plume, a local celebrity. A more important comic hit was scored when he played Shakespeare's Petruchio for the first time.

Such training was of incalculable value to the young actor. It developed his confidence, his range, and his sensitivity to audience response. Booth testified to the efficacy of his early training in a letter to his daughter written in 1873. He said: "When I was learning to act tragedy, I had frequently to perform comic parts, in order to acquire a certain ease of manner that my serious parts might not appear stilted. . . ." [5] Later on, in a letter of advice to a young actor, he wrote:

A frequent change of role, and of the lighter sort . . . is the best training requisite for a mastery of the actor's art.

I had seven years' apprenticeship at it, during which most of my labor was in the field of comedy,—"walking gentlemen," burlesque, and low comedy parts,—the while my soul was yearning for high tragedy. I did my best with all that I was cast for, however, and the unpleasant experience did me a world of good. Had I followed my own bent, I would have been, long ago, a "crushed tragedian." [6]

After Booth's apprenticeship in California, he returned to the East and immediately scored an enduring triumph. Although his art was not yet fully developed, he was successful enough to be hailed as "the hope of the living drama." An interesting picture of his qualities at this time is given by William Winter, who writes:

Those who saw him at that time saw a young man of extraordinary grace, robust yet refined vigor, and a spirit ardent with the fire of genius. In the form of his acting there were defects . . . but it was felt that in the soul of Booth's acting there was spontaneous passion, imaginative power, —the nameless beauty which thrills, entices, and enables, and which is the inseparable attribute of inspiration. [7]

From the time of Booth's eastern debut in 1856, until his death in

1893, he remained a star of the first magnitude. At the peak of his career, after Forrest had passed his prime, he was universally acknowledged to be America's greatest tragic actor.

The major premise in Booth's artistic creed was his belief that art should interpret, exalt, ennoble. He felt, like Sir Joshua Reynolds (who had influenced the Kembles), that art should appear natural and illusionistic but not by copying all the literal details of life or by exalting the drab and the commonplace. Art should reveal the higher reality, the universal essence of people and problems. It should achieve naturalness by interpreting and elevating nature.

To achieve his high ideal in acting, Booth utilized all his physical and mental endowments. Edwin Forrest had been criticized for relying on the physical and omitting the spiritual. James Murdoch was accused of over-intellectualizing his roles. But Booth, it was claimed, had the ideal combination of mind, voice, and body. Winter said he was endowed with "profound and intense power equally of emotion and of intellect." [8]

There can be no doubt but that Booth was richly endowed by nature. His voice had superb quality, range, and carrying power. Towse thought that his tones lacked "the organ-like volume of Salvini's" but that Booth's voice was "a rich and beautiful instrument upon which he played with great skill." [9] Henry Austin Clapp describes his delivery in these words: "Faultless pronunciation, an enunciation distinct, clean, and clear, without formalism or apparent effort, an exquisite feeling for the sweetness of words, and a delicate sense of their relation to one another, unite to give his delivery exemplary distinction, and to make it a model and a standard." [10]

The revelation of mood and meaning which Booth could achieve through the tone of his voice alone is shown by the success of his acting in Germany. In 1883 he fulfilled a sensationally successful engagement at the Residenz Theatre in Berlin. He spoke his lines in English while the supporting cast used their native German. In spite of this, Oscar Welten in the *Taglishe Berliner Rundschau* wrote: "Booth is the best Hamlet I have ever seen. . . . You can understand . . . perfectly, although you may not know a single word that he utters." [11]

Booth was a man of average height, endowed with agility and excellent coordination. He was always praised for the eloquence of his movements. His slim build and graceful manner made him the ideal Hamlet but were a handicap to him in roles like Macbeth and Lear.

Towse believes that such characters require "massive grandeur in emotion" based on rugged physique and that Booth's firm intellectual grasp of the roles could not compensate for the advantage which physically powerful actors like Forrest and Davenport possessed in the crises of emotion.

When it came to intellectual and spiritual grasp, Booth was never equalled. His power to illuminate his characters through imaginative, poetic insight was his chief glory. Strang called him "the foremost poet of his profession," [12] and Winter declares: "the distinctive quality that illuminated his acting was the personal one of poetic individuality." [13]

The revealing, spiritual quality of Booth's acting was felt by everyone, but it was hard to analyze and describe. Henry C. Pedder, writing in *The Manhattan* magazine for April 1884, comes close to an acceptable explanation when he says:

> In the portrayal of human passion it is possible to be at times strong and terrible and yet human. And in this essential human quality Mr. Booth never fails. There are times when the heroes and heroines of Shakespeare cry aloud in their pain . . . yet we never seem to lose the sense of a harmonizing unity which is always present, and which, when adequately interpreted, strikes the keynote to the deep, mysterious undertone of life.

Booth's penetrating, spiritual insight, Pedder thinks, always struck the keynote and thus was able to illuminate "the darkness of the moment by the calm beauty of a comprehensive consciousness." Winter says, "Poetry in acting cannot be carried further. . . ." [14]

Booth's style of acting was shaped by his natural gifts: a beautiful voice, a graceful though not a powerful physique, and a penetrating, poetic mind. The result was acting which excelled in consistency and lack of mannerism. His art was smooth, even of texture, and marvelously relaxed. It never depended for its effect upon tricks or explosions. Nat Goodwin, who specialized in burlesquing famous people, was once asked why he never tried an imitation of Edwin Booth. He replied: ". . . what's there to hang a caricature on? His art's round like a ball. . . . You can't be funny by exaggerating something that is not in the first place a little overdone. . . . No, I won't tackle Booth. I couldn't be funny caricaturing perfection." [15] George William Curtis, the editor of *Harper's Magazine,* had the same impression of Booth's art. In reviewing a performance of *Hamlet,* Curtis wrote: "His playing throughout has an exquisite tone, like an old picture. . . . It is not any particular scene, or passage, or look, or movement, that conveys the impression; it is the consistency of every part with every other. . . ." [16]

The beauty and perfection of Booth's playing were the result, not only of great natural talent, but also of careful preparation and lifelong study. He was a keen observer of nature and copied many effects from actual life. For example, in preparing for the mad scenes of *Hamlet* and *King Lear,* he visited hospitals and asylums all over the country and carefully studied the behavior of the patients. However, consistent to his artistic ideals, he did not literally reproduce the behavior he witnessed. Rather, he selected the ideas and elements which suited his purpose and incorporated only these into his characterizations.

His art was never static. He studied his parts as long as he played them, tirelessly probing for deeper meanings and more effective expression. He scrutinized the texts of Shakespeare and tested every possible interpretation of the lines. He studied all the commentaries, and personally consulted the best Shakespearean scholars. Observers noted that his Macbeth changed with the years, becoming more robust and massive as the actor grew more mature. His Lear mellowed and strengthened as the actor passed through the ordeal of personal suffering. His portraits of Richelieu and Iago gained in profundity from season to season. His Hamlet, always one of his best roles, grew and developed until it became his masterpiece. Clapp, in praising Booth's tireless improvement of his roles, says: ". . . through his shifting ideals, as they were embodied from year to year, the spectator could discern the extraordinary variety of treatment which Shakespeare's creations, because of their many sided humanness, will permit." [17]

Shylock was a character which challenged Booth all of his life. He acted the role during his first season in California and played it successfully many times after that. He portrayed Shylock "sometimes as a fierce money-catching old clothes dealer. . . . Sometimes as a majestic Hebrew financier and lawgiver; sometimes . . . in the just mean between the two extremes. . . ." [18] Yet Booth was never satisfied. As late as 1885, only eight years before his death, he was still studying the part. Writing to Harold H. Furness, he complains:

Shylock haunts me like a nightmare: I can't mount the animal—for such I consider Shylock to be.

I made an effort to get at him through G. F. Cooke's notes on his own acting of the part, but was surprised to find out how he was influenced by tradition. . . . My effort was a vain one. I will try again before the "call boy" summons me to work.[19]

Two years later Booth again wrote to Furness, announcing joyfully:

Hold on! The Jew came to me last evening, just as I was leaving Pittsburgh and stayed with me all night, on the sleeping car, whence sleep was banished, and I think I've got him by the beard, or nose, I don't know which; but I'll hang on to him a while, and see what he'll do for me. I'll have his pound of flesh if I can get it off his old bones.[20]

Evidently Booth did hang on until he achieved a remarkable characterization, for at a late date the judicious Towse writes that Booth's skillful blend of prejudice, hate, avarice, dignity, craft, and abject defeat created a "perfect picture, finished to the nails." "One is inclined to apply to it," continues Towse, "the certificate given to old Macklin's 'This is the Jew that Shakespeare drew.' " [21]

As a means of gaining truth and conviction in his performances, Booth tried to "think himself" into his roles. He attempted, imaginatively, to *become* the characters so he could better understand how they felt. On nights when he could not sleep, he let the moods of his roles "flood through his mind." Before a performance, he tried to avoid distractions which might break his mood. One night in the "Tubal scene" of *The Merchant of Venice,* the actress playing Jessica watched the scene from the wings where Booth could see her. When the scene was over, Booth asked her never to do it again, explaining: "I go into that scene with a clear picture of Jessica. My own flesh and blood has betrayed me. . . . I am deserted. . . . I am hopeless—alone. I charge my voice with Shylock's agony, and then look up and see you—my daughter—standing before me, come back to me. My picture breaks up! I lose my scene!" [22]

Booth was, to some extent, a temperamental actor and at times depended too much on thinking himself into the proper mood of his role. If he could not summon the necessary emotion, his acting could be cold and formal; when thoroughly aroused, he could enthrall his audience with the beauty and fire of his performance.[23] However, it should not be assumed that Booth habitually "let himself go." There is abundant evidence to show that he had learned to exercise a critical, artistic control over his emotions at all times. "When I am enrapt in a character I am impersonating," he once said, "there seems to be another and a distinct individuality, another me, sitting in judgment on myself." [24]

It is sometimes said that Booth was indifferent to the quality of his supporting players and to the *mise en scène* in which he appeared. It is also said that he deliberately surrounded himself with inferior actors so that his own genius would shine more brilliantly. There is little evidence to substantiate these claims. During his career Booth acted with all the leading stars—Salvini, the Italian; Irving, the Englishman; Cushman, Janauschek, Modjeska, Barrett, and Murdoch—and he always welcomed comparison with them. When he built his own theatre and organized his own company, he surrounded himself with the best talent available. He dazzled New York with a series of sumptuously mounted and historically accurate Shakespearean revivals. As a manager and stage director, he spent endless hours planning, rehearsing, and supervising every element of his productions. Katherine Goodale, who toured with him in 1886–87, tells how he scrutinized every detail of her costumes and make-up, suggesting changes and improvements, and—on one occasion—making her completely re-do her make-up as one of the apparitions in *Macbeth*.

During the many years of his life when he was a traveling star, Booth was forced to accept whatever support was provided for him. Often both the scenery and the players were wretchedly poor, and then he had to carry the play by his own virtuoso efforts. If the support happened to be good, he took full advantage and responded eloquently to the actors around him. He could "listen" well, and he could respond to any emergency or challenge. Many stories relate how supporting players improvised new business or gave surprise readings to their lines just to see how skillfully Booth could meet the situation.

Among the great players of the nineteenth century, Booth was the finest artist; he was also one of the most versatile. It should be remembered that in his apprentice days, he made several hits in farce and burlesque; he acted the comedy roles of Petruchio and Benedick many times and kept them in his repertory almost to the end of his career; [25] he played Romeo, Don Caesar, and several other romantic heroes. But it was in the field of tragedy that his real versatility was displayed. He acted with striking success heroes and villains of every age and every temperament. In this field, says Strang, his art "was magnificently full and comprehensive. It encompassed the mental enigma of the intellectual Hamlet and the brutal animalism of the jealousy-mad Othello; it exemplified the very essence of evil in the diamond-like brilliancy of Iago, and the fullness of pitiable pathos in the . . . physically and mentally warped Bertuccio." [26] William Winter confirms this judgment when he says: "Booth can pass with ease from the boisterous levity of Petruchio to the height of Hamlet's sublime delirium. . . . Othello, the Moor, Iago, the Venetian, Richelieu, the French priest, and Don Caesar, the Spanish gallant—emblems of a great variety of human nature and experience—are all, as he presents them, entirely distinct individuals." [27] Booth's greatest creation, Hamlet, tended to obscure the numerous other characters which he could act with equal skill. Yet the discriminating critics were well aware of his versatility. Otis Skinner remarks: "With such gentleness as his it was singular that his greatest effects should have been made in parts of sinister and diabolic character—Iago, Richard, Bertuccio, Macbeth, Pescara, Shylock. . . ." [28] Katherine Goodale records how shocked she was when she saw Booth act Sir Giles Overreach for the first time and realized that her idol could create a horrifying portrait of "a monster without one redeeming trait." Booth himself enjoyed playing the villains. During long runs of *Othello,* he alternated between Iago and the title role, and confessed that he much preferred Iago. Skinner relates how Booth remarked to him one evening: "This fellow (Benedick in *Much Ado About Nothing*) is a lover . . . I loathe the whole pack of them. Always did. Even as a youngster I loved the villains." [29]

The art of Edwin Booth can be summarized as follows: Acting, to him, was not entertainment. It was the revelation of the beauty and wisdom contained in great dramatic poems. To interpret these masterpieces worthily, he tirelessly cultivated his talents. He realized that his physique was limited but that his voice was richly expressive and that his poetic temperament was capable of illuminating many roles. He built his technique upon these strengths, and was able to act a wide variety of parts with great distinction.

He learned from nature, but he never believed in a literal transcription of life. He repudiated extravagant displays of passion and theatrical trickery. He studied his parts continually, and sought to identify himself with his characters without ever losing control of his emotions. His playing, at its best, was harmonious, unmannered, and "round as a ball." "When he made his final bow," wrote Towse, speaking for a host of admirers, "the curtain—so far as the American stage was concerned—fell also upon the legitimate drama." [30]

JAMES E. MURDOCH

In the winter of 1830, Edwin Forrest was playing a star engagement in Augusta, Georgia, under the management of Vincent DeCamp. One morning at a rehearsal of *Damon and Pythias,* Forrest became so disgusted with the wretched performance of the actor playing Pythias that he stopped the rehearsal and refused to continue until a better actor could be found. DeCamp protested that the present Pythias was the best his company could offer. "No," said Forrest decisively, "he is not. You have a man named Murdoch in your company whom I once saw act in Philadelphia. Give the part to him." [31] This was the beginning of James E. Murdoch's rise to eminence in his profession.

The name of James Murdoch is not often linked with that of Edwin Booth, and yet they were leaders in their profession during the same years and held the same artistic ideals. Murdoch was twenty-two years older than Booth, yet each reached the zenith of his acting career in the third quarter of the nineteenth century. In 1853 they acted together in San Francisco. In 1856, while Booth was winning New York, Murdoch was conquering London. In the ensuing years, their paths crossed many times. Both men died in 1893 within a month of each other.

Murdoch was a far less gifted actor than Booth, and his name does not retain the luster of his younger colleague's. Yet Murdoch was the more influential of the two in shaping the style of American acting. Whereas Booth wrote no treatise on the art of the stage, and left no successors or disciples, Murdoch recorded his theories in three different books; [32] he became an eminent teacher of elocution; his methods and beliefs influenced the course of dramatic instruction throughout the whole United States.

Murdoch was born in Philadelphia in 1811, the son of a bookbinder and paper-ruler—a profession which young Murdoch was expected to follow. But early in his life he joined a local dramatic group and began the study of elocution under two popular instructors: Lemuel G. White, who had been the teacher of Edwin Forrest, and Dr. James Rush, the author of an influential book on elocution. In 1829, Murdoch forsook the book-binding business, much to his father's disappointment, and made his debut at the Arch Street Theatre in Philadelphia. Shortly thereafter, he joined the first of several dramatic troupes which were to guide him during his apprenticeship. He worked steadily, studied diligently, and rose in his profession. In 1842 he retired from the stage for three years to lecture, to teach, and to write a book on vocal culture. He returned to the stage in 1845 and during the next fifteen years he established a national reputation as a versatile player who could perform excellently in a wide variety of parts. During this period, he starred for 110 consecutive nights at the Haymarket Theatre in London. When the Civil War began, Murdoch abandoned the professional stage and devoted his talents to entertaining Union troops in camps and hospitals. Following the war, he made a farewell tour of the principal cities, then retired to his farm in Ohio. His retirement was not absolute, for he reappeared on at least two occasions. However, more of his time between 1865 and 1893 (the year of his death) was devoted to writing and teaching than to acting.

Murdoch shared with Booth a noble conception of the art of acting. He believed the true actor possessed a creative capacity as great as any other artist. To be sure, fidelity to the poet's image must be uppermost in the actor's mind, and he is not free to distort or to improvise according to his own whim. Yet, to understand and grasp the poet's vision requires a "receptive power" which, Murdoch declares, "is by no means the passive and servile thing which a superficial criticism would make it . . ." and "it demands an assimilating and cooperative soul, a positive genius to develop it." [33]

Besides the "receptive faculty" the actor must have a genuine expressive faculty, for he must project the poet's image and convince the spectator of its truth and beauty. Murdoch believed that such a task requires a creativeness which is equal to the dramatist's.

In projecting a "vivid impress" of the poet's conception, an actor must keep his portrait true to nature. Like Booth, Murdoch believed that truth to nature is not to be found in harsh reality but rather in an idealized rendering of it. "The exaggerating attempts . . . to make everything in dramatic representation seem as real as possible," says Murdoch, "proceed upon the assumption that nature is found only in the actual and real, while the natural in expression lies ever nearest to the ideal." [34]

The confusing of individuality with human nature is another misconception to be avoided. Murdoch believed that too many actors cultivate mannerisms which are natural only to themselves, and in so doing destroy the illusion of dramatic character. An actor who exploits his own idiosyncrasies under the mistaken notion that he is being natural "appropriates both the stage and Shakespeare to himself, and swallows them up in the inordinate self-esteem of the individual." [35] Murdoch cautions his fellow actors to remember that the plays of Shakespeare mirror the universal truths of nature, and if an actor is to communicate them, he must universalize his impersonations in such a way that he reaches the hearts of all his spectators.

In preparing a role, Murdoch believed—like the rest of the versatile tragedians—that careful study and sound scholarship were necessary. He also recommended the cultivation of the imagination. Without specifically naming the imaginative process, Murdoch states that an actor should "pass out of self consciousness" and should "take on the fresh and deep impression" of the poet's thought. In preparing a role, an actor must put himself "under the influence of a poetic spirit"; in so doing, "he loses self in the picturing of the mind," and by means of such "mental workings" a convincing portrayal emerges. The process of cultivating the imagination is further described when Murdoch states that an aspirant training for the stage "must study the profoundest forms of thought, the noblest moods of sentiment, the most vivid emotions of the soul, and dwell upon them until their full power and value are deeply felt, and their intensity glows into expression." [36]

It is interesting to note that Murdoch's belief in imagination seems to be the same as that which characterized the influential teachings of S. S. Curry some two generations later. Both men believed that imagination can be cultivated, and that when it is strong enough it can stimulate the voice and the body to effective expression. Murdoch, however, eventually adopted a system of voice cultivation which prescribed precise rules for vocal expression. In Curry's opinion, he thus cut off the inspiration of the imagination and substituted a system of dead mechanics.

Although an actor should cultivate a vivid, glowing imagination, he should not forget his own identity and try to become the character he represents. Murdoch believed that complete absorption in a role destroys the critical detachment which is necessary for the finest acting. Two other pitfalls which an actor should avoid are the extremes of either monotony or ranting. The impulse to strut and roar and posture is one of the "prominent vices" of the stage, says Murdoch. The other is sermonizing. An actor who seeks to avoid excess often becomes "a mere elocutionist and declaimer." "Words, words, words," says Murdoch, "form the sum and substance of his performance . . ." and "such a counterfeit presentation of a passion . . . falls down to the monotonous delivery of a sermonizing lecture or the recitation of a school boy's task." [37] The ideal player, Murdoch believed, sought a careful and honest revelation of the poet's vision through balance and proportion in his acting.

Despite his belief in balance, Murdoch had a definite bias toward the importance of vocal expression in dramatic art. He firmly believed that gesture and movement were decidedly inferior as means of expression. Early in his discussion of acting he says: "To . . . personal bearing, modes of action and gesture—I shall only refer in a passing way; such being the mere physical attributes of the performers, and of less importance to the public than the more intellectual qualities of voice and speech." [38] On rare occasions, Murdoch praised the effect of pantomime and physical action, as when he commended Garrick for having a body which was capable of "answering readily to the manifestations of fancy or will." [39] In general, Murdoch was so personally engrossed in the study and teaching of elocution, and he so despised the "pantomimic ranters" with whom he was often surrounded, that it is not surprising for him to have written:

The only way by which the reader or actor can reach the sympathies and affections of the human heart is through the magnetic power of the voice. When that delicate organism, which produces the broad effects and nice distinctions in kind and degree of expressive vocality, is subjected to true feeling and good taste and judgment, then may Shakespeare's creations be transformed from the dead letter of the printed page to that stage of action where they first drew breath and looked and moved as living things. [40]

In his own acting, Murdoch tried conscientiously to illustrate the validity of his theories. He studied his roles carefully and cultivated his own powers of imagination. He attempted, creatively, to idealize and universalize the characters he played and thus to avoid the literalness of commonplace reality. He practiced a critical self-possession even in scenes of violent passion, and he shunned both rant and verbosity. Above all, he cultivated the expressive powers of his voice and developed an elocution which, at its best, was a delight to the listener. [41] Alfred Ayres ranked him fourth in achievement after Forrest, Cushman, and Edwin Booth. Indeed, says Ayres, "If versatility would make greatness, he would rightfully have been counted great." [42]

Like Booth and the other versatile tragedians, Murdoch acted successfully in comedy, tragedy, and romance. The great tragic roles—such as Hamlet, Macbeth, and Othello—were all popular features of his repertory. His portrayal of romantic characters like Claude Melnotte in *The Lady of Lyons* was widely acclaimed. In the roles of artificial comedy, Murdoch was even more successful. Many critics affirmed that he had no peer in such parts as Young Mirabel in *The Inconstant,* Charles Surface in *The School for Scandal,* Rover in *Wild Oats,* Don Felix in *The Wonder,* and Vapid in *The Dramatist.* He acted Benedick and Petruchio with great credit, but he was more praised in roles where he could use his gift for artificial comedy.

All of Murdoch's acting, from farce to tragedy, was characterized by sincerity, intellectuality, imagination, and finesse. Early in his career, *The Spirit of the Times,* New York, praised his portrayal of Hamlet in these words:

The pervading quality of the performance was grace and propriety of conception and delivery: relieved by electric flashes on passages of a more elevated character. All our contemporaries concur in acknowledgement of his manly bearing, the beauty of his voice, and his admirable reading. . . . A performance freer from rant, more entirely with good discretion throughout was never presented.[43]

More than thirty-five years later, when Murdoch was seventy-one years old, Otis Skinner saw him play the same role and he wrote:

No longer able to look the Prince of Denmark, he yet contrived to convey in his bearing much grace and courtliness, and his reading was a delight. In watching his Hamlet from the wings, I found myself shutting my eyes . . . leaving my ear to drink in the clarity and music of his elocution.[44]

Murdoch earned high rank among nineteenth-century players for the distinction and versatility of his acting. He also won renown as a pioneer in the teaching of elocution. His long activity and wide influence in this sphere deserve additional comment.

Murdoch acquired a lively interest in the study of elocution from his first teacher, Lemuel G. White. Shortly thereafter he came under the influence of Dr. James Rush and eventually became a devoted disciple of the Rush theories of vocal instruction.

In 1827, Rush had published a work entitled *The Philosophy of the Voice.* It was a ponderous book, long, complicated, and full of scientific terminology. Many people found it incomprehensible. A few, like Murdoch, saw beneath the verbiage an exciting new approach to the art of elocution. The young actor studied the text avidly and discussed its principles with the author. The theories it advanced fitted his own predilection and practice. He came to believe that it was "the most complete system ever offered to the student of elocution." A burning ambition rose in him "to see these principles universally recognized and accepted in their integrity." The fulfillment of this ambition accounts for his temporary retirement from acting in 1842 and for his subsequent interest in teaching and writing.[45]

The Philosophy of the Voice presented a theory and a method which, Murdoch felt, had never before been successfully outlined. Among the contributions of the book were a scientific terminology for speech instruction, and a system of notating speech sounds. The need for such a system was keenly felt by many actors. Elocution teachers and dramatic coaches were accustomed to describing the effects they wanted in general terms like "fervent expression," "modulation," "tone of feeling," etc. Such vague instruction led generally to unsatisfactory results. Rush declared:

> We seem not to be aware that no describable perceptions are associated with such terms until required to illustrate them with some definite discriminations of vocal sounds. . . . The studious inquirer has long wanted a language for the meaning of the voice he has always felt. . . . The few and indeterminate designations of the modes of the voice in reading, compared to the number and accuracy of the terms in music, imply the different manner in which ease has been cultivated.[46]

Rush, building on the earlier work of John Walker and Thomas Sheridan, developed a comprehensive system of nomenclature and notation which defined and labeled every speech sound. The system employed the musical staff to indicate pitch, and symbols to represent each syllable, its duration in time, and the direction and variation of its pitch. Additional symbols represented metrical pauses, heavy and light accents, and a variety of other vocal effects. Also, an extensive descriptive vocabulary was used preceding each selection, so that directions like the following were found: "Moderate movement. Natural Quality. Middle Pitch. Gentle Force. Waves and Intervals of a Second and Third" [47] or, "Slowest Movement. Low Pitch, Slightly Aspirated. Suppressed Force. Median waves. The Refrain here is Semitonic." [48]

Rush also advanced a "theory of correspondence" between the inner feeling of the performer and the vocal sign. This theory, which Murdoch admits was not entirely new but was scientifically explored by Rush for the first time, was based on observable physical phenomena. Thoughts, sentiments, passions—said Rush—affect the muscles of the body, among them the vocal muscles. Thus, in natural speaking the tone of the voice is automatically altered to correspond to the inner feelings. Murdoch asserts that:

. . . the great fundamental principle of Dr. Rush's philosophy of spoken language, and overlooked in anything like scientific detail . . . in former systems, was that *every state of mind* had its corresponding vocal sign in *some of the varied forms of pitch, force, time, and quality.* These vocal signs he observed and recorded, not only . . . with reference to their individual form and character, *but classified them on the principle of this natural relation to the mental phenomena of which they are the audible* indication.[49]

Rush's system was not intended to constitute an arbitrary, iron-clad scheme. The "scoring" of a speech or a poem according to this system was simply a means of stimulating and inspiring the student. "The principles which the notations illustrate," says Murdoch, "are positive, but the notation itself only suggestive of the means of attaining the desired end of natural effect in the utterance of premeditated language." [50] Also, the notations were to serve the purpose of giving the student "command, through the practice it affords, over the different vocal movements it indicates." [51]

Murdoch firmly believed that the Rush system of elocution was the only "true method." S. S. Curry, and other teachers of a later generation, found the system hopelessly mechanical and productive of pedantic, artificial expression. However, before the system was abandoned, it exerted wide influence throughout the country. Murdoch used it to train many actors who played with him or sought formal instruction from him. His text book was used for years in American schools and colleges. Some of the terms he employed and techniques he advocated still appear in manuals of dramatic instruction. Many of his pupils gained prominence in the field of education and profoundly influenced the development of speech training in American universities. Among the most noted of his students were Robert I. Fulton, who became Professor of Elocution and Oratory in the Ohio Wesleyan University,

Interior of the Park Theatre, New York, as painted by John Searle in 1822. Courtesy of the New York Historical Society, New York City.

Edwin Forrest at the age of twenty.
Portrait by Samuel Lawrence.

Yours sincerely,
Edwin Forrest

(left) Exterior of the Park Theatre, New York, in 1799. This theatre was the leading playhouse in New York for almost fifty years.

Mary Ann Duff.
From the Harvard Theatre Collection.

John McCullough.

Fanny Janauschek in 1894. From the
Ross Theatre Collection, University of
California Library at Berkeley.

Mary Anderson.
Photograph by Bradley and Rulofson.

Edwin Booth as Richelieu in Bulwer-
Lytton's play. From the Ross Theatre
Collection.

Charlotte Cushman.
(top) From the Harvard Theatre
Collection. *(bottom)* From the
Hoblitzelle Theatre Arts Library.

Edwin Booth. Portrait by John Singer Sargent. Courtesy of the Walter Hampden Memorial Library at The Players, New York City.

(right) Anna Cora Mowatt as Rosalind in *As You Like It*. From the Harvard Theatre Collection.

Lawrence Barrett as Count Lanciotto Boker's *Francesca da Rimini*. From the Ross Theatre Collection.

(right) James E. Murdoch in Kotzebue's *The Stranger*. From the Ross Theatre Collection.

Mrs. Leslie Carter. From the Theatre
Collection, University of California Library at Berkeley.

Fanny Davenport.
Photograph by Sarony.

Clara Morris, "Queen of Spasms."
From the Ross Theatre Collection.

Thomas C. Trueblood, who became Professor of Elocution and Oratory in the University of Michigan, S. S. Hamill, who became Professor of Rhetoric, English Literature, and Elocution first at Illinois Wesleyan University and later at Illinois College, and Professor John R. Scott, who became head of speech instruction at the University of Missouri.

James E. Murdoch, as actor, teacher, and writer, demonstrated an impressive range of talents and, like Edwin Booth and the other versatile tragedians of his day, enriched the offerings of the American Theatre.

EDWARD L. DAVENPORT

Edwin Forrest is said to have called E. L. Davenport "the best actor on the American stage." [52] Lewis Strang described him as "entitled to rank next to Edwin Booth, Charlotte Cushman, Edwin Forrest, and William Warren, as the most brilliant product of the stage in the United States." [53]

This gifted player, whose very versatility tended to obscure his brilliance, was born in Boston in 1815 and twenty years later made his professional debut in Providence, Rhode Island. He served a distinguished apprenticeship in theatres up and down the east coast for more than ten years until, in 1846, he became the leading man of Anna Cora Mowatt, who had made her sensational debut only the year before. In 1847, Davenport accompanied Mrs. Mowatt to England and remained there for seven years. During the first few of these years, Davenport remained with Mrs. Mowatt—much to the satisfaction of that talented lady, who praised him in these words:

His moral character, his unassuming and gentleman-like manners, his wonderful versatility and indisputable talents, caused him to be selected as the person who was to travel with us during my second year on the stage. Upon his selection, every succeeding month and year gave us new cause for congratulation. The prominent position he has since won upon the English stage, and the honors he has received from fastidious English audiences, are just reward of intrinsic and *unostentatious* merit.[54]

Mrs. Mowatt might also have mentioned the fact that he *looked* like a leading man. He possessed an unusually distinguished face, a graceful walk and carriage, and a voice which was soft and musical but capable of great range and power. All his photographs, both as a young man and as an old one, show him to be handsome, aristocratic, and manly.

In January, 1851, while he was still in England, Davenport was chosen to support the eminent English tragedian, William Charles Macready, in a series of farewell appearances and won high honor for himself. Shortly afterwards, he acted with James H. Hackett, who was then performing as a star.

Davenport returned to the United States in 1854 and made his reappearance at the Broadway Theatre in New York. During the ensuing months and years, he acted everything from Bill Sykes to Hamlet and from Sir Lucius O'Trigger to Othello. On a single evening he is known to have presented three acts of *Hamlet,* one act of *Black-Eyed Susan,* and finally a farce in which he impersonated a stage-struck Yankee.

On several occasions during his career, Davenport tried his hand at managing a theatre but he was never very successful. Although he possessed both energy and taste, he also possessed the sort of liberality which made him generous to everyone but himself. In casting a play, he first took care that all members of the company were satisfied with their parts and then, if there was anything left, he assigned it to himself. Often he succeeded in making these minor studies noteworthy, but his constant minimizing of his own ability had a deteriorating effect on his reputation. However, he scored many triumphs during the years of his maturity. His career culminated in the famous production of *Julius Caesar* at Booth's Theatre in 1875–76, in which Davenport played Brutus, Lawrence Barrett played Cassius, and Frank C. Bangs played Marc Antony.

It was during the long run of this play that Davenport demonstrated once again the consideration and thoughtful kindness for others which always endeared him to his fellow actors. He was suffering so painfully from rheumatism in one of his hands that he could not bear anyone to touch it and yet, it is said, he concealed his suffering with genial gaiety and had a good word and a pleasant smile for everyone around him. "His kind and amiable disposition," wrote one of his fellow actors, "endeared him to his associates, while his great abilities as an actor won their unbounded admiration." [55] Another actor wrote: "In all the relations of life, he was a gentleman, courteous in every sense to those with whom he came in contact, walking the earth as if he loved it, and ever ready to extend the right hand of fellowship to anyone who sought his aid. . . ." [56]

The season of 1876–77 was Davenport's last. During that year he acted many roles, among them Richard III, Edgar in *King Lear,* and a sturdy blacksmith in *Dan'l Bruce*—again demonstrating the wide versatility he possessed. He died on September 1, 1877, but his name was not soon forgotten. His beautiful daughter, the talented Fanny Davenport, achieved great fame as an actress of the emotionalistic school.

Davenport's acting was always praised for its smoothness and polish. He studied his roles carefully before enacting them, with the result that every detail of characterization and every aspect of motivation were revealed in his performances. In his hands a role had symmetry and balance from first to last, and was always presented with grace and repose. He didn't aim to be sensational or to win the applause of his audience. All his effects were governed by good taste. His elocution was always exemplary. H. D. Stone summarizes his excellences in these words:

He does not seek to take his auditors by storm; he is content with *winning* them. In his impersonations, calm judgment controls his impulses; his action and declamation are never measured and gauged by popular applause, but regulated by his own correct taste. He appears utterly unconscious of the presence of his audience. . . . His conception of character, matured in his closet, is produced upon the stage as he was learned to understand it. He leaves nothing to chance-thought. Of course, like every man of genius, he is not insensible or unaided by the inspiration of the hour. In reviewing any one of his delineations one is struck with its harmony. None of its local lights and shades will be found to have been exaggerated, but the various parts appear so duly balanced that the impression left upon the mind is precisely that produced by a well-drawn, well grouped, and well colored picture.[57]

On certain occasions during his career, Davenport was criticized for lacking fire. One critic said that his Hamlet was "tame" and "never excited any real emotion." Clara Morris, who saw him in his last years on the stage, said that his followers "delighted in the beautiful precision and distinctness of his reading" of the part of Hamlet, but, she said, "He always seemed to me a Hamlet cut in crystal—so clear and pure, so cold and hard he was." [58] Other critics disagree with these estimates and praise Davenport for the power and fire he could display when he felt it was appropriate. One of his most memorable roles was that of Sir Giles Overreach in *A New Way to Pay Old Debts*—a character which, early in his career, he had seen acted by the elder Booth. Davenport performed the part off and on during his whole career and is said to have been peerless in the role. His performance had force, intensity of passion, subtlety, malignancy, and furnished a "terrible picture of the grasping, avaricious father" whose final collapse was played with an intensity which was "almost fearful." Mrs. John Drew, a notable actress herself and the mother of a whole line of actors, declared that Davenport, as Sir Giles, "surpassed even the Elder Booth, and to those who remember that great actor nothing can be said beyond that." [59]

Davenport was universally praised for his great versatility, but this gift was, to some degree, a handicap. Because he seemed to be good in everything, nothing stood out as memorable—at least in the mind of the general public. Clara Morris explained the apparent contradiction by saying that Davenport

. . . was wonderfully versatile, but though versatility is a requisite for any really good actor, yet for some mysterious reason it never meets with great success outside a foreign theatre. The American public demands specialists —one man to devote himself solely to tragedy, another to romantic drama and duels, another to dress-suit satire. One woman to tears, another to laughter, and woe betide the star who, able to act both comedy and tragedy, ventures to do so; there will be no packed house to bear witness to the appreciation felt for such skill and variety of talent.[60]

The hallmark of Booth, Murdoch, Barrett, and many lesser players was versatility, yet their merits received greater acclaim than Davenport's—despite the opinion of Clara Morris. But perhaps within a wide range of parts they specialized to a degree—and certainly, also, they were less self-effacing than Davenport.

Whatever the reasons, E. L. Davenport never received the rank and the acclaim which seem rightfully to belong to him. Yet the record of his achievement is proof that he thoroughly merits the high praise given him by his discerning followers.

LAWRENCE BARRETT

Perhaps the least gifted but certainly the most persevering of this group was Lawrence Barrett. His great success in the theatre is a testament to the efficacy of consuming ambition, unremitting industry, and stubborn intelligence. He began his career ignorant and penniless, without education or influence, and possessed of only the meagerest physical and vocal equipment. Yet he became an outstanding actor, the leading scholar of the American stage, and a man whose "lasting influence on the theatre of this country was far beyond that of Davenport and nearly equal to that of Booth." [61]

Barrett was born in Paterson, New Jersey, April 4, 1838, the son of ignorant Irish immigrants. At the age of ten he ran away from home. At the age of fourteen he became call boy at the Metropolitan Theatre in Detroit. Fired with ambition to become an actor, he began his theatrical education by studying the only book he possessed—a battered copy of Webster's Dictionary. He practically memorized the dictionary, and he literally memorized the plays of Shakespeare as soon as he could lay his hands on them. He plagued the manager to give him bit parts, and whenever he received one, performed with an awkward intensity which was ridiculed by the rest of the company. But he persisted, and with no encouragement except his own ambition and effort, he developed slowly and fumblingly. After two years he secured a humble place in a Pittsburgh stock company. He went from here to New York—where he almost starved to death before any manager would give him a chance. Finally, in 1857, at the age of nineteen, he obtained an engagement at Burton's old Chambers Street Theatre and was successful enough to win a permanent position. With passionate zeal and single-minded intensity, he studied dramatic literature, disciplined his mind and body, exercised his voice, and pushed his claims with every friend and every manager. He rose slowly but surely, fiercely proud of his accomplishments, and keenly jealous of those who were more talented or successful than himself. He eventually became a leading man, then a star, and—as a climax to his career—arranged the famous partnership with Edwin Booth, during which, as manager and co-star of the combination, he achieved the prestige of equal billing with America's greatest tragedian. His career ended on March 18, 1891, when he insisted upon filling an acting engagement even though he was suffering from pneumonia. He collapsed during the performance and died the next day.

Barrett was a man of medium height and slight physique. His principal physical grace was "the curve in his back," of which, says Otis Skinner, he was "quite vain." [62] His features were not handsome, but his deep-set, burning eyes gave his face an intensity which reminded Skinner of a monk. The voice of the actor was not naturally full and rich, but assiduous effort gave it strength and flexibility. By the time Barrett had reached his prime, his voice was described as an instrument "of unusual range . . . compelling and powerful" in its effect.[63]

The lack of schooling and cultural training in his early life gave Barrett a deep reverence for scholarship. As soon as he gained access to books, he became a diligent student and soon acquired a reputation for wide reading and sound learning. Like Booth, Murdoch, and Davenport, he studied his roles thoroughly, acquainting himself with all the history and commentary associated with them. No part was ever undertaken without intensive and painstaking research, a research which included study of the broad backgrounds of the drama as well as scrutiny of the individual role. So widely and thoroughly did Barrett venture in the realms of scholarship, that before he died he was credited with being an authority on the history of the stage, an expert in every branch of English literature, and "pre-eminently the scholar of the American theatre."

Barrett's zeal for improvement and his arduous self-training could not compensate, however, for limited endowments. His acting never achieved the poise, the grace, and the naturalness of a great artist. It was always studied and somewhat artificial. Otis Skinner, who acted with Barrett many times, thought he was "one of the most mannered men the American stage ever produced," [64] and wondered where in the world he had ever acquired such a style. Another critic said he performed like a scientist, solely with his brain, revealing a character "with the watchful precision of a botanist at work on a delicate flower." [65] Because the mechanism of his art was always apparent, he rarely seemed spontaneous and he never assumed "the convincing dash of a master."

Barrett's elocution was the most artificial element in his acting. In the actor's anxiety to perfect himself, he practiced his elocution assiduously, but always in the direction of precision and elegance. The result was pedantic enunciation and a monotonous, deliberate reading of the blank verse. Alfred Ayres says: "He was a chanter, a sing-songer; his mind was always more occupied with the tones he was making than with the thoughts he was speaking." [66] Barrett, incidentally, was unconscious of the way he sounded. The jibes of the critics offended him, and he is said to have remarked stiffly: "It would not become me to say that they are wrong; I will say this however: if my elocution is as bad as they say it is . . . I am not conscious of it." [67]

In addition, Barrett lacked a warm, attractive stage personality. He commanded respect and admiration but he very rarely inspired affection. Audiences were not charmed and warmed by his personality as they were by actors like Booth and McCullough. Without a popular play and strong support, Barrett could not draw large crowds to a theatre. In the season of 1871–72, for example, he starred in *Man O'Airlie* for over four weeks at Booth's Theatre, with a resultant loss to the management of $8,500. Barrett was angered when the play was withdrawn, and even more angry when Edwin Booth tried tactfully and sympathetically to point out his deficiencies.[68]

But the acting of Lawrence Barrett was not without its excellence. All his roles were illuminated by two virtues: intelligence of conception, and earnestness of purpose. The actor's studious analysis of his characters always resulted in a coherent and logical delineation which revealed appreciation of the dramatist's purpose and a firm grasp of his design. Intelligent treatment of this sort was recognized by Barrett's audiences and appreciated by them. Also, they never failed to perceive the earnestness in his work. The actor was passionately devoted to his profession and fiercely ambitious for fame and fortune. In pursuance of his goals, he acted with a sincerity and an intensity which raised many a performance from mediocrity to success. Alfred Ayres wrote: "His position as a player was due mainly to his ability to be in earnest, a faculty that often blinds the millions to every shortcoming. . . ."[69]

Barrett's acting, although mannered and formal, was not without its moments of excitement. When a scene demanded passionate display he was capable of rising to the challenge and thrilling an audience with vehemence and force of feeling. Sometimes these displays sounded calculated; at other times they appeared to be the natural overflow of powerful emotions. Otis Skinner tells us that despite the artificiality of his style, on occasions "There was a tempestuous, torrential character . . . in many of his parts that swept his audiences into enthusiasm" and that sometimes he displayed a "high pitch of nervous intensity" that caused him to "shoot through his parts like a race horse."[70]

During his career, Barrett acted all the great Shakespearean roles such as Hamlet, Macbeth, Othello, etc., and in these he was considered more than adequate. With Booth he played "seconds," appearing as Horatio, Macduff, Iago, etc., and was highly successful. Perhaps his outstanding characterization was that of the "lean and hungry" Cassius in *Julius Caesar*. Barrett's looks and temperament exactly fitted this role. Many spectators felt that the tense, ambitious Cassius had actually come to life when the tense, ambitious Barrett strode onto the stage. The actor's skill at presenting "stinging, biting . . . passion, . . . anger suppressed but struggling for an outlet" [71] found ample scope in the part of Cassius, and won high critical acclaim for the performer.

Barrett's acting was always overshadowed by the peerless art of Edwin Booth,[72] but Barrett contributed to the American theatre in other ways. He demonstrated superior ability as a manager and promoter: he had a sharp sense of business, he cared about details, and he was a tireless worker. During his lifetime, he not only promoted himself, but he also promoted the cause of good drama throughout the United States. He hated what was cheap and sensational on the stage, and tried to maintain the popularity of the classic repertory. He encouraged new playwrights and sponsored the first presentation or the revival of many plays which he considered to have literary and dramatic merit. His revival of Boker's *Francesca da Rimini* was noteworthy, and he could take credit for many other successful presentations such as *Yorick's Love, Pendragon,* and *Ganelon.*

One of his most valuable contributions to the theatre was his creation and management of the Booth-Barrett combination in the 1880's. By this time, Edwin Booth, worn out physically and emotionally, was in the closing years of his career. The great tragedian had been battling personal tragedy and business disasters for more than thirty years, and now was too tired to care about fame or reputation. His acting had become empty and mechanical. The form was there but the fire was gone. Barrett realized that the fire was not quenched but merely smouldering and, under favorable circumstances, could flare up again— much to the profit of anyone who stoked it. He proposed to stoke it himself, as a service to American drama and to himself, and so he arranged a partnership between himself and Booth—in which he assumed the complete responsibility of business and artistic management, while Booth had no obligations or worries except his own acting. Barrett became, as Clara Morris has described it, the "agent, manager, stage-manager, friend, co-worker, and dramatic guardian angel" of Edwin Booth, and "all he asked of him in return was to act." [73] The results were epochal. Booth responded with a splendid revival of his old-time genius; Barrett reaped high honor and profit for himself; and American audiences enjoyed an Indian summer of great drama greatly acted, the like of which is rarely seen.

For his services in this undertaking, and for his many other contributions to the well-being and high standing of the American theatre, Lawrence Barrett well deserves the tribute written by William B. Laffan: ". . . Mr. Barrett has done more than anyone else in America to present the higher drama under conditions of artistic completeness, and to stimulate the literary and artistic development of a stage impressed with his own character and taste." [74]

There were other capable actors, more limited in talent and less eminent in position than Booth, Murdoch, Davenport, or Barrett, who played the same roles and demonstrated to a lesser degree the same range of versatility. Among the actors who belong in this group are several who made noteworthy contributions to the American stage.

GEORGE C. VANDENHOFF

Son of an eminent English actor of the Kemble school, George C. Vandenhoff made his American debut in 1842 and remained in this country, except for occasional visits to Great Britain, until his death in 1884. Vandenhoff's first role in the United States was Hamlet and in the part he was praised for grace and dignity, for correctness of delivery, and for the poetic elegance of his style. In the other parts he played, such as Richard III, Hotspur, Marc Antony, Mercutio, Macbeth, Benedick, and Claude Melnotte, these same excellences were extolled, and, at the same time, a certain deficiency of passion and lack of fire were noted. Evidently, refinement and polish were his forte while strength and power were somewhat lacking. His feeling for refinement and his disappointment at what he considered to be a decline in taste for good drama led him to withdraw from regular stage appearances in the middle years of the 1850's, after which he devoted his life to teaching elocution and to reading Shakespeare in public. One of his pupils was Mary Anderson who took ten lessons from him, the only instruction in dramatic art she ever received. But Vandenhoff returned to the stage on occasions; one of his last appearances was in 1874 when he played Macbeth to Charlotte Cushman's Lady Macbeth in Miss Cushman's farewell appearance in New York City.

EDWIN ADAMS

Edwin Adams (1834–1877), a native-born American, is remembered as a light comedian, but he had sufficient scope to warrant his inclusion here. It is true that Adams played romantic comedy with dash and brilliance, but early in his career his emotional power was noted and encouraged. Mrs. John E. Owens, wife of the famous comedian, records that in 1855, two years after Adams' debut, he made a hit as Edward Mapleton in *The Merchant and His Clerks* and in the portrayal he "developed such force and emotional power that Mr. Owens advised him to devote attention to tragedy, feeling sure that his talent was great for that line of drama." [75] Apparently Adams took this advice, because in 1860 he played Hamlet and three years later he was the leading man in H. L. Bateman's company where he acted all the top roles in tragedy and romance. In 1869 when Booth's Theatre opened in New York, Adams played Mercutio to Edwin Booth's Romeo. He remained in the company as a leading man, acting such roles as Iago to Booth's Othello, Rover in *Wild Oats,* Claude Melnotte in *The Lady of Lyons,* and many of the chief roles in Shakespearean tragedy. He was efficient and capable as a tragedian but his greatest strength seemed to lie in romance and comedy. He created the role of Enoch Arden in a play based on Tennyson's poem, and was considered such a perfect embodiment of the character that other actors hesitated to attempt the part. He excelled as Mercutio, and was the first portrayer of Robert Landry in *The Dead Heart.* William Winter says that "next to E. L. Davenport, he was the best Mercutio I have ever seen." [76] Clara Morris goes farther and declares that as a portrayer of Mercutio "no greater ever strode than . . . Edwin Adams." [77]

Adams, unlike the greatest of the tragedians, was not a careful scholar nor a skillful analyst of motives and character. However, he had a dramatic instinct which was unerring and a vitality and charm which "thrilled the feelings and fired the imagination" of his audience. His voice, too, enhanced his appeal. All of his contemporaries praised it as "superb," as "rich, soulful, lovely," or as "one of the most melodious and sympathetic ever heard."

Evidently Adams' joyous charm, his winning vitality, and his engaging manliness were an intrinsic part of his personality. He was liked and admired as much off the stage as on. Joseph Jefferson says that "As a man he was loving and beloved. . . ." [78] And William Winter, lamenting his early death at the age of forty-three, writes that "He was one of those rare men who refresh mankind by spontaneous, shining exposition of the loveliness which is an inherent element of human nature." [79]

CHARLES W. COULDOCK

Charles W. Couldock (1815–1898) was another Englishman who became identified with the American stage and who during more than sixty years of acting contributed many well-loved portraits to our theatrical gallery. The actor was brought to America by Charlotte Cushman in 1849 and made his United States debut as leading man in her production of *The Stranger* on October 8 at the Park Theatre in New York. He was an immediate success and continued as a star for many years. He played heroes and villains in both comedy and tragedy but was best, perhaps, in romantic melodramas like *The Willow Corpse, The Chimney Corner,* and *Hazel Kirke.* He is not remembered for the great roles of tragedy—although William Winter lists him as one who could play Hamlet in an efficient and thoroughly satisfactory manner—but he is remembered for having given brilliant life to such roles as Abel Murcott in the original United States production of *Our American Cousin* and Dunstan Kirke in the original New York production of *Hazel Kirke.* William Winter calls him one of the "shining names" which "brightly spangled" the last half of the nineteenth century.

JOSEPH HAWORTH

Joseph Haworth (1855–1903), who was born and reared in Cleveland, Ohio, made his debut there and served his early apprenticeship in John Ellsler's Cleveland company. As a young man he acted with Edwin Booth, John McCullough, Lawrence Barrett, and many other great players. From them he learned to know and love the Shakespearean repertory and he eventually played the great roles of Hamlet, Othello, Richard III, etc. His Shakespearean characters were always soundly conceived, carefully worked out, and performed with skill and effectiveness. When he became a star, he followed the trend of the times and appeared less often in Shakespeare and more frequently in the romantic drama and melodrama of the late nineteenth century. He was admired for his force, his technical control, and his theatrical effectiveness in such plays as *The Christian, The Bells, Ruy Blas,* and *Paul Kauvar*. He died at the age of forty-eight and is remembered as one of the very good actors of his time but not as a great one.

Following are some other actors of lesser stature whose names are associated with the versatile tragedians.

John Howard Payne (1791–1852) is best known as the author or adapter of over sixty plays. He was hailed as the "American Roscius" when he made his debut as a child prodigy in 1809 although he was seventeen years old at the time. For the next five years he acted such roles as Hamlet, Romeo, Petruchio, Edgar in *King Lear,* and a variety of romantic heroes, but after 1813, when he went to England, his active career as a player virtually ended. His principal occupations for the rest of his life were playwriting and government service.

Peter Richings (1797–1871), born and reared in England, spent his entire professional life in the United States as an actor and a manager. His style in such roles as King Claudius in *Hamlet,* Henry Bertram in *Guy Mannering,* and Sikes in *Oliver Twist* was considered artificial but effective.

William Wheatley (1816–1876), son of the famous comedienne Sarah Ross Wheatley but best known as a manager and as the producer of *The Black Crook,* was an actor of repute who played such roles as Hamlet and Romeo but was far more successful in showy, romantic parts like Claude Melnotte in *The Lady of Lyons* or in stuffy comic roles like Captain Absolute in *The Rivals*.

Charles Barron (1843–1918), for many years the leading man at the Boston Museum, was famous for his portrayal of Bill Sikes as well as for many other characterizations among the more than five hundred parts he played during his lifetime. His great versatility in both classic and modern roles earned him the admiration of his fellow players, one of whom declared: "I never knew a man who could play so many parts so well, and play them so easily." [80]

STEELE MACKAYE, DISCIPLE OF
FRANÇOIS DELSARTE

James Morrison Steele MacKaye, eccentric genius and jack-of-all-arts, can hardly be said to have been a "master" of any single activity but he succeeded, to a degree, in every theatrical activity he tried. Among his talents were: scene designing, stage lighting, the invention of stage machinery, directing, managing, teaching, acting, and playwriting. Perhaps he is best remembered as a dramatist, for he wrote or adapted or collaborated in the writing of thirty plays, of which the best known is *Hazel Kirke*. However, it is his contribution to American acting which concerns us here. This contribution is more indirect than direct. That is, his introduction to America of the Delsarte theories of expression and his establishment of the first dramatic school in the United States, which later became the American Academy of Dramatic Arts, exerted more influence on the development of American acting than did his own professional appearances on the stage.

MacKaye, who was born in Buffalo, New York, in 1842, evidenced talent and artistic temperament at a very early age. His father, an affluent and influential attorney, encouraged the artistic ambitions of his son, sending him to Paris at the age of sixteen to study painting and placing "unlimited funds at his disposal." But neither painting nor an unrestricted bank account were sufficient to hold the interest of the restless, volatile young man. Within a year he returned to the United States, and shortly after the outbreak of the Civil War, he joined the Union forces. It was in the Army, of all places, that he first demonstrated his theatrical talents. During the month of August, 1862, in the barracks of the Seventh New York Regiment, then stationed in Baltimore, Maryland, he played five Shakespearean roles: Othello, Antonio, Hamlet, Cassius, and Shylock. He was supported by a cast of fellow soldiers.

After the war, he deserted his newly found love of acting and tried his hand at a variety of enterprises, all of which proved unsuccessful. He eventually returned to Paris and began the serious study of singing and acting with François Delsarte. He became Delsarte's best student, avidly absorbing the master's teaching and brilliantly demonstrating his principles. Then, with characteristic enthusiasm, MacKaye returned to the United States eager to reform the American stage through an application of the system he had just discovered. He became the high priest and chief representative of the Delsarte principles in this country. He lectured on them, he taught them to other actors who sought his guidance, and he made them the basis for the dramatic school he established in connection with the Lyceum Theatre in 1884. It was this school which was later to evolve into the American Academy of Dramatic Arts under the leadership of Franklin H. Sargent.

MacKaye's professional debut as an actor occurred in New York in January of 1872 when he performed the leading role in a play written by himself and Francis Durivage entitled *Monaldi*. The supporting cast of this production was composed of MacKaye's pupils to whom he had been imparting the principles of Delsartism. Fired anew with a zeal for acting and, apparently, desiring additional instruction in the art, MacKaye returned to Paris later in 1872 and placed himself under the tutelage of François Régnier, Director of the Théâtre Français. He appeared as Hamlet in the Paris Conservatoire late in 1872, acting the role in French. The following spring he played the part in London, acting it in English—the first American ever to perform the role on the British stage. This seems to be the high point of MacKaye's career in acting, for shortly thereafter his enthusiasms were directed elsewhere. During the rest of his life he occasionally assumed roles in his own plays or appeared in benefit performances for other actors. But he did not develop his talents as a tragedian or as an exponent of Shakespearean drama. In the twenty years between his return from England in 1874 and his death in 1894, he made brief appearances in only sixteen different plays, eleven of which were his own dramas. The "wayward genius," described by William Winter as "impetuous, capricious, volatile, prone to extravagant fancies and bold experiments," [81] directed his restless energies into playwriting, teaching, theatrical management, the rebuilding of playhouses, the invention of stage machinery, and into grandiose schemes such as those for a "Spectatorium" to embellish the Chicago World's Fair of the 1890's.

MacKaye's achievements as an actor were not sufficient to exert much influence on the development of American acting. But his teaching of the Delsarte principles of expression both to private pupils and to the classes he established exerted considerable influence—some of it good, much of it bad.

What were the main principles of Delsarte which MacKaye found so stimulating? They were chiefly concerned with action and gesture as a means of expression and not with speech. "The text is only a label," writes the Abbe Delaumosne, one of Delsarte's disciples. "The sense lies not in speech but in inflection and in gesture. Nature institutes a movement, speech names the movement. . . . Speech is only the title of that which gesture has announced; speech comes only to confirm what is already understood by the auditors." [82] With such a belief in the primacy of movement, Delsarte proceeded to establish a "science of movement." He declared that man's fundamental nature has three aspects: physical, mental, and moral. These aspects are conditioned and modified by man's normal, concentric, or eccentric states of being. The normal state is the calm state of the individual; the concentric inclines him toward concentration and inversion, while the eccentric state impels him toward expansion and extroversion. The fundamental aspects of man's nature, modified by his state of being, have a special apparatus for their expression in which each organ of the body participates. Every thought, sentiment, emotion, or sensation arising from man's triple nature is reflected and expressed in a characteristic way through his physical body.

On the basis of this general theory, Delsarte proceeded to examine the reactions and movements of each physical organ and to analyze their roles in the expression of thought and feeling. The movements of the head, the torso, and the limbs are all classified and described according to their meaning and significance. The result is a series of charts where, for instance, one can see illustrated the position of the eye in exaltation, aversion, astonishment, and every other emotional state. The same careful classification of response is given to the arms, the legs, the hands, and each expressive part of the body.

It may be surprising to many readers to learn that this theory of expression, which later became so mechanized and distorted, was designed to produce greater sincerity and naturalness in acting. MacKaye introduced the system to America believing that it would render an actor more life-like and would eliminate the posturing and artificiality too often observed on the stage. Indeed, Delsarte had evolved his system as a revolt against the teachings of the Paris Conservatoire which he found to produce a conventionalized and unnatural style of performance. The purpose of Delsarte's research was to discover natural physical movements, the responses of real people in real situations. To this end, he studied anatomy and physiology, he visited hospitals and dissecting rooms, he spent endless hours observing people in all walks of life, and he scrutinized the masterpieces of painting and sculpture in the Paris galleries. The aim of the system which resulted from his research was the elimination of the artificial and mechanical in movement and the substitution of the real and the true as nature revealed them.

When MacKaye applied Delsarte's principles in his own acting, he impressed his audiences as being sincere, natural, and free from artificiality. The reviews of his performances all praise him for quiet intensity, for the absence of rant, for movement and gesture which were simple and "true to nature." MacKaye transmitted Delsarte's aims and methods, with embellishments of his own, to his classes and to his private pupils. Many of them found the instruction rewarding and productive of greater sincerity and naturalness in their own acting. Perhaps the outstanding example of the success of MacKaye's teaching was the popular tragedian, John McCullough, whose early style of performing, as has been noted in a previous chapter, was patterned after the heroic, muscular school of Edwin Forrest. In 1877, after twenty years on the stage, he took some lessons from Steele MacKaye and the results were notable. The period of his finest acting ensued. The critics now praised him for "tempered emotion," for "discipline and control," for "more repose, more dignity, more grace." McCullough was generous in crediting his improvement to Steele MacKaye, for he reported to A. C. Wheeler: ". . . that teacher, MacKaye, has taught me more in three months than I could have learned otherwise in twenty years, and I don't care who knows it." [83]

The Delsarte principles benefited many performers, but these principles were easily distorted and misapplied. Unhappily there was as much misapplication as there was sound teaching, so that today the principles are remembered for the grotesqueries they spawned rather than for the good they did. Delsarte's science of movement became a system of gymnastics. (MacKaye abetted this perversion by adding "harmonic gymnastics" to the Delsarte exercises.) Delsarte's system of gestures became elaborate pantomimes accompanied by music and recitations. His aim to reproduce the truth of nature became a mechanical distortion of nature which was so absurd as to discredit the art of elocution for several decades. American acting was influenced for the worse in many cases.

Perhaps the best effects of MacKaye's teaching, aside from his assistance to certain actors like John McCullough, was the stimulation given to three students who eventually became prominent teachers of expression and acting. These were Samuel S. Curry, who became the author of many books and the head of the Curry School of Expression; Dr. Charles W. Emerson, a pupil of a pupil of MacKaye's, who became head of the Emerson College of Oratory; and Franklin H. Sargent, a pupil and co-worker of MacKaye's, who became President of the American Academy of Dramatic Arts. These men freely acknowledged their indebtedness to MacKaye and to the stimulation they received from the Delsarte principles. But these principles, in their hands, were altered, refined, and expanded according to their own research and experience and thus evolved into quite different approaches to acting than the one created by Delsarte.

In general, these leaders rejected the practice of teaching attitudes and gestures or of specifying particular vocal devices for the revelation of emotion. They felt that life-like creation of expression can only develop from within. Thus they emphasized the cultivation of imagination and sensitivity, and they sought to develop not only the intellectual and physical faculties and functions, but "the powers of personality itself—the inner and deeper natures . . . the temperamental and imaginative, instinctive, and conceptively original powers of feeling." [84]

The teachings of these three leaders, and of other responsible students of MacKaye, were absorbed by several generations of students and performers, many of whom became teachers themselves in American universities and in professional schools of dramatics. Thus the original inspiration of the Delsarte principles, as transmitted by Mac-Kaye in his classroom rather than in his own performances, came to exert a widespread but indirect influence on the development of American acting.

[NOTES ON THE SETTING]

Later Nineteenth Century

BY THE MIDDLE OF THE NINETEENTH CENTURY THE colorful cultural backdrop before which Edwin Forrest and his colleagues had made their entrance in 1820 had shifted to reveal a new and altered landscape before which the American actor played his part.

The most notable feature of the new landscape was its astonishing increase in size. The territory of the United States had grown enormously. The Louisiana Purchase had been made in 1803, three years before Forrest was born, and Florida had been acquired a year before Forrest made his debut as an actor. During the succeeding years, while Forrest was climbing to stardom, the Texas and Oregon territories were annexed, and then—following the War with Mexico—a vast western empire was acquired, later to be carved into the states of California, Nevada, Utah, Colorado, Arizona, and New Mexico. By 1850, some form of dramatic activity stretched from the Atlantic seaboard across the wilderness for three thousand miles to California.

In mid-century, this enormous territory was being opened to settlement, to trade, and to theatrical enterprise by the rapid development of the railroads. As early as 1854 several lines had crossed the Mississippi, and in 1869 the first transcontinental line, joining New York with San Francisco, was completed. Now the stars and traveling companies—instead of bumping over hazardous roads in wagons and stagecoaches, as their predecessors had done—could move from town to town both quickly and comfortably.

Within this greatly expanded country population was growing and industry was booming. In 1820, when Forrest made his debut, there were over nine and one half million inhabitants in the United States. Thirty-six years later, when Edwin Booth made his first appearance in New York City, the population had grown to thirty million and large numbers of these citizens were congregated in cities where they could be easily lured into the playhouses. New York City, in 1850, with a population of over 600,000, boasted seven legitmate theatres and the Astor Place Opera House plus many halls and gardens devoted to concerts, vaudeville, and minstrel shows. Boston and Philadelphia each had several excellent theatres as did many other cities in the East and South. New Orleans was a thriving theatrical town, Chicago and Cincinnati were building playhouses, and in San Francisco Thomas Maguire opened the Jenny Lind Theatre with the enthusiastic support of a population of 50,000. Almost every village, hamlet, and town had some kind of a playhouse. In 1850, there were more than fifty stock companies opening in American cities, and by 1880, according to William Winter,[1] there were in the United States and Canada about 3,500 towns in which plays were regularly given. Distributed in these towns were approximately 5,000 playhouses supplied by more than 250 companies and stars drawn from no less than 5,000 professional players.

The country, as a whole, was vigorous and prosperous. There were recurring financial panics and depressions which slowed down all business, including show business, but the set-backs were temporary. Even the growing tensions which were to culminate in the Civil War did not seriously impede the steady progress toward greater wealth and leisure—both of which were of major importance to show business. The Puritan prejudice against the theatre as a center of sin and depravity was not dead by any means, but the prejudice was weakening. When ladies of virtue and social position, like Mrs. Anna Cora Mowatt, became actresses and conducted themselves with exemplary propriety, thousands of citizens decided that the theatre might not be so sinful after all.

A significant portion of the growing population of the country were immigrants speaking a babel of tongues. Often they crowded into the cities in such great numbers that it was profitable to open foreign language theatres for their entertainment. New York City had two German theatres by 1866 and later on a Yiddish, an Italian, and a Chinese theatre. New Orleans had French theatres, and San Francisco was soon to have both a Chinese and an Italian theatre. But the real influence of the many-tongued population showed itself in the tremendous growth of the "popular" theatre. The polyglot population began to give enthusiastic support to minstrelsy, vaudeville, burlesque, the circus, and every form of variety entertainment which could be enjoyed without an understanding of any language. During the second half of the nineteenth century, these forms of popular theatre gained immense appeal.

In the legitimate playhouses, Shakespeare was still standard fare, and so were the plays of Goldsmith, Sheridan, and other writers of "old comedy." The reigning contemporary playwrights were all foreign, and they were turning out romantic tragedies and sentimental melodramas with great appeal to American audiences. Native playwriting was still suffering from prejudice and an inferiority complex, and American dramatists were still copying foreign models—even though Anna Cora Mowatt had written a sparkling comedy of social satire called *Fashion,* and George Henry Boker had produced what was perhaps the best American romantic tragedy with his drama, *Francesca da Rimini.* Other Americans had written Yankee plays or comedies of life-in-the-big-city or farces, but the slapstick, rough-and-tumble farces—which for years had been played as afterpieces following the main drama of the evening—were now being eliminated.

In mid-century, the metropolitan theatres which presented the plays of the time had become elaborate structures with ornate lobbies, upholstered seats, and every form of luxury known to the period. Often they were of immense size. New York's Bowery Theatre, rebuilt in 1845, seated 4,000, and even P. T. Barnum's "Lecture Room" was remodeled in 1849 to hold 3,000. The shape of these theatres had not changed since the debut of Edwin Forrest. Proscenium doors were disappearing and the forestage was diminishing in depth, but the picture frame stage still faced an auditorium with boxes and galleries suspended in a horseshoe curve above a pit or orchestra floor. Both stage and auditorium were lighted by gas.

As yet, most of the scenery which surrounded the players on the stage was composed of elaborately painted wings and drops. But now there was occasionally seen the exciting new "box" type setting introduced by Dion Boucicault. This energetic, versatile Irishman is credited with introducing the interior setting composed of three walls and a ceiling which gave the illusion of an actual room. Moreover, the floor was carpeted, the doors and windows were the "working" type —not painted on canvas—and the furniture and properties were numerous and practical. Such scenery earned Boucicault the title of "the upholsterer of the stage," and it was the type of realistic setting which, with increasing refinement, has dominated the American stage ever since—varied and transformed only occasionally by the art of the "New Stagecraft" introduced in the twentieth century by Gordon Craig and Adolphe Appia. In the middle of the nineteenth century, the realistic box setting was a novelty.

Boucicault is credited with another innovation which was to have far-reaching effects upon the American theatre, that is, his introduction of the "combination" or road company. Until about 1860, the only actor who traveled was the star. He journeyed from town to town acting with one of the resident companies in each city. He chose the plays he wished to give and the resident company provided the complete supporting cast as well as all the other elements of the production. On the whole it was a good system because it encouraged strong resident companies in each city and it provided immense and varied experience for the members of these companies. About 1860, Boucicault saw the economic advantages of organizing a cast to perform a single popular play and then dispatching the entire company on a tour of the nation. The local community was now asked to supply only the playhouse and the facilities but no supporting actors. The system, proving profitable to the manager or impresario, quickly gained in popularity and soon began to destroy the venerable institution of the resident company.

However, in mid-century and for twenty years thereafter, the resident companies were strong and prosperous and the actor dominated the theatrical scene. These were the so-called "palmy days" when the star player was king. He evolved his own style, worked out his own characterizations, designed his own make-up and costumes, and performed in the manner which *he* felt was effective. The actors of the supporting cast had the same independence to a lesser degree, because there was no director or régisseur to tell them what to do. The company manager or the stage manager rarely if ever ventured to give advice to the player. It was not until the advent of such men as Augustin Daly and David Belasco, at the end of the century, that the concept of the modern director emerged. In the palmy days the star actor was supreme.

In 1860, who were the players who thus dominated the theatrical scene? Edwin Forrest, John McCullough, and other actors of the heroic school were still active and popular. Forrest did not retire until 1872, the year of his death. But he had formidable rivals. Booth was the new sensation of the tragic drama; Murdoch and Davenport were established favorites; Barrett was beginning his rise to prominence. Mary Ann Duff, the first great classic actress, was dead, but Charlotte Cushman was still acting her superb tragic roles and was to continue for another fifteen years. Two other classic actresses, who were to adopt the United States as their homeland, were flourishing in Europe: Helena Modjeska was the leading actress in Poland and not due to make her American debut until 1877; Fanny Janauschek, a star in Germany, would appear in the United States in 1866. Of the actresses of the emotionalistic school, Laura Keene and Matilda Heron were enjoying great popularity; Anna Cora Mowatt had made her sensation and was now retired; Clara Morris, Fanny Davenport, and other actresses of the emotionalistic school had not yet begun their careers and neither had the great ladies of the personality school —with the exception of Clara Fisher, who had ended her reign as a child prodigy and was now playing adult roles with charm and effectiveness. Great comic performers were flourishing more vigorously than perhaps at any other time in the history of American drama. Such superb character comedians as William Warren, Henry Placide, John Gilbert, and Mrs. John Drew were at the height of their powers, and they were surrounded by a host of other players almost as good. Comic specialists like Joseph Jefferson III and John T. Raymond had already made names for themselves and so had other unforgettable characters like Francis Chanfrau, E. A. Sothern, and George Holland. In addition to the legitimate theatres playing the standard repertory of tragedy and comedy, melodrama and farce, there were hundreds of halls, saloons, tents, and playhouses where the public was enjoying vaudeville, minstrelsy, burlesque, circus, and productions of *Uncle Tom's Cabin*. It was, indeed, a luxuriant and prosperous time for American acting, and it was due to last for many more years. The Civil War was to provide a temporary setback, and the tragedy at Ford's Theatre in Washington was to force Edwin Booth into retirement for several months. But neither war nor the assassination of a President were to impede seriously the progress of the theatre or the development of the colorful careers of American players.

IV

THE SCHOOL OF EMOTIONALISM

DURING THE SECOND HALF OF THE NINETEENTH CENTURY, WHILE the actresses of the classic school were demonstrating their art in the great roles of the standard drama, another group of actresses was winning popular acclaim as purveyors of emotionalism. Developing their style through different methods, and usually exercising their appeal in tearful domestic melodramas adapted from French or German dramatists, these actresses constitute a group which can be called the school of emotionalism. This kind of acting was developed almost exclusively by female performers for the simple reason that emotionalistic roles were not often written for men. It would have been unthinkable for a male, in the American theatre with its Puritan, Anglo-Saxon background, to exhibit the kind of emotionalistic behavior which seemed probable and acceptable when coming from a lady in distress. The actresses who specialized in playing the lady in distress and who were the most notable exponents of the emotionalistic school included, among the early representatives, Anna Cora Mowatt, Laura Keene, and Matilda Heron; among the later the most famous were Clara Morris, Fanny Davenport, and Mrs. Leslie Carter.

As a manner of performing, emotionalistic acting could be recognized by three dominant characteristics.

First of all, the actress of this school actually experienced the feelings and passions of her role and surrendered herself to these emotions. She did not simulate but actively participated in the agonies of the mimicked character.

Secondly, she cultivated a lush, overt display of the passions she was feeling. Her performance was marked by sobs, tears, screams, shudders, heavings, writhings, pantings, growlings, tremblings, and all manner of physical manifestations. Sometimes these reactions were reproduced fully and realistically. This was the case with Clara Morris and the later representatives of the school. Sometimes the reactions were subdued and sentimentalized, this being the case with Laura Keene and the early representatives of the school.

The third major characteristic of the emotionalistic school was neglect of technique. In surrendering to emotion and cultivating lavish, overt expression, the emotionalistic actress disregarded discipline and control. Her elocution, gestures, movement, and performance of stage business were likely to be impromptu, unstudied, and haphazard. She relied on inspiration rather than art.

Every actor and actress will recognize that emotion is an indispensable ingredient of acting, and almost all players will testify that every performer who is worth his make-up feels the emotions of his role to some degree, although players differ greatly in the amount of feeling they experience and in the length of time it takes them to summon this feeling. The actress of the classic school certainly experienced the emotions of her roles to a greater or lesser degree, but at the same time she exercised artful discipline and control over her own emotional output. In contrast, the emotionalistic player abandoned control and surrendered herself entirely to the emotions of the part.

In any performance, the emotion of a role must be communicated by voice, gesture, movement, and facial expression. The actress of the classic school selects those details which best suggest the emotions of the situation and suppresses others. Only the most significant physical manifestations are projected and these in a conscious pattern for, as George Henry Lewes has written, "the internal workings must be legible in the external symbols; and these external symbols must also have a certain grace and proportion to affect us aesthetically." [1] The emotionalistic player, in contrast, exercises little selectivity but includes in her performance the maximum number of "external symbols."

No actor performs without some technique. But whereas the actress of the classic school uses it as a means of refining and controlling her emotional output, the emotionalistic player considers it of minor importance and relies, instead, upon uncontrolled feeling to gain her effects.

In addition to these three dominant traits, certain correlaries are significant.

Apparently, youth, beauty, and personal magnetism are absolutely essential in successful emotionalistic acting. The careers of members of this school indicate that youth is necessary to insure the actress an abundance of fresh and vigorous emotion, for with advancing age the well springs of passion appear to dry up. Beauty and magnetism are needed to charm the eye and touch the heart of the spectator so that he suspends his critical faculties while he revels in the personal spell of the player. It is true, of course, that these qualities are helpful in every style of acting. They can always be utilized on the stage to good advantage. However, those performers who earned a lasting reputation as great players did not rely on youth, beauty, and magnetism alone but developed powers which were independent of these—powers which served them well into old age and won them plaudits long after they had passed their physical prime. Among the actresses of the classic school, Mary Ann Duff, Charlotte Cushman, Helena Modjeska, and Fanny Janauschek are outstanding examples of players who succeeded greatly long after their youth was gone. On the other hand, it will be seen that the actresses of the emotionalistic school usually sank into disfavor and obscurity when they lost their youth and beauty.

Emotionalistic acting also needs a certain kind of play for its fullest development. All the actresses who gained fame in the emotionalistic school utilized dramas which are characterized by abundant sentiment, melodramatic action, and contrived emotional crises. The plays of Kotzebue, Bulwer-Lytton, Dion Boucicault, Bronson Howard, Augustin Daly, and David Belasco are all examples of this kind of drama. Such fervid works as Sardou's *Fédora* and *La Tosca,* which were unusually popular in the late nineteenth century, typify the vehicles in which the emotionalistic actresses were notably successful. When they attempted to act in plays of a different type—for example, the plays of Shakespeare or, later on, the dramas of Ibsen and Chekhov—they were notably unsuccessful. The careers of a few exponents of this school are surveyed below.

MRS. MOWATT (ANNA CORA OGDEN MOWATT RICHIE)

In May, 1845, Mrs. Anna Cora Mowatt suddenly decided to become an actress, and three weeks later her debut became the sensation of the New York season. For nine years she illumined the dramatic heavens, and then she withdrew as suddenly and as unexpectedly as she had appeared. Her career is significant because it marks the beginning in the American theatre of the school of emotionalism. Mrs. Mowatt was the first of a long line of actresses who achieved success primarily through personal charm and emotional exhibitionism.

Anna Cora Mowatt was an unusual and remarkable woman. Born into a household of twelve children, the daughter of well-to-do and socially prominent parents, she showed signs of precocity at an early age. When she was ten she had read the whole of Shakespeare's plays many times over. At the age of fifteen she married a wealthy New York lawyer. At the age of seventeen she published an epic poem, and when the critics condemned it as worthless, she refuted the critics in an effective verse satire. At eighteen she was threatened with consumption and went abroad for fifteen months to recover her health. While she was recuperating she found energy to write magazine articles, visit the theatre, take lessons in Italian, and compose a play in blank verse. When she was twenty-one, her husband lost his fortune, whereupon she launched a successful career as a public reader after only two weeks of training. When her health forced her to abandon the platform, she retired to her study and wrote magazine articles, novels, a life of Goethe, a life of Madame D'Arblay, and books on Housekeeping, Cookery, Embroidery, Etiquette, and Marriage. When she was twenty-five, a friend suggested that she try playwriting. The result was her famous comedy *Fashion,* which was submitted to the Park Theatre and was produced immediately with outstanding success. A few weeks later, because her husband had suffered additional financial reverses, she decided to become an actress. She allowed herself three weeks of preparation and one rehearsal. On June 13, 1845, she made a triumphal debut at the Park Theatre, New York, as Pauline in *The Lady of Lyons.* She shocked her genteel friends, but delighted the playgoing public. Her acting career, once started, prospered enormously. During her first year on the stage she appeared in all the principal cities of the United States, acting for more than two hundred nights in such roles as Lady Teazle, Mrs. Haller, Lucy Ashton, Katherine, Julia, and Juliet. In view of this prodigious activity and phenomenal success, Laurence Hutton declares: "In the history of the stage in all countries there is no single instance of a mere novice playing so many important parts so many nights, before so many different audiences, and winning so much and such merited praise, as did this lady during the first twelve months of her career as an actress." [2]

For nine years Mrs. Mowatt performed successfully and prosperously in Great Britain and the United States. Then, in June, 1854, when her appeal was still great and her charms unimpaired, she suddenly withdrew from public life and never appeared on the stage again. However, her busy private life continued until her death in 1870.

Mrs. Mowatt's great success, achieved without training or apprenticeship, seems to refute the belief that good acting is the result of careful preparation and long practice. The home theatricals, in which Mrs. Mowatt had participated since the age of five, and her brief career as a public reader, gave her a modicum of experience, but these activities cannot be considered adequate preparation for an acting career. To what can her quick success be attributed, and how praiseworthy was her style of acting?

There can be no question but that Mrs. Mowatt was a remarkably gifted person. She had unusual intelligence, keen aesthetic perception, thorough education, wide cultural experience, an excellent speaking voice, and beauty of face and figure—all of which are invaluable endowments for any actress. In addition, Mrs. Mowatt had an emotional sensitivity which enabled her to "abandon herself to a role," to "live the part," and this ability, added to her other endowments, was sufficient to win her success on the stage for nine prosperous years.

Edgar Allan Poe was a warm admirer of Mrs. Mowatt's acting (although he was a harsh critic of her dramaturgy). He describes her physical charms in these words:

Her figure is slight—even fragile—but eminently graceful. Her face is a remarkably fine one, and of that precise character best adapted to the stage. The forehead is the least prepossessing feature, although it is by no means an unintellectual one. The eyes are gray, brilliant and expressive, without being full. The nose is well formed, with the Roman curve, and strongly indicative of energy; this quality is also shown in the quality of the chin. The mouth is somewhat large, with brilliant and even teeth, and flexible lips, capable of the most effective variations of expression. A more radiantly beautiful smile we never remember having seen. Mrs. Mowatt has also the personal advantage of a profusion of rich auburn hair.[3]

In analyzing Mrs. Mowatt's acting, Poe singles out certain qualities for special commendation. He praises her ease and self-possession, her graceful movement, her richness of voice, and her distinctness of utterance. But, says Poe, "the greatest charm of the . . . acting . . . is its naturalness. She moves, looks, and speaks with a well-controlled impulsiveness as different as can be conceived from the customary rant and cant—the hack conventionality of the stage." [4] In amplifying his praise of Mrs. Mowatt's "well-controlled impulsiveness," Poe notes that she is able to make her bosom heave, her cheek grow pale, her limbs tremble, and her eyes fill with "nature's own tear" when she is called upon to portray feelings which are generous, noble, or unaffectedly passionate. Poe feels that this "freshness of the heart" and this "well of deep feeling" from which she draws so naturally, are gifts which distinguish her from the usual actress of the day and which enable her "effectively and unimpededly" to "lay bare to the audience the movements of her own passionate heart." [5] Poe was obviously much impressed by the emotionalistic aspects of Mrs. Mowatt's acting.

Other critics besides Poe were struck by the natural emotional quality of Mrs. Mowatt's portrayals. One English reviewer, in commenting on her performance in her own play *Armand,* said: "There seems no acting, but the direct and spontaneous expression of individual character." [6] Other critics mention her lack of exaggeration, her ability to enter into the spirit of a part, her gift for balancing "sensitivity and mirth," and the sincere appeal of her "poetic fervor."

Mrs. Mowatt comported herself gracefully and confidently on the stage—as she did in life—but she was never able to simulate emotions which she did not feel. As Poe observed, she was an impulsive, emotional actress, and she needed both a warm heart and a warm head to achieve her effects. She could not arouse an audience unless she herself were deeply stirred. Describing her very first appearance on the stage, she writes: "I gave myself up to the part, and acted with all the *abandon* and intensity of which I was capable." [7] On many other occasions she affirmed that she had to lose herself in a role before she could act effectively.

It is clear that the appeal of Mrs. Mowatt's acting came from her ability to arouse emotions in herself and, at the same time, to communicate these to an audience in a manner which seemed natural and graceful. Her lack of rant, and her personal beauty, charm, and refinement added to her appeal. Despite these abilities, it is unlikely that she ever mastered the subtle physical and vocal skills of the seasoned professional, or the technical facility to appear convincing when her own inspiration was at low ebb. Joseph Jefferson, always a perceptive critic, makes the following comment on her style:

I am of the opinion that "once an amateur, always an amateur." There are many good actors that have this peculiar, raw quality who have been on the stage for years; and it is because they began their careers by acting leading characters. Mrs. Mowatt and James H. Hackett were examples of many in our profession who have committed this fatal error. No matter how bold and dashing they may appear, there is a shyness and uncertainty about everything they do. It exhibits itself in the casting of the eyes down upon the stage in an embarrassed way just after they have made a point. This is very disastrous. When a strong effect is made the eye, the pose, the very feeling, should be, for an instant only, a picture, till the public digest it. If it is disturbed by some unmeaning movement the strength is lost, and the audience will at once discover that they are not looking at a master. This characteristic of the amateur may wear off in some instances, but I do not remember any.[8]

Mrs. Mowatt recognized that there were at least two schools of acting, which she described in somewhat extreme terms as follows: "The actor of the one school totally loses his own individuality and abandons himself to all the absorbing emotions that belong to the character he interprets. His tears are real, his laughter real, as real to himself as to the audience."[9] In contrast to this school stands the actor who "exercises perfect command over the emotions of the audience . . . but not a pulse in his own frame beats more rapidly than its wont."[10] Mrs. Mowatt was perfectly aware that she belonged to the first school, and furthermore she declared that this type of acting could not be called "the highest school of art." At the end of her discussion of acting she writes:

No amount of study or discipline could have enabled me to belong to the grand and passionless school. I never succeeded in stirring the hearts of others unless I was deeply affected myself. The putting off of self-consciousness was, with me, the first imperative element of success. Yet I agree with those who maintain that the highest school of art is that in which the actor, Prospero-like, rises or stills tempestuous waves by the magical force of his will—produces and controls, without sharing, the emotions of the audience.[11]

Although Mrs. Mowatt's stage career was meteor-like in both its brilliance and brevity, she nevertheless exerted a strong influence on the theatre of her day. In one respect, her influence was unfortunate. Her quick success set a false standard and encouraged countless amateurs to try their luck in a profession for which they had no qualifications except an ardent desire and a pretty face. Laurence Hutton notes that "There have been *debutantes* enough in New York since the *debut* of Mrs. Mowatt to fill to overflowing the auditorium of any single city theatre . . . but the great majority, dispirited and disheartened, have gone back to the private life from which they sprung, without song, without honor, and without tears, except the many tears they have shed themselves." [12]

Mrs. Mowatt's acting, whose chief appeal was feminine charm and emotionalism, undoubtedly confirmed a trend which became a major style in American acting. Feminine emotionalism of some kind and in some degree can be found in all periods of acting from the time the first female actress, Mrs. Coleman, performed on an English public stage in 1656, until the present day. However, Mrs. Mowatt is the first American actress of stature to use feminine emotionalism as her principal method and appeal. Undoubtedly the force of her example and the effect of her success influenced many other actresses to adopt her style. This aspect of her influence cannot be called beneficial. However, other aspects of her influence were entirely praiseworthy. The sincerity and naturalness which she displayed in her emotionalism encouraged many players to develop these qualities in their own acting. Furthermore, Mrs. Mowatt's very presence on the stage, whatever her style of performance, did great service to the profession of acting and helped to weaken the Puritan hostility toward the American theatre. Being a well known woman of wealth, education, and social position, Mrs. Mowatt's decision to go on the stage invoked the wrath of countless puritanical people. Yet for nine years she conducted herself with all the virtue, dignity, and graciousness of a born lady, and when she retired thousands of people throughout the nation had revised their opinions of the sinfulness of the theatre. As Arthur Hobson Quinn remarks, Mrs. Mowatt "took into the profession her high heart, her utter refinement, her keen sense of social values, and her infinite capacity for effort, and her effect was a real and a great one. . . . Her career as related in the steady sparkle of her Autobiography makes any compatriot who reads it thankful that she has lived." [13]

LAURA KEENE

Another woman of strong will and varied abilities, who made her American debut just two years before Mrs. Mowatt quit the stage, was the imperious beauty, Laura Keene. Like Mrs. Mowatt, Laura Keene had boundless energy, abiding self-confidence, and enough ability to demonstrate competence in several fields. She was a charming and graceful actress, a successful manager, a respected business woman, and an able enough student of aesthetics to lecture occasionally on the fine arts and to edit, for a brief time, a magazine devoted to the fine arts. Though she made no lasting impression on the American theatre and though her popularity and success declined long before she quit the stage, her name is associated with the careers of many great stars of the American theatre, her acting was a worthy example of feminine charm and emotionalism, and her name is forever linked with American history because she was the star of the play being presented in Ford's Theatre the night Abraham Lincoln was assassinated, and she was the one who recognized John Wilkes Booth as he made his escape and who, it is said, held the dying President's head in her lap until he was carried from the theatre.

Laura Keene was born in England sometime between 1820 and 1830 and received her early theatrical training in Madame Vestris' London company. It is thought that she acquired two traits from Madame Vestris: (1) A taste for lavish stage ornamentation, and (2) a haughty and imperious manner in directing a company. Both of these traits were prominent in Miss Keene's management of her own theatre.

Miss Keene was "discovered" in 1852 when James W. Wallack visited England in search of a leading lady for his theatre. Struck by her beauty and talent, Wallack engaged her at once. She accompanied him to the United States where she made a brilliant debut on September 21, 1852. Henceforth her theatrical career was exclusively American, and her name must be included in the history of American, not British, acting.

During the season of 1852–53 at Wallack's Theatre, Laura Keene acted such roles as Lady Teazle, Lydia Languish, Lady Gay Spanker, Beatrice, Portia, and Rosalind, and was greatly admired for her looks, her gentility, and her deft comic touch. Though slight of figure, she had a fine carriage and admirable grace in all her movements. Her large expressive eyes were set in a face of "exquisite pallor" and topped by a mass of auburn hair. In addition, Odell says she had "temperament and magnetism" and, to the audiences at Wallack's, was "irresistible." [14]

Her acting at the time—and throughout her entire career—was marked by delicate taste and feminine charm. She did not so much draw details of character as suggest them, so that Kate Reignolds declared that her acting "was not photography or labored art, but a water color sketch, full of light and grace." [15]

After one highly successful season at Wallack's, Miss Keene departed abruptly without even giving notice to Mr. Wallack. She spent the next two years acting in Baltimore and San Francisco, and also in Australia where her touring partner was the young Edwin Booth. She returned to New York in 1855 and opened a theatre of her own called "Laura Keene's Varieties." The following year she moved into a new theatre built for her by John Trimble and called "Laura Keene's New Theatre." She remained there as manager and leading lady until 1863. Finally tiring of her managerial chores, she relinquished her theatre and became a traveling star. But her career began to decline and her health began to fail. She tried theatrical management again, she gave public lectures, she edited a magazine, but though her courage and sense of humor were unimpaired, her health and talent were not. After several years of declining fortune, she died of consumption on November 4, 1873.

The years from 1856 to 1863 were the most successful in the career of Laura Keene. Before evaluating her acting as another example of the school of emotionalism, it is interesting to note her activity as a manager and her influence as a tutor of other players.

As manager of her own theatre, she delighted New York with a series of comedies and extravaganzas which were elaborately mounted and which reflected the feminine grace and poetic tastes of the producer. The entire scene of one of her plays, for example, was composed of the finest white lace to be found on the market and cost Miss Keene several hundreds of dollars. Other scenes in other plays were praised for their novelty, ingenuity, or splendor.

Miss Keene, as manager, not only designed and painted scenery; she also made costumes, trained actors, directed publicity, wrote or adapted scripts, and tried to encourage native Americans to write for the stage. At one time she offered a prize of $1,000 for the best American play submitted to her.

Miss Keene presided over all these activities with the imperious manners of a dictator; her word was law, and no opinion but her own was tolerated. Even her husband and business manager, John Lutz, if on the stage during rehearsal, was brushed away by a wave of the hand, according to the testimony of Frank Mordaunt.[16] Miss Keene's haughty temper often resulted in tiffs and quarrels with her actors, who called her "the Duchess," but underneath her dictatorial manner she was loyal and kind hearted, and won the respect and admiration of her fellow workers. Joseph Jefferson, who acted for some time in her New York company, recognized her basic charity and goodness of heart and affirmed that he "never heard her speak ill of anyone but herself." [17]

An indication of Miss Keene's high repute as a manager and worth as a person is found in the distinguished company of players she attracted to her theatre. Joseph Jefferson, E. A. Sothern, Kate Reignolds, Dion Boucicault, Agnes Robertson, John T. Raymond, Charles M. Walcot, Stuart Robson, W. J. Florence, and Charles W. Cauldock—all of these acted under the aegis of Laura Keene and many of them graduated to stardom from her theatre. It may be true that Miss Keene, as a manager, often presided over warring elements in her company, and it also may be true, as Odell says,[18] that her theatre lacked policy or "idea"—an audience never knowing what to expect of any announced new play—still, from 1856 to 1863, Miss Keene's energy and talents made her theatre one of the most popular and successful in New York.

Laura Keene not only managed and directed the multifarious details of her company; she also played all the leading feminine roles. The beautiful face, graceful figure, and musical voice which had won her great applause during her first season at Wallack's, were unimpaired in the years from 1856 to 1863. These endowments served her well in roles which ranged from high comedy to emotional melodrama. William Winter admired her versatility, pointing out that she did equally well as the cruel selfish beauty in *The Marble Heart* and as the simple, artless maiden in *The Heir-At-Law,* and he noted, with approval, one of the pecularities of her acting, "a swift, gliding movement, which was remarkably effective." Winter was not so enthusiastic, however, about another of her mannerisms—"the singular expedient," he called it, "of rapidly and continuously blinking her eyes" by way of expressing emotion.[19] Joseph Jefferson praised her for "the rare power of varying her manner" from "the rustic walk of a milkmaid" to "the dignified grace of a queen," [20] and John Creahan, her worshipful biographer, declared she was "a master of high classic comedy" and "equally great in pastoral, spiritual, romantic, pathetic, poetic, and the emotional school of acting." [21] Other critics felt that her charming, sprightly portrayal of Florence Trenchard in *Our American Cousin* represented her best comic style. Certainly this play, which she introduced to America, was her most successful production and will be long remembered not only because of the parts played in it by Miss Keene and Joseph Jefferson but because of the stardom it gave to E. A. Sothern for his creation of the role of Lord Dundreary.

Although Laura Keene began her American career by successfully acting a variety of parts, including roles in Shakespearean drama and in "Old Comedy," she soon limited her range by specializing in plays where personal charm and emotional display were the primary attractions. The character of the plays, which she produced with increasing frequency, is indicated by their titles. *Mary's Birthday, Two Loves and a Life, Birds of Prey, The Elves,* or *The Statue Bride, Blanche of Brandywine, Old Heads and Young Hearts, The Wife's Secret, Plot and Passion, Rachel the Reaper, Camille,* and *Judith of Geneva*— these are only a few samples of the kind of dramas in which Miss Keene was the star. William Winter dubbed such plays "ultra-emotional drama of the hydrostatic order" [22] and deprecated the fact that Miss Keene blighted her talents by identifying herself with this kind of drama.

There is no record of how keenly Miss Keene felt the passions she portrayed or how extravagantly she may have embroidered the emotional fabric of her roles. It is clear, however, that her feminine charm and emotionalism were the primary attractions in her acting. It is also clear that after a brilliant beginning as a versatile actress she limited her talents largely to emotional and sentimental histrionics and subsequently lost her hold on the public. As William Winter said in

1915, ". . . it is scarcely possible, even at this long distance from the time of her feverish exploits and melancholy end, to think of her without a certain sense of regretful disappointment." [23] She died before she reached the age of fifty,[24] leaving the memory of talents which never fully matured but also leaving a record of activity, energy, and versatility which made her, for a time, an outstanding woman of the theatre.

MATILDA HERON

As early exponents of the emotionalistic school, Mrs. Mowatt and Laura Keene emphasized feminine charm and sentiment in their acting. They occasionally indulged in exhibitions of tears, rage, and hysteria, but such exhibitions were not their stock in trade. Moreover, the roles they played and the tastes of the time caused them to subdue and to idealize, in some degree, their emotional pyrotechnics. They were content to suggest the overt responses of emotion and to suppress ugly details. Their successors, however, shunned idealization and exploited other traits of the emotionalistic school. With the rise of such performers as Matilda Heron, Clara Morris, and Mrs. Leslie Carter, primary emphasis was placed on extravagant displays of the more violent feelings. Moreover, the representation of these feelings became realistic and naturalistic. Instead of refining or sentimentalizing their emotional exhibitions, the later actresses reproduced the overt manifestations of passion in detail and with clinical accuracy. By these means they shocked and fascinated their audiences and won notoriety for themselves.

The first influential actress of this branch of the emotionalistic school was Matilda Heron. Her contribution to American acting is represented in her single outstanding role: Camille. This is the role which brought her fame and fortune. In this role she most effectively displayed her naturalistic, emotional style of acting. This is the role which influenced many other actresses to join the school of emotionalism. And this is the role which was remembered at the time of her death: on her coffin was engraved the single word "Camille."

Miss Heron, Irish by birth but American by adoption, had gained a name for herself before she discovered *Camille*. Her career had begun in traditional fashion. She had been trained in an elegant style of elocution by Peter Richings. She had made her debut, February 17,

1851, in the standard role of Bianca in *Fazio*. She had played other standard roles such as Juliet, Parthenia, and Mrs. Haller and had been highly successful. She had traveled to San Francisco and made a great hit in that city. Then in 1854 she went to Paris and saw Mme. Doche act in Dumas' *La Dame aux Camélias*. The American actress was fascinated. She returned to the play night after night and memorized every detail of the production. She bought a copy of the play and made her own translation. By the time she returned to the United States, she was ready to act the Matilda Heron version of *Camille*. This she did in New Orleans in 1855, but the results were unsensational. It was not until two years later, when she staged her production at Wallack's Theatre in New York, that the furor began. She and *Camille* became the rage. Her picture appeared in all the journals; she was pursued, serenaded, and lionized. Poems were dedicated to her, and music was written in her honor. Her *Camille* ran for one hundred nights at Wallack's and was repeated with phenomenal success all over the United States. Before she sank into obscurity, the play netted her at least $100,000.

Matilda Heron was not the first Camille America had seen, but she was by far the most sensational. The play she had adapted from Dumas afforded her wide scope for the display of both emotionalism and naturalism. Her *Camille* was written in a far more realistic style than the standard drama of the period. It did not deal with courtly or poetical figures but with more familiar human beings. The passions exhibited were not noble or exalted; they were the visceral emotions of sexual love and physical suffering. Miss Heron developed on her own a style of acting compatible with this type of drama. Helen Ormsbee said: ". . . from neither Cushman nor Forrest, nor from the many inferior copies of them, could Matilda Heron have got her naturalistic method. She must have thought it out herself." [25]

The naturalism of Miss Heron's acting had several characteristics new enough in the mid-nineteenth century to cause excited comment. Miss Heron did not make her entrance with her face to the galleries and wait for a "reception"; she walked in naturally and ignored the audience. She did not raise her voice or project her words perceptibly, but spoke in what seemed to be a commonplace, conversational tone. On occasions, she even dared to turn her back to the audience. She utilized a multitude of realistic details. She made no attempt to idealize or refine her character; she did not even select and arrange her effects, but included commonplace business of every sort, no matter how awkward or distracting it appeared. And finally, she portrayed physical and clinical reactions which were rarely if ever exhibited on the stage of that period. Many of her scenes were called repulsive and revolting. Her death-bed scene was considered especially painful. But all of the "disgusting minutiae" added to the fascination of the play and attracted thousands of spectators.

Miss Heron was impulsive and sentimental by nature, given to such foibles as writing on the wall of her St. Louis hotel room, in immense crayon letters: "Easter Sunday. God bless St. Louis! Matilda Heron." [26] On the stage she had an animal vitality and a wildness of passion which she displayed freely and extravagantly. She projected all the passions and agonies of a woman's heart with a vivid sense of reality. Her emotionalism was the realistic passion of the boudoir and the sickroom unrefined by poetry or idealism.

Although she exhibited limited imagination or intellect, Miss Heron's stage personality had an irresistible magnetism which could hypnotize an audience. As long as her magnetism was potent, she retained her hold on the public, but when her youth and animal vitality waned she apparently did not have sufficient art to sustain her and so sank rapidly into disfavor and obscurity. She will be remembered not only because of the sensational success of her *Camille* but because she developed a style of acting which influenced American actresses for many years to come. Her attraction as a performer is aptly summarized by William Winter when he says: ". . . if she was not a great artist, she certainly was a very remarkable example of elemental power. She had a wildness of emotion, a vitality in embodiment and many indefinable magnetic qualities . . . no spectator of her acting ever—till her powers were on the wane—missed the sense of an original, vigorous, brilliant, and startling personality." [27]

CLARA MORRIS

In the first volume of her reminiscences, Clara Morris asks the question: "What could *you* do to make yourself cry seven times a week for nine or ten months a year?" And then she wonders: ". . . did I ever do anything else? For it seems to me I have cried steadily through all the years of my dramatic life. Tears gentle, regretful; tears petulant, fretful; tears stormy, passionate; tears slow, despairing; with a light patter, now and then, of my own particular brand. . . ." [28] It was precisely this ability—to weep all kinds of tears at every single performance for season after season—that distinguished the acting of Clara Morris. She was the Mistress of the *Ductus Lachrimalis,* the Queen of the Streaming Eye. She wept her way to stardom; she maintained her position by weeping; and her unending rain of tears earned her the large fortune which, dissipated too soon, brought forth new showers of tears from both the actress and her sentimental public. The kingdom of Robert Bruce is said to have been founded on a spider's web. The dramatic empire of Clara Morris was founded on a drop of water.

Miss Morris's career in emotionalistic acting was longer and more varied than the careers of her predecessors. Laura Keene, Matilda Heron, and Mrs. Mowatt, the early representatives of the emotionalistic school, all enjoyed a relatively brief popularity; Matilda Heron succeeded brilliantly in only a single role. Clara Morris, in contrast, played many parts and her career lasted for more than thirty years. She is the outstanding representative of a later group of emotionalistic actresses which included Fanny Davenport and Mrs. Leslie Carter, all of whom practiced the style of acting described in the careers of their predecessors—with emphasis, however, on a fervid naturalistic display of emotion rather than on a suggested or sentimentalized display.

Miss Morris's affiliation with the theatre began in 1862 when, at the age of fourteen she became a ballet girl for John Ellsler, manager of the Cleveland Academy of Music. The only theatrical instruction she ever received was a lesson in make-up, given her by an older actress of the company. The rest of her knowledge was gained by observation, and by playing every kind of part, large or small, comic or tragic, in Ellsler's company. While still in her teens she acted Gertrude to the Hamlet of Edwin Booth, and Emilia to the Othello of E. L. Davenport. Her apprenticeship lasted seven years, and ended when she became leading lady at Woods Theatre in Cincinnati. But she remained in Cincinnati for only one season. The encouragement she received from critics and friends led her to apply for a position in Augustin Daly's New York company. Daly engaged her, at a nominal salary, with the idea of making a comedienne of her. "Your forte is comedy, pure and simple," he told her after studying her face.[29] But Clara Morris never acted comedy for Mr. Daly. When Agnes Ethel refused the feminine lead in a play called *Man and Wife,* Miss Morris was given the part. It was an emotional role in a domestic drama, and the young actress from the West played it with triumphant success. Henceforth, she became a specialist in domestic emotionalism. Parts in comedy or high tragedy were abandoned for the tearful heroines of contemporary French melodrama. She played so many of these roles, and she identified herself so completely with them that when, later on, she tried to extend her range and play Lady Macbeth or Evadne or Jane Shore, she was criticized for converting these heroines into "incongruous women of the present day."

Typical of the plays with which Miss Morris became identified, and in which she scored her triumphs, were *L'Article 47, Alixe,* and *Miss Multon,* all of them adaptations from the French. In the first of these, the heroine, Cora, is the mistress of a young Frenchman, who shoots her in a fit of passion, leaving a hideous scar on her face. He then marries a "pure" woman and Cora devotes her life to winning him back and plotting revenge. *Alixe* is the spectacle of a young girl tortured almost to madness by the loss of her lover, then rent with double anguish by the discovery that her rival is her own sister, and finally driven to suicide by the discovery of her mother's past dishonor. *Miss Multon* is a version of *East Lynne,* in which a wife abandons her children for a lover then, repenting, returns in disguise to become their governess, is finally discovered, and dies with her children sobbing around her.

In such plays as these, Miss Morris won the title of "Queen of Spasms." She was always the "soiled dove," the woman who dies a heartrending death after several acts of sinning and suffering. In her ability to portray the required emotions, Miss Morris was unmatched. No actress could equal her flashes of scorn, her overpowering grief, or her tumultuous passion. At times she was feverish and cat-like; at other times she was a human volcano "lighting up the stage with blazes of emotional lightning." But more successful yet was her portrayal of the inner struggles which manifest themselves in the quivering lip, the heaving breast, and especially the streaming eye. Miss Morris's power to manufacture stage tears was phenomenal. She could weep any time the dramatic situation demanded it. The tears were real, too, not simulated by trickery or illusion. They flowed whenever the actress turned her thoughts to sad or pitiable things. She tells us it was necessary for her to feel actual sadness before she could weep, but apparently she was able to summon a tearful mood quite easily. If the role she played had lost its sadness through frequent repetition, she stimulated her emotions by imagining her own death, or by recalling a tragic book, poem, or incident from real life. "Thus," she tells us, "in *Alixe* it was not for my lost lover that I oftenest wept such racing tears, but for poor old *Tennessee's Partner* as he buried his worthless dead. . . . While in *Camille* many and many a night her tears fell fast over the memory of a certain mother's face as she told me of . . . returning from the burial of her only child. . . ." [30]

The sympathetic appeal of Miss Morris's tears was enhanced by the personal situation of the actress. When she was young, she had met with an accident which injured her spine and caused her considerable suffering for the rest of her life. In her public writings she also complained of her "chronic neuralgia" and the malaria which she never "got out of her bones." These ailments, and Miss Morris's courageous endurance of them, were well advertised to the public. Audiences knew she carried bottles of medicine with her on the stage and had a physician in attendance to minister to her between acts, so when the actress appeared to suffer torments as Alixe or Miss Multon or Camille, the audience suspected she actually was feeling great physical pain and enduring it for the sake of her performance. Miss Morris encouraged this belief by taking prolonged intermissions between each act of her plays. Sometimes these waits were as long as forty-five or fifty minutes each, and a performance lasted far, far into the night. During these waits, audiences imagined that the brave Miss Morris was backstage battling for strength enough to continue her acting. It is true that sometimes she was ill and was forced to rest and take treatment between the acts, but very often—according to Vivia Ogden, a fellow actress—she simply refused to hurry and frittered the time away while the audience waited with pity and admiration growing in their hearts.*

Even without such devices, Miss Morris could make an audience weep and suffer with her. Spectators experienced an immediate and strong empathic response to her acting; they identified themselves personally with her struggles. Few actresses have ever possessed so much personal magnetism. Sometimes the spell which Miss Morris exerted amounted to actual hypnotism. For example, in the mad scene of *L'Article 47* the actress would seat herself on a chair, put her elbow

* Despite her frail health, Miss Morris lived to the respectable age of 77.

on her knee, and play her scene gazing straight into the eyes of the spectators—with the result that invariably women in the audience would faint or become hysterical. Even the actors and actresses playing with Miss Morris felt the potency of her spell. The man who played Gaston to her Camille usually was weeping when he left the stage. Louis James, who played with her in *Miss Multon,* was so overcome by her mimic agony that he couldn't speak until she prompted him. Vivia Ogden, acting in the same play, burst into tears and could hardly control herself enough to continue the scene.[31]

Almost everyone felt the unusual magnetism of the Morris personality, but no one could explain it. Most of the critics agreed that her appeal defied analysis. In 1885, for example, "Nym Crinkle" (the dramatic critic, A. C. Wheeler) wrote: "I give it up. Critics have wrestled with that condition in and out of season—how she can play upon all sensibilities and sweep as with supernatural fingers the whole gamut of emotions passes critical knowledge." [32]

In stimulating the emotions of her spectators, Miss Morris was aided by a keen sensitivity to their moods and reactions. She detected the feelings of an audience and she played upon these feelings as a musician plays upon his instrument. In her *Life on the Stage* she declares: ". . . I possessed that curious sixth sense of the born actress, and as a doctor with the aid of his stethoscope can hear sounds of grim warning or of kindly promise . . . so an actress, with that stethoscopic sixth sense, detects even the *forming* emotions of her audience, feeling incipient dissatisfaction before it becomes open disapproval, or thrilling at the intense silence that ever precedes a burst of approbation." [33]

Like Matilda Heron, Clara Morris practiced a naturalistic type of acting. Her scar in *L'Article 47* was copied from a hideous disfigurement she saw on a woman who sat opposite her in a street car. Her simulation of death by heart disease in *Miss Multon* was copied from the horrors she watched when a physician friend of hers paid a sick patient to run up a long flight of stairs so that the actress could observe the actual symptoms of a heart attack. Incidentally, Miss Morris reproduced these symptoms so realistically in her performance that she alarmed several medical men who sat in the audience.

Miss Morris rendered other death scenes with equal realism. Her acting in *Camille* was criticized for including too much revolting detail. The poisoning scene in *The Sphinx,* another play adapted from the

French, was described by a contemporary critic as follows: ". . . anything more ghastly, terrible, and realistic than her death scene has not for a long time been seen upon the stage. . . . A visible shudder went through the audience, and horror was depicted upon every face. Mingled with this was a sensation of disgust. It is evident, however, that this scene is to prove the sensation here, as it was in Paris, that will crowd the theatre." [34]

Clara Morris's unique power to make the spectators feel the womanly emotions she displayed was her supreme dramatic talent, and it covered a multitude of deficiencies. She did not have a particularly beautiful face or graceful figure. In her middle years she was sometimes described as being stout and ugly. Her voice was ordinary and her elocution was faulty. She was frequently criticized for her nasal twang and her barbarous pronunciations. *The Spirit of the Times,* on December 18, 1880, went so far as to suggest that if she were planning to act in London she had only one chance of success. "Let her be advertized as an Indian star who speaks Choctaw, while the rest of the company speaks English . . . and the novelty may be a sensation."

Miss Morris was crude in her stage technique, too. Her gestures were monotonous, her movements were often careless and awkward and she had many irritating mannerisms. Yet she triumphed. In spite of all her sins and deficiencies, in spite of the melodramatic claptrap in her plays, she mesmerized both the public and the critics. She gave them a thrill. Her emotional pyrotechnics made them shudder and weep, and this power was enough to win her a large and devoted following.

It is clear that Miss Morris's acting was instinctive and intuitive. A few critics, especially in her early years, claimed that she was a careful artist who prepared her effects and exercised "the art that conceals art" but the evidence is against this point of view. We know that she never acted in rehearsals. "Only foreigners do that," she said contemptuously. Before each new play, Augustin Daly, her director, was in terrible suspense not knowing what she would do in performance. Often he begged her to give him some inkling of the way she planned to play a scene, but she always said it was impossible for her to act without an audience. In preparing the role of Cora in *L'Article 47,* Miss Morris tells us that she did not know how she was going to act the part until the night before the opening. After the final rehearsal, she was so worried that she retired to her own room, locked herself in, and spent several hours devising a walk and a crouch for Cora, choosing a certain tone of voice, and determining where her climaxes should come.[35] With this last minute preparation, she was ready to act the part on the following day. Such a confession does not suggest careful artistry but rather an habitual reliance upon inspiration—an impression which is confirmed by the way her performances varied according to her moods and impulses.

One would expect that an actress who wept real tears and who, according to her own testimony, felt every emotion she portrayed, would have little control of herself while she was in the grip of these passions. Evidently this was not the case with Clara Morris. Her head was relatively cool even when her heart seemed to be breaking. In this trait she was not typical of the usual actress of the emotionalistic school who completely lost herself in the emotions of her role. In contrast, Miss Morris was able to maintain a particular state of mind which she describes as follows: "There are, when I am on the stage, three separate currents of thought in my mind; one in which I am keenly alive to Clara Morris, to all the details of the play, to the other actors and how they act and to the audience; another about the play and the character I represent; and, finally, the thought that really gives me the stimulus for acting. . . . As to really losing one's self in a part, that will not do: it is worse to be too sympathetic than to have too much art. I must cry in my emotional *roles* and feel enough to cry, but I must not allow myself to be so affected as to mumble my words, to redden my nose, or to become hysterical." [36]

Evidently Miss Morris could remain detached even in impassioned scenes. When Louis James was overcome by her agony in *Miss Multon* and couldn't force himself to speak, the actress—in the midst of her tears—muttered, "I say, what ails you. . . . Are you dumb?" [37] When Miss Morris and one of the child actors were performing a tearful scene in *Miss Multon,* the actress let the child weep for a while, then she leaned over, "her own face strained with tears, and agony in every line of it" and murmured: "Shut up now, and give me a show." [38] Often in a tense scene when the audience was dissolved in tears, Miss Morris would turn upstage and whisper something so spontaneous and witty that it was almost impossible for her fellow actors to keep a straight face. One of Miss Morris's hostile critics relates that in *Alixe* during the best scene with her mother, Miss Morris, as Alixe, "sawed one arm across the other as a sign to the leader of the orchestra to start the music, and during one of her mother's most impassioned appeals, she walked to the wings and gave an order off stage!" The critic adds the horrified comment, "Fancy Alixe directing a fiddler and chatting with a stage-carpenter during one of the climaxes of her sufferings!" [39]

During the early years of Miss Morris's career, she enjoyed an immense popularity. Audiences had never seen anything like her opulent display of womanly emotions. Her ability to weep was the talk of the nation. Any faultiness in her stage technique was forgotten in the hypnotic spell she was able to cast. So long as her inspiration was strong and her emotions youthful and vigorous, she maintained a loyal following. As she grew older and stouter and failed to develop in versatility or artistry, and as public taste shifted away from the Sardou-type drama, the critics began to ridicule her methods. In the 1880's she was billed as "America's Greatest Living Actress." By 1902 the newspapers referred to her as "America's once famous actress." In 1876, her performance in *Miss Multon* received the following review in the *Spirit of the Times:* "Her great intensity was astonishingly effective, her pathos genuine and unaffected, and throughout she held her audience, so to speak, in the palm of her hand. . . . Her acting was superb. . . . Before such a rare manifestation of genius, criticism is perforce silent. Can we give greater praise? We have no fault to find. Not one blemish is to be discovered even by the most critical eye. . . ." [40] By 1888, the *Spirit of the Times* had lost its breathless admiration, and reviewed Miss Morris's *Renée de Moray* as follows: "She cries and makes her audience cry; she has long waits between the Acts and makes her audiences wait; she is the same Clara Morris and attracts the same admirers of stage hysteria and disease. It is as impossible to improve her by criticism as to reform the morphia habit by sensible advice. We can only wonder and pity and pass on." [41] And finally, the ultimate damnation was uttered in 1902 by Alan Dale who, after listening to a lecture by Clara Morris, wrote: "I not only found no symptoms of greatness, but though I tried hard, persistently, strenuously, I could not discover any one single peg upon which to hang the barren possibility of one solitary great moment." [42]

Ill health and, perhaps, waning popularity forced Miss Morris to retire from regular stage appearances in the 1890's. For several years thereafter, she was seen occasionally in vaudeville and revivals, and kept very much in the public eye by her lecture tours and her writing.

Three volumes of stage reminiscences came from her pen, and she was a regular contributor to the Sunday supplements with articles on such subjects as "Temptations of the Stage," "Why Men Don't Go to Church," and "If I Were a Girl Again." In 1903, 1909, and again in 1911 she received wide publicity because, according to the newspapers, the mortgage on her home was about to be foreclosed while the old actress was lying inside at death's door. Each time, Miss Morris's health revived, and each time the actors of New York came to her rescue with a splendid benefit. Miss Morris finally did lose her old home and went to live with relatives, but she did not die until 1925.

Probably the fairest estimate of the acting of this unusual woman can be found in an essay by John R. Towse, the noted dramatic critic of the New York *Evening Post*. In reviewing her career, Mr. Towse says:

It is by no means easy to define her place in any coldly critical category. She was, first and last, a natural born actress. If judged by her artistic equipment only, she could not establish a claim to any very high place in the ranks of her contemporaries. She was far behind many of them in artistic cunning, but she distanced all of them in flashes of convincing realism and in poignancy of natural emotion. She was often barely respectable as an elocutionist, she was habitually crude, and occasionally unrefined, in pose, gesture, and utterance; she had distressful mannerisms, she could not or did not attempt to modify or disguise her individual personality, her range was limited—she could not soar into the upper regions of tragedy—but, nevertheless, she showed, especially in emotional crises, a strong grasp of diversified characters within her own boundaries and illuminated them, at intervals, with such a blaze of vivid truthfulness that, for the moment, she seemed to be perfectly identified with them. . . . As she never really succeeded, or came very near to success, in any great part, she can never be called a great actress. . . . But she was great as a realist in the exaggerated, false, or morbid emotionalism of the current French plays of her period, and displayed high intelligence in a considerable range of English drama.[43]

FANNY DAVENPORT

When Agnes Ethel refused the leading role in Augustin Daly's production of *Man and Wife,* the part was entrusted to Clara Morris and her success in the role launched her career as the queen of domestic emotionalism. However, there was another actress in the company who might have been given the role, and who might have proved equally successful in it. This was Fanny Davenport. She had been engaged by Daly in 1869, a year before Miss Morris joined the company, and had already established herself as a charming, vivacious comedienne. However, Daly feared she did not possess the emotional power for the lead in *Man and Wife* so, after some backstage finagling,[44] she was assigned the comedy role of Blanche and Clara Morris got the emotional role of Anne. Perhaps Daly was right in believing that Fanny Davenport could not play the role of Anne, yet before this actress ended her career she had metamorphosed from a sparking comedienne in such plays as *London Assurance, The Belle's Stratagem,* and *Merry Wives of Windsor,* to an emotional star in four melodramas by Victorien Sardou. Thus it is fair to say that in her early career Miss Davenport belonged to the personality school of Viola Allen, Julia Marlowe, and Ada Rehan, but during the last fifteen years of her acting she firmly established herself as a leader of the school of feminine emotionalism. It is as an exponent of this school that she is best remembered; ". . . when the name of Fanny Davenport is mentioned," says Mary Caroline Crawford, "it is of her Sardou period . . . that most of us think—such power and passion, such a wealth of artistic temperament did she display in these roles." [45]

Eminent and successful as was the career of Fanny Davenport, she set no styles in acting, established no school, and never achieved unanimous acclaim as a "great" actress; yet her solid success and her wide popularity deserve inclusion in the list of representative actresses of the school of emotionalism.

"Miss Fanny," christened Fanny Lily Gipsy Davenport, was the eldest child of the great American tragedian, E. L. Davenport, and literally grew up in the theatre and with a love for the theatre. As a child she appeared in many of her father's productions, and made her adult debut at the age of twelve, playing the role of Charles II of Spain in *Faint Heart Never Won Fair Lady.* The fact that she was always robust and big for her age enabled her, in her early career, to play boy's parts and parts beyond her years. Soon after her adult debut, she left her father's company and acted in Louisville and Philadelphia. In 1869 she attracted Augustin Daly's attention, and soon made her appearance in his Fifth Avenue Theatre as Lady Gay Spanker in *London Assurance.* Thereafter she acted a variety of roles in Shakespeare, old comedies and new comedies, and, under Daly's tutelage, she established herself as an actress of charm, vitality, and sparkle. Her abundant physical endowments added to her appeal. William Winter, always appreciative of wholesome physical allure, described her as "a voluptuous beauty, radiant with youth and health, taut and trim of figure, having regular features, a fair complexion, golden hair, sparking hazel eyes, and a voice as naturally musical and cheery as the fresh, incessant rippling flow of a summer brook." [46]

Fanny Davenport's acting, before her Sardou period, was sprightly, high spirited, charming, and feminine. Her effectiveness was largely the result of her lavish physical endowments and captivating personality. John R. Towse says she was "a superb creature physically, in form and feature a thing of perfect beauty. . . . Her personal charms formed no small proportion of her theatrical assets." [47] In reviewing her roles, Towse always points out the defects of the actress's techniques, yet he always notes the compensating charm of her looks and personality. As Letitia Hardy in *The Belle's Stratagem,* for example, Towse says that Miss Davenport ruined the earlier scenes by grotesque exaggeration "but she was a bewitching vision." [48] As Peg Woffington in *Masks and Faces,* the actress was "In personal fascination . . . the equal, doubtless, of Peg herself. . . ." But "The tone of the comedy and the manners of the period she disregarded." [49] In *As You Like It,* "Fanny Davenport was a lovely Rosalind to the eye, was spirited, arch, gallant, and coquettish, but the poetic side of the character eluded her." [50] Brander Matthews, another perceptive critic, says that he remembers Fanny Davenport as the most satisfying Lady Teazle he ever saw, yet Matthews, too, adds the qualifying statement that "perhaps . . . her youth and her beauty, her high spirits and her enjoyment of life made me credit her performance with more merit than it had." [51]

During the first half of her adult career, Fanny Davenport relied upon beauty and personality for the success she achieved. During the last half, she forsook romantic and comic roles for more emotional and tragic parts, and became a leading actress of the emotionalistic school. Her developing dramatic power was first noted in 1873, when she played Madge, the tramp, in W. S. Gilbert's *Charity.* Augustin Daly, always ready to capitalize on the talents of his company, recognized Miss Davenport's new potentialities and, in 1876, wrote for her a play called *Pique.* In this drama Miss Davenport was asked to exhibit a considerable emotional range. She succeeded brilliantly, and

Pique ran for 238 consecutive performances. Shortly thereafter, Miss Davenport formed her own company and toured the United States as a star, accumulating a repertoire which included more and more emotional roles. In 1883 she secured the American rights to Sardou's *Fedora,* and from then until her death in 1898 she was strictly a devotee of "Sardoodledom." *Fedora* lasted for five seasons, and was followed by *La Tosca, Cleopatra,* and *Gismonda,* all of which were enormously successful.

In the emotional melodramatics of the Sardou drama, Miss Davenport used her imposing physique and her great vitality to good advantage. But instead of the coquetry and charm of her early acting she now displayed violent emotion—rage, jealousy, grief, hatred, and lust. That she succeeded in the portrayal of these passions is shown by the public reception of her plays and by the critical comments she received. The reviewers praised her "dramatic explosions," her "well-simulated frenzies," her "terrible struggles," and her "power and passion." Montrose Moses deplored her lack of "quietude and repression" and declared that she made her roles great "through exertion, not through unconscious inspiration." [52] At any rate, these emotional exertions captured the public fancy and earned rich financial rewards for Miss Davenport. She died a wealthy woman—albeit much too young—and will be remembered as a good, though not a great actress, who succeeded both as an exponent of the personality school and as a leader in the field of feminine emotionalism.

MRS. LESLIE CARTER

The school of feminine emotionalism found another prominent exponent in Mrs. Leslie Carter. This actress, whose career extended well into the contemporary period, can be considered as one of the last successful practitioners of this type of acting. Although feminine emotionalism of some kind will always be seen on the stage, the naturalistic exhibitionism practiced by Matilda Heron and Clara Morris was eventually obliterated by the demands of the Ibsen-Chekhov drama and by the ideals of acting, established in the United States by Minnie Maddern Fiske and in Europe by the Moscow Art Theatre. However, before the new ideals of acting gained dominance, Mrs. Carter triumphed in the field of feminine emotionalism and, although she eventually changed her style to fit a new kind of drama and a changed public taste, she can be considered as a prominent representative of a vanishing school.

The emotional performances of Mrs. Carter attracted much notoriety; so did her private life and the plays in which she appeared. She was born Caroline Louise Dudley in Lexington, Kentucky, on June 10, 1862, and at the age of eighteen married the prominent and wealthy Leslie Carter. The marriage lasted nine years, ending in a divorce suit which was the sensation of the period. Left without a means of support, Mrs. Carter determined to try the stage. Since she had no experience or training, her only assets were (1) the publicity received from her divorce suit; (2) her determination; and (3) the beauty of her face and voice. David Belasco described her as "a pale, slender, red-haired girl with a pair of green eyes, gleaming under black brows, who alternately wept and smiled, whose gestures were full of unconscious grace, and whose voice vibrated with musical sweetness." [53]

After her appearances in two Broadway productions—*The Ugly Duckling* in 1890 and *Miss Helyett* in 1891—in which she did not achieve any particular distinction, Mrs. Carter retired for two years and placed herself under the tutelage of David Belasco. Her training during this period was unique. Belasco recruited a company whose sole purpose was to rehearse with Mrs. Carter. With only Belasco as critic and audience, the would-be actress prepared and acted forty roles ranging from Shakespeare to French melodrama, and from old comedy to modern farce. It is said that every one of the parts was studied, rehearsed, and acted as carefully and completely as though a crowded house was to see the performance. It is further said that Belasco used such teaching devices as dragging his protégé about the floor by the hair and kicking her in the spine so she could experience the sensations of physical suffering.[54]

Mrs. Carter emerged from this training in 1895 to act the leading role in Belasco's production of *The Heart of Maryland*. She was sensationally successful and played the role for three years. Then followed her triumphs in Belasco's *Zaza, Du Barry,* and *Adrea*. The first two plays received as much notoriety for their "lurid" and "immoral" subject matter as for the emotional pyrotechnics of Mrs. Carter's performances.

In 1906, Mrs. Carter defied the wishes of her tutor and manager, Mr. Belasco, and married an obscure actor named William L. Payne.

There ensued a sensational break between the actress and her manager, with charges and recriminations on both sides and with reams of
publicity in the tabloids and Sunday supplements. Mrs. Carter never
again acted for Belasco. Her career, however, continued for twenty-
five years under other directors or under her own management. Although she flourished to a degree, her subsequent success was never so
brilliant as it had been under Belasco. Her last stage appearances were
in 1929, and she died eight years later at the age of seventy-five.

The bases for Mrs. Carter's success as an actress are clear. She had
striking beauty: a mass of red hair "one shade hotter than Titian," an
exquisitely pale complexion, soft blue eyes, and a slender, shapely figure; she had a mellifluous, musical voice, capable of great range and
variety and trained for clarity and cadence; she had a fiery temperament to match her red hair; and, finally, she had the ability to lose
herself in the emotions of her role and to involve an audience in the
hysteria of her own feelings.

There is much evidence to illustrate the emotional nature of Mrs.
Carter's acting. One scene in *The Heart of Maryland* required her to
race up a flight of stairs and swing from the clapper of a bell to prevent its ringing. In rehearsal she tried running up the spiral stairs but
found that the ascent made her dizzy. She refused to rehearse the
scene, declaring that she could never do it except under the excitement
of actual performance. This proved to be the case. Whenever there
was an audience to stimulate her, Mrs. Carter could perform her gymnastics with admirable success, but without an audience she was unable
to act.

The same situation prevailed in Mrs. Carter's performance of the
sensational play *Zaza*. Her force and effectiveness, says Lewis Strang,
came from a state of semi-hysteria. There was, he said, "an exciting
spirit of gamble about Mrs. Carter's impersonation. One paid his
money at the door, not knowing exactly what was coming to him in
return for it. He might be favored with a wholly absorbing exhibition
of hysterical theatrics; he might get merely a mildly interesting speci-
men of mechanical acting." [55]

On the opening night of *Zaza*, Mrs. Carter pulled all the emotional
stops and gave a performance which stirred her audience with as much
passion—almost—as she herself had been experiencing. Franklin E.
Fyles describes this debauch in the following words: "Finally, the
audience could no longer contain itself, and it burst into mad applause

and cheers, drowning the last words of the hysterical woman before them. As she fell back against the mantelpiece exhausted and trembling, the tears streaming down her face, . . . all over the house people rose, some standing on their chairs, waving handkerchiefs and programmes in fanatical irresponsibility." [56] Mrs. Carter was called upon for a speech, but, reports the New York *Herald* for January 10, 1899, she was "too overwrought for more than a mere expression of thanks."

This kind of exhibitionism characterized Mrs. Carter's acting in all her roles. Whenever she was able to throw herself into a state of semi-hysteria, she stirred and titillated her audiences; when the mood escaped her, she failed to make an impression. Thus it followed that her early performances in any role were generally her best; the longer she played a part the more mechanical it became because, with each repetition, she was less able to lose herself in the appropriate emotions.

William Winter despised the "lewdness and cheapness" of Mrs. Carter's roles, and he also ridiculed her reliance on physical and emotional exhibitionism. In commenting on her performance in *Du Barry,* Winter says: ". . . the method of Mrs. Carter . . . was to work herself into a state of violent excitement, to weep, vociferate, shriek, rant, become hoarse with passion, and finally to flop and beat the floor." [57] Although Winter disliked such a method, he nevertheless recognized the "executive force and skill" in Mrs. Carter's performances, and when she acted the role of Adrea in 1904, Winter had high praise for "the depth of tragical feeling" and the "power of dramatic expression" [58] which she revealed—to Winter—for the first time.

It is clear, therefore, that the main attraction of Mrs. Carter's acting, on which her fame largely rests, was her emotional pyrotechnics. In her early roles under Belasco these exhibitions won her great acclaim and gained her the reputation of having "shed tears over every square foot of all the older stages in America. . . ." [59] Besides her ability to emote, she had the assets mentioned previously: beauty of face and figure, clarity and purity of speech, and a large measure of feminine magnetism. However, these were used as adjuncts to her emotional exhibitionism and were always considered subsidiary to her main appeal. In her later years on the stage, after she broke with Belasco and after her youth and emotional powers had declined, she changed her style to fit her roles in such plays as Pinero's *The Gay Lord Quex* and

Maugham's *The Circle*. However, it is as a successful emotional actress in plays such as *Zaza* and *Du Barry* that Mrs. Carter earned her place as a successor to the vanishing tradition of Mowatt, Keene, Heron, Morris, and Davenport.

V

THE PERSONALITY SCHOOL

THE LADIES OF THE EMOTIONALISTIC SCHOOL ENJOYED WIDE POPULAR-
ity but they were not without rivals. Competing for public esteem was
a group of young players, mostly women, whose style of performance
was different and who appeared in plays that were a sharp contrast to
the fervid emotional dramas favored by Clara Morris and Mrs. Leslie
Carter. This group of performers, whose most prominent representatives at the end of the nineteenth century were Maude Adams, Julia
Marlowe, Viola Allen, and Ada Rehan, constituted a group which can
be termed the personality school. Its outstanding characteristic was the
appeal of the personality of the individual player. Personality, to be
sure, is an ingredient in the appeal of every performer. It flavors and,
in some degree, shapes each role which a player creates. At times, a
performer's personality, added to the dramatist's conception of a character, may effect a synthesis which creates a performance of memorable quality. Thus, Edwin Booth's personality helped to illuminate the
character of Hamlet and to shape his performance of that role into a
portrayal of unusual dimension. Charlotte Cushman's personality enabled her to complete and project the character of Queen Katherine as
few actresses have ever done. However, in neither case did the performer substitute himself or herself for the dramatic character. Booth's
Hamlet was Shakespeare's character plus Edwin Booth; Cushman's
Queen Katherine was the poet's ideal plus certain aspects of Charlotte
Cushman's personality.

In contrast to this kind of creative synthesis is the method of the
personality school: the substitution of the performer's personality for

the dramatic character, or the portrayal of dramatic characters which fit the performer's personality so exactly that performer and character are practically identical. In either case, the effect is the same: the basic appeal of the acting comes from the individual personality of the player.

The typical actress of the personality school based her acting on the appeal of personality and, moreover, on a particular kind of appeal: that of womanly loveliness and feminine virtue, unsullied by coarseness or passion. The actress of this school had usually undergone a thorough training and apprenticeship and, like the actress of the classic school, had performed a wide variety of roles in the standard drama, including parts in comedy and high tragedy. In her maturity, however, she confined herself to roles which were sweet, wholesome, and refined—like the actress herself. If she performed Shakespeare, it was not Lady Macbeth or Queen Katherine but Rosalind or Viola. If she acted in contemporary plays, they were not the social problem plays of Ibsen or the sexy melodramas of Sardou, but romantic and sentimental dramas like *The Christian, When Knighthood Was in Flower,* and *Peter Pan.* The great tragic roles of the old standard drama were avoided in favor of charming, romantic roles. The portrayal of strong passion was shunned in favor of sentiment and wholesome feeling. The actress aimed to charm her spectators with her feminine loveliness and to uplift and ennoble them by the moral appeal of her personal character and the wholesome effect of the role she was acting.

Typically, too, the actress of the personality school was assisted in her appeal by a lovely face and figure, by a rich or appealing voice, and by great competence in stage technique. She was, in short, a deft and artful performer with unusual personal magnetism who used the stage as a means of projecting her feminine charms to inspire her audience with a feeling of purity and optimism.

Although the personality school, as here defined, flourished most prominently at the turn of the nineteenth century, it was ably represented much earlier in the history of American acting. Two early and notable exponents of the style were Clara Fisher and Maggie Mitchell. They were worthy predecessors of the Adams-Marlowe-Allen-Rehan group, and illustrate the fact that the kind of acting whose chief appeal resides in the personality of the individual player can be found in every period of dramatic history. These two actresses will serve as the prototype of hundreds of other players of the same school who have enlivened the theatrical scene but whose achievements are less worthy of review.

Clara Fisher was the actress whom Noah Ludlow termed "the most fascinating woman on the stage or in private life that I remember to have ever met in the profession." [1] Singularly gifted both as an actress and a singer, Miss Fisher appears to have owed more success to her sparkling, vivacious personality than to her considerable histrionic ability. Some critics might group her with the classic actresses because of her range, her mastery of the techniques of her art, and her occasional appearance in such roles as Ophelia and Desdemona. Or she might be classed as a variety artist like Lotta Crabtree because of her gift at mimicry, her skill in entr'acte singing and dancing, and her direct, spontaneous appeal. Indeed, she was a clever, versatile performer whose long career and varied talents relate her to several styles and schools. Still, it was her fascinating personality which attracted most comment and which enlivened all her roles. Hence it is not unreasonable to consider her an early representative of the personality school.

Clara Fisher, like Mary Ann Duff and many other American actresses, was English born, but she adopted America as her home in 1827 when she was sixteen years old and spent the remaining seventy-one years of her life in the United States. She was already a star when she arrived in New York in 1827, for at the tender age of six she had appeared in a children's production at Drury Lane Theatre in which she had acted several characters, including Richard III. She was such a sensation that she became "the wonder of her times." Joseph Ireland declared that as a juvenile performer she "eclipsed all predecessors and has been surpassed by no successor." [2]

As a juvenile, Clara Fisher amazed her public by appearing to grasp the concept of her author and to understand the motives and psychology of the adult characters she played. Laurence Hutton records that when she acted with an adult cast she was never dwarfed by the contrast with them but, instead, made them appear to be entirely out of proportion.[3] However, it was as a young lady almost seventeen years old that Clara Fisher made her American debut, and the qualities which captivated her audience on this occasion—and which continued to captivate them for many years—were her beauty of person and her irresistible buoyancy of personality. Ireland describes the physical charms which dazzled her first night audience in these words:

Though not possessing strict beauty of feature, she was . . . one of the most bewitching specimens of feminine creation that eyes have ever looked on. Her person, below the medium height and just reaching an agreeable plumpness, was exquisitely formed, her manners were sprightly and vivacious, yet perfectly natural and artless, her expression arch and intelligent, her cheeks dimpling with smiles. . . .[4]

During her early years on the American stage and, indeed, throughout most of her career, Clara Fisher impersonated a wide variety of characters, both male and female, but won greatest acclaim in those parts where her natural vivacity and charm were exploitable: rollicking boys and girls, saucy chambermaids, and coquettish belles. This type of character is well illustrated in the roles she performed oftenest, among which were Albina Mandeville in *The Will,* Letitia Hardy in *The Belle's Stratagem,* Maria in *The Actress of All Work,* Little Pickle in *The Spoiled Child,* and the Four Mowbrays in *Old and Young.* Miss Fisher was also a popular vocalist and often appeared in light opera or entertained her audience with entr'acte songs. Although her singing voice had limited range, she put over a song with resounding success by means of her varied facial expressions, her expressive gestures, and her amazing ability to act out the number while she was singing it. She was able to project her personality even in her singing.

Miss Fisher also parallels the later members of the personality school in the reputation she established for exemplary moral conduct. In her heyday she was the idol of the male population but she avoided temptation and maintained a spotless reputation. After she married the musician, James G. Maeder, she became a faithful wife and a devoted mother. James Murdoch called her "a lady of refined manners and irreproachable character" [5] and Charles Congdon, a journalist of the period, wrote that "those who talk foolishly about the immorality of the stage may be surprised and perhaps pained to learn that she was a good wife, a good mother, and a good woman altogether." [6]

Miss Fisher remained on the stage for many years, for she did not retire finally until 1880, but her appeal steadily diminished as she lost her youthful vivacity and allure. She eventually played classic parts and old lady roles in which her experience and technical skill were great enough to make her successful. However, it was in the sprightly, youthful roles which fitted her sparkling, joyous personality that she made her greatest success and she deserves, therefore, to be called one of the earliest and brightest stars of the personality school.

MAGGIE MITCHELL

Another representative of this school, whose appeal was similar to that of Clara Fisher, was Margaret Julia Mitchell, beloved throughout the nation as Maggie Mitchell. Like Clara Fisher, Maggie began her career as a child and won acclaim for portraying three different male characters—Claude Melnotte, Richard III, and Young Norval—in a single evening. Also like Clara Fisher, Maggie captivated her audience with her sprightly dancing and, more importantly, with her elfin, roguish appeal—an appeal which was always presented in a wholesome, uplifting fashion. Her career extended from 1851 to 1891, and while it was not quite so long nor nearly so varied as Clara Fisher's, it was notable for its sustained success.

For most of her life, Maggie Mitchell specialized in roles which suited her wholesome vivacity and hoydenish charm. By far her most popular vehicle was a piece called *Fanchon the Cricket,* a dramatization of George Sand's story, *La Petite Fadette.* Maggie stumbled onto the play in 1861 and from then until the end of her career, Fanchon remained the most popular character in her repertory. Other plays like *Little Barefoot, The Pearl of Savoy, Mignon,* and *Jane Eyre* were presented with success but the public always demanded a return of *Fanchon the Cricket.* In all these vehicles, Maggie projected her own engaging personality. As Oral Coad and Edwin Mims remarked, "Her sketches were not careful studies, but pleasing improvisations," and the secret of their success was "naturalness and a seeming absence of art" [7] combined with youthful animation which she never lost even in her mature years. "She had," wrote Luther L. Holden, "the rare faculty of painting the picture of maidenly purity and nobility of soul most deftly; and her audience laughed when she laughed, and wept when she wept." [8] As a purveyor of personal charm for forty years, she is a colorful representative of a style of acting which has been seen in every age of the American theatre but which flourished as a school after Maggie Mitchell left the stage.

A SISTERHOOD OF SWEETNESS AND LIGHT

The actresses who made the personality school a dominant force in the American theatre at the turn of the nineteenth century were four outstanding performers: Maude Adams, Julia Marlowe, Viola Allen, and Ada Rehan. This quartet of charming and virtuous ladies form a "sisterhood of sweetness and light." In contrast to the ablest players of other schools, their achievement was not the greatest. For example, none of them attained the stature of Charlotte Cushman and none of them possessed the elemental emotional power of Clara Morris. Yet all of them won great popularity and acclaim; all of them were admired for their personal refinement and uplifting influence; and all of them provided superior examples of the kind of acting characteristic of the personality school.

The Misses Adams, Marlowe, and Allen were born within six years of each other and made their adult debuts within six years of each other. Maude Adams and Viola Allen were children of theatrical parents and both of them practically grew up in the theatre. Julia Marlowe, who was born in England and came to America when she was four, began her theatrical career at eleven, playing children's roles in musical shows. The first two ladies learned their art through practical experience, while Miss Marlowe, in addition to practical experience, had a three-year course of training with a retired actress, Miss Ada Dow, who took the girl into her home and administered a thorough, old-fashioned course in how to prepare and how to act the great feminine roles of the standard drama.

Miss Marlowe made her adult debut as Parthenia in the old-fashioned tragedy of *Ingomar*. For the ensuing nine years she acted nothing but classical roles. Then, bowing to popular taste, she appeared in modern romantic comedies and played in them for six years. Returning to the classics, she began starring in Shakespearean drama with E. H. Sothern, and from 1914 until her retirement in 1924, she and Sothern became famous as the leading exponents of Shakespearean drama in the United States.

Miss Allen, like Julia Marlowe, received her initial training in the classics. Her second adult role was Desdemona, which she played to the Othello of John McCullough. She also supported McCullough in *Virginius, The Gladiator,* and *Richard III*. She continued her theatrical education by playing engagements with Lawrence Barrett and Tommaso Salvini, after which she acted for two seasons in "Old Comedy" with Joseph Jefferson, W. J. Florence, and Mrs. John Drew. Such early and thorough experience in the standard drama of the mid-nineteenth century gave Miss Allen's style an elevated, poetic quality which she never lost. It enabled her in later life to succeed admirably in romantic drama but handicapped her in the performance of modern comedy.

In the training they received, the Misses Marlowe and Allen represent the survival of the classic repertory in the American theatre, but Miss Adams, who exceeded both of them in popularity, was identified almost exclusively with contemporary drama. She began her career acting modern roles and scored her greatest triumphs in the plays of James M. Barrie. Whereas we remember Miss Marlowe for her Rosalind and Miss Allen for her Viola, we remember Maude Adams for her Lady Babbie and Peter Pan.

None of the sisterhood of sweetness and light can be called great in her art. Adams, Allen, and Marlowe were accomplished actresses who served their professions with integrity and devotion, but all three were limited to roles which suited their own personalities. They could claim a modest versatility, but when they attempted the greatest tragic roles or the greatest comic roles, either they failed completely or they achieved only a moderate success.

Within their own range they were remarkably effective. They triumphed through the potency of their individual charms and through the appeal of their admirable womanhood. Personality and character were the secrets of their success, a success which illustrates, as one critic has remarked, how manner and temperament can eclipse the claims of genius.

Maude Adams, the most popular of the three, was the top moneymaking star in the entire United States. During her most active years, the public paid over a million and one half dollars to see her in Chicago and Boston, while almost twice as much was spent in New York City. She was, at the peak of her career, "the most conspicuous figure upon the English speaking stage, the most notable woman in a nation of a hundred million people. . . ." [9] And yet she could not claim either dramatic genius of the first order or great beauty of face and figure. She was merely "a little home-like woman, with gentle intimate graces, a fanciful, elfin humor, retiring, shy, and unworldly" but whenever she appeared, the theatres were packed—not only with seasoned playgoers—but with thousands of people who never entered a play-house except to see Maude Adams.

The attraction of Miss Adams was the irresistible appeal of joyful-ness, of goodness, of optimism, and of eternal youth. She symbolized all that was fine and pure and hopeful. Her acting filled the spectator with a clean, sweet sense of happiness and well being. The spectator identified himself keenly and joyfully with Miss Adams' creations and the experience seemed to satisfy his hunger for better things. The affec-tionate relationship between actress and spectator which Miss Adams created in her portrayal of Lady Babbie is typical of her unique ap-peal. Lewis Strang writes:

Babbie was to us some dear friend, a cherished companion, whom we loved very much, whom we wished always with us, whose happiness was our greatest pleasure, whose sorrows awoke in us keenest sympthy; a friend whom we felt that we could trust to the end of time, who never dis-appointed nor wounded us, who never fell from our ideal, who returned sentiment for sentiment, who inspired us to look up and seek beyond, whose sympathy was rich, full, and complete, whose influence was en-nobling, purifying, and broadening.[10]

Miss Adams avoided roles which portrayed the seamy side of life, and she very rarely attempted parts which included the fierce, ele-mental passions of hate, jealousy, anger, or sex. When she played Juliet, she was admired for the convincing sweetness of her portrayal, but her performance lacked the depth and strength of high tragedy. William Winter said she presented "A balcony scene without passion, a parting scene without delirium of grief, and a potion scene without power." [11] It was in the realm of sentiment, of wholesome ideals and heart-warming charm that she excelled. Her appeal in this field was unique. Rarely has the power of an actress been described in such evangelistic terms as are used in the following summary of Miss Adams' influence: "She is building hope in the hearts of the despair-ing, courage in the souls of the conquered, and reviving beauty and joy and love in the lives of those whom misery and sin have crushed." [12]

The appeal of Viola Allen was also one of wholesomeness and up-lift. This actress had a refined, ladylike charm which added a touch of nobility to all the roles she played. She was unusually competent in her art, studious in her approach to any role, and well grounded in the techniques of her profession. Her appeal was not directly to the hearts of her audience, like that of Maude Adams, but she touched the minds of her spectators, she pleased the critics with her well-rounded performances, and she satisfied the moral aspirations of a large segment of the public. She played many Shakespearean roles, and was greatly admired as Viola. But perhaps her most successful play was a piece called *The Christian* which, although universally acknowledged to be an "uncommonly bad drama," nevertheless drew audiences for two full seasons because of the uplifting nature of its message and the wholesome charm of its star.

Julia Marlowe, the third member of the sisterhood of sweetness and light, was perhaps the most versatile of the group. She played almost all the heroines of Shakespeare, including Cleopatra and Lady Macbeth, and she even attempted the role of Prince Hal. However, her success in the latter parts was negligible, whereas her achievement in such roles as Rosalind, Viola, and Juliet was admired and praised in both England and America. The latter roles suited Miss Marlowe exactly, for she was the epitome of womanly virtue and feminine loveliness—the foremost romantic actress of her time. She was careful and studious like Miss Allen, but possessed more warmth and personal magnetism. Arthur Symons, the English poet and critic, called her "warm and engaging" and said that "she fills and gladdens you with a sense of the single human being she is representing." [13] She did not, however, equal Maude Adams in arousing fervent loyalty and adoration. In an Adams performance, the spectator identified himself completely with her joyous, heart-warming youthfulness, whereas in a Marlowe performance, the spectator was content to sit back and enjoy the spectacle of winsome, lovely womanhood. Miss Marlowe always evoked such comments as "admirable, graceful, and sweet," "a beautiful, appealing, and poetic portrayal of a sweet character," "the very quintessence of femininity," "an enthralling influence of sweet and lovely womanhood."

An important element in Miss Marlowe's appeal, in addition to grace of person, was beauty of voice and delivery. Her tones were varied and flexible. Sometimes they were rich and satin-like or tender and appealing; at other times they could be hard and impervious or sharp and pitiless. In reading her lines, Miss Marlowe was always distinct and fluent and, according to Winter, she showed a fine discrimination for the meaning of words and a nice ability to "make her speeches seem the utterance of thoughts prompted by words addressed to her. . . ." [14] Even higher praise was given her elocution by Arthur Symons who declared that there was no actor on the British stage who could speak English or English verse as beautifully and effectively as could Julia Marlowe and her partner Edward Sothern.[15]

Critics of an older generation who watched Miss Marlowe in her Shakespearean roles felt that she was always worthy but never great. She did not equal the famous Shakespearean performers of the mid-nineteenth century, but in an era when modern comedy had supplanted the standard repertory, she was welcomed and lauded for maintaining the Shakespearean tradition. Through long and devoted effort and, perhaps, for lack of competition, she won universal recognition as the foremost Shakespearean actress of her time. William Winter said: "She was not a Siddons, a Cushman, or a Faucit, but she is a superb actress. The sum of her influence has been distinctly and strongly helpful. . . ." [16]

For the first time in the history of American acting, uplifting influence became a major element in the appeal of popular stage performers. Audiences were attracted by the individual virtues of these ladies and by their reputations as moral leaders. Miss Allen was widely known for her activity as a Sunday School teacher. She refused to include any but virtuous characters in her repertory and made her greatest success as the noble heroine of *The Christian*. Miss Marlowe, too, specialized in virtuous roles and guarded her productions against coarseness or profanity. In the romantic play, *When Knighthood Was in Flower*, she refused absolutely to say the word "damn" on the stage even though the script called for it. Like Miss Allen, she maintained a spotless personal reputation and identified herself with many worthy philanthropies.

Maude Adams also set an example of purity and goodness in her personal life. She was a shy and reticent person who, in her heyday, never submitted to a press interview and never mingled in the world of fashion. On one occasion a certain magazine offered her $35,000 for a single article of biographical interest, but she refused the offer on the ground that her private views were of no consequence and should not be imposed on the public. She was a woman who guarded her integrity and her high ideals, who felt deep sympathy for all human suffering, and who dreamed of a world where beauty and goodness and happiness might be shared by all mankind. These aspirations, well illustrated in the roles Miss Adams acted, inspired and ennobled the many thousands of people who flocked to see her. David Gray epitomized her influence when he wrote: ". . . Maude Adams must be accepted as an evolution-working personality, luminous with sweetness and light, even more than an artist; as a public influence even more than an actress. . . . The main current of her force is ethical rather than aesthetic." [17]

Maude Adams, Julia Marlowe, and Viola Allen were not great creative performers nor pioneers in any branch of theatrical art, but their admirable talents and their high moral influence, projected through charming personalities, give them high rank as exponents of the personality school.

Ada Rehan began her career a few years before her "sisters" and retired while they were still in their prime, yet Miss Rehan is closely related to them in the style and appeal of her acting and in the influence she exerted. Like them, Miss Rehan's range of parts was limited; she excelled in roles which suited her own personality; feminine charm and personal magnetism were strong elements in her appeal; and she was admired for her industry, her virtue, and her wholesome influence.

Ada Rehan was not a native American. She was born in Limerick, Ireland, April 22, 1860, but when she was five years old her family moved to Brooklyn, and there she grew up and went to school. Except for professional trips abroad, she lived her whole life in the United States, and died in New York City on January 8, 1916.

She received a sound, practical training in her profession. Her elder sisters had gone on the stage, so it was natural for Ada to consider a career in the theatre. She made her debut in Newark, New Jersey, at the age of thirteen, and two years later, through her sister's influence, she secured a place in Mrs. Drew's famous stock company at the Arch Street Theatre in Philadelphia.[18] She played stock there and in other eastern theatres for the next four years, and received a well-rounded training in the standard repertory of tragedy and old comedy. Like so many other young actresses of the period, she was called upon to support various traveling stars in their local appearances, and thus she had the opportunity of playing Ophelia to the Hamlet of Edwin Booth, and Virginia in John McCullough's production of *Virginius*. But Miss Rehan's career was not to be in tragedy; she was destined to shine for twenty years as the bright star of Augustin Daly's company, and to make her reputation as America's representative comedienne in certain Shakespearean roles and in the comedies and melodramas which Daly adapted from contemporary German playwrights.

Augustin Daly first took note of the acting of Ada Rehan in 1877. He observed her several times thereafter, and in 1879 engaged her as a permanent member of his own company. Miss Rehan became his leading lady and remained in this position until Daly's death in 1899. During this time she played over two hundred parts and played them all with a skill, a charm, and a magnetism which placed her in the front rank of American comediennes.

The two outstanding qualities of Miss Rehan's acting were vivacious humor and womanly charm. All the reviews of her acting laud these qualities in an amazing variety of phrases. Miss Rehan was always "sweetly reckless," "ardently impetuous," or "piquantly alluring." In all her roles she displayed "kindly vivacity," "ingenuous glee," "demure archness," "bewitching reserve," or "roguish charm." Whatever the female she portrayed, a basic womanliness and feminine appeal shone through. In her acting of Katherine in *The Taming of the Shrew*, "the crown of the assumption was woman-like charm." [19] As Valentine in *The Railroad of Love,* the outstanding trait was "tantalizing, delicious feminine caprice." [20] The chief beauty of her Julia in *Two Gentlemen of Verona* was "womanlike loveliness and grace." [21] And, as the leading lady in Tennyson's *The Foresters,* "the crowning excellence of her art was its expression of essential womanhood." [22]

Miss Rehan's looks, voice, and temperament enabled her to project and enhance her two outstanding qualities of vivacious humor and womanly charm. William Winter, a fervent admirer, says her physical beauty was "of the kind that appears in portraits of women by Romney and Gainsborough—ample, opulant, and bewitching." [23] She was tall and generously proportioned, with gray-blue eyes and a mass of brown hair. Many of her admirers considered her goddess-like in beauty, while others felt that it was her charm and vitality and not the perfection of her features which created the illusion of beauty. Walter Prichard Eaton says she was "not conventionally beautiful but arch, piquant, incessantly alive, with great feminine charm. . . ." [24] A study of her photographs reveals a face which a modern critic would call fresh, wholesome, and pleasing—but certainly not beautiful in the way Lillian Russell was beautiful.

As to the beauty of her voice, there was no disagreement. Everyone praised it for roundness, fullness, richness, and clarity, and many critics were struck by what they termed its "caressing" quality. Otis Skinner said that Miss Rehan's voice "melted and caressed as it drawled," [25] and George Bernard Shaw, who witnessed her London performance in 1895, said: "When she is at her best, the music of her voice melts in the caress of the emotion it expresses." [26]

Another accomplishment on which there was little disagreement, was the clarity and grace of Miss Rehan's elocution. William Winter spoke of the "delicious purity" of her articulation and believed that her delivery of English verse was "the most melodious" then heard upon the stage. Even the London critics praised her "distinct enunciation" and the "perfect delivery" of her lines. A minority opinion was expressed by John R. Towse, who declared that: "Her delivery of verse, whether blank or rhymed, was always curiously monotonous and inexpressive." [27] The majority of critics and playgoers, however, agreed with George Bernard Shaw who, after witnessing her performance of Helena in *A Midsummer Night's Dream,* described her elocution in admiring terms, as follows: "Her treatment of Shakespearean verse is delightful after the mechanical intoning of Sarah Bernhardt. She gives us beauty of tone, grace of measure, delicacy of articulation: in short, all the technical qualities of verse music, along with the rich feeling and fine intelligence without which those technical qualities would soon become monotonous." [28] Evidently Miss Rehan's elocution made a lasting impression on Shaw because several years after her death he still classed her and Forbes Robertson as "the best speakers you could find on the stage." [29]

But perhaps the outstanding appeal of Miss Rehan's acting was the personal magnetism she exerted. Her exuberance and wholesome animal spirits coupled with her innate sweetness and tenderness were strong enough to captivate her audiences. Miss Rehan possessed the fortunate and somewhat rare power to impress her rich, warm personality on a single visitor chatting in her dressing room or, with equal force, on a thousand spectators sitting in a darkened auditorium. Undoubtedly her success on the stage was as much attributable to this personal magnetism as to her theatrical technique.

In the techniques of her art Miss Rehan was accomplished. Her training in stock and her association with the mature stars of the classic repertory gave her skill and assurance and taught her a style which perfectly suited the parts she acted. It was a deft, artificial style in which graceful movement and gesture, artful timing, and fluent, musical delivery were so combined as to give the effect of spontaneity and naturalness. Augustin Daly, who monopolized Miss Rehan's talents for twenty years, capitalized on this style. The plays he chose for his star were not the modern, realistic dramas of Ibsen, then beginning to reshape the theatre. Rather, they were old comedies like *The School for Scandal* and *The Belle's Strategem,* or carefully selected and adapted comedies of Shakespeare, like *The Taming of the Shrew, Twelfth Night,* and *As You Like It,* or, most often, they were farces and melodramas borrowed from German dramatists and reworked by Mr. Daly. The following plays are examples of this latter group: *Red Letter Nights,* in which Miss Rehan played an amiable but mischievous girl; *The Transit of Leo,* in which the leading lady must alternate between "piquant playfulness" and "rueful self-censure"; *The Two Escutcheons,* which offered Miss Rehan another "arch and gay" part; and *The Countess Gucki,* which is described as "a fabric of comic complexities and playful colloquy." [30]

In all of these plays Miss Rehan was able to exploit her vivacious humor and womanly charm. She was also able to use her sprightly, artificial style of acting. As she was absolute mistress of this style, it won her great applause and wide popularity. But continued repetition of the same kind of role in the same style of acting eventually arrested Miss Rehan's growth as an actress and limited her range of accomplishment. George Bernard Shaw, in 1895, warned Miss Rehan that if she persisted in playing only the light, artificial roles which Daly selected, her style would become increasingly rhetorical and unreal. Shaw urged her to leave Daly's management, to espouse young ideas, and to seek plays with real women's parts in them. But Shaw's advice went unheeded. Miss Rehan remained faithful to Daly, acting in the plays he chose for her until his death. Then the situation, foreseen by Shaw, came to pass. Miss Rehan was unable to adapt her style to the demands of twentieth century realism. The years, too, had taken their toll, and Miss Rehan's youthful buoyance and charm were no longer strong enough to captivate her audiences. In the season of 1903–4, when Miss Rehan toured with Otis Skinner in a repertory of three of her best roles, Skinner sadly records: "From the opening rehearsal it was evident that the exquisite comedienne with whom I had the happiest memories of five years' association, was no more." [31]

In 1905, at the age of forty-five when she should have been in her prime, Miss Rehan made her final appearance on the stage. She died eleven years later. As an actress she had provided wholesome pleasure for thousands of playgoers; she had brought to life a whole gallery of sprightly, charming, attractive women shaping them into likenesses of her own radiant personality; but certain of her techniques, suitable for poetic plays and artificial comedy, were not flexible enough to meet the needs of the new naturalistic drama. Her style became rhetorical and unreal as the years passed; and so, to the regret of many playgoers, Miss Rehan's appeal vanished with her youth and with the outmoded repertory of the Daly company.

VI

THE COMIC STAGE

THE SECOND HALF OF THE NINETEENTH CENTURY MIGHT BE CALLED
the golden age of comic acting in America. During this period there
flourished a host of players who were prodigal both in number and in
comic genius. Their enormous versatility, their unending variety, and
their astonishing achievements are enough to dazzle an admirer who
studies their careers a full hundred years after their great performances.
They can honestly be called comedians without peer, consummate
artists, and the greatest comic performers in the history of the American stage. In order to understand the unique kind of acting they
achieved in their time, one must glance at the type of comic acting
which is seen today.

Many of the comedians of the twentieth century fall, roughly, into
two classes. There are the clowns and gagsters, like Bob Hope, Jack
Benny, and Red Skelton, and there are the sophisticates like Noel
Coward and Cary Grant. The first group includes the men who have
created a unique stage personality for themselves and who exploit it
largely through verbal gags, and absurd situations which lead to gags.
Bob Hope, for example, is always the exuberant, ingratiating smart
alec, rolling his eyes and delivering rapid-fire wise cracks; Jack Benny
is always the egregious tightwad bragging about himself and exchang-
ing insults with his colleagues; Danny Kaye (with rare exceptions) is
always the irrepressible clown, singing, dancing, cavorting, and double-
talking his way in and out of scrapes. In cinema, television, or living
theatre, the roles played by these comedians are always the same, and
the programs are always tailored to fit the players. Bob Hope, Jack

Benny, Danny Kaye, and their fellows are enormously successful because the public enjoys the characters they have created for themselves, and the players behind the characters are expert in manipulating themselves through an endless succession of situations.

The sophisticated comedians seen on the recent American stage are a somewhat different breed. They are not clowns, gagsters, and entertainers like the Hopes and the Bennys. They are charming, polished, urbane drawing-room heroes with a dash of romantic appeal. They appear on stage, screen, and television in sprightly comedies like *Mary, Mary* or *The Moon is Blue.* Generally they do not vary their roles but play their attractive and clever selves over and over again.

The great decades of the nineteenth century had clowns and sophisticates, but it had, in addition, a group of expert actors whom I shall call character comedians. These gifted players were quite different from the clowns and sophisticates because they could change their personalities with their roles; they could produce uproarious laughter through careful portrayal of character; and they could and did create rich galleries of unique comic portraits.

To understand the kind of character acting they developed and the versatility they achieved, one should recall the extensive comic repertory of the period. First of all, there were the comedies of Shakespeare, which were part of the standard repertory and which offered such challenging roles as Bottom, Dogberry, Falstaff, Malvolio, Sir Andrew Aguecheek, etc. Secondly, there was so-called "old comedy," best represented by the plays of Goldsmith, Sheridan, and Farquhar, and offering such popular parts as Sir Peter Teazle, Sir Anthony Absolute, Bob Acres, Sir Lucius O'Trigger, Tony Lumpkin, and a galaxy of other characters which no comedian could resist. A third group of plays, which furnished some of the most popular vehicles of the century, were the dramas and adaptations of recent or contemporary playwrights. A few of the best known examples are Boucicault's adaptation of *Rip Van Winkle,* which provided Joseph Jefferson with his greatest role; Morris Barnett's *The Serious Family,* which included the character of Aminidab Sleek; Tom Taylor's *Our American Cousin,* which included the roles of Asa Trenchard and Lord Dundreary; and George Coleman's *The Heir-at-Law,* which featured the popular characters, Dr. Pangloss and Zekiel Homespun. A final group of plays, providing further tests for the skill of the comedians, were the farces which generally appeared as afterpieces to the main drama of the evening. Representative examples are the lively inventions of J. Madison Morton such as *Slasher and Crasher, Betsey Baker,* and *Poor Pillocoddy.* A character comedian in the mid-decades of the nineteenth century customarily played a major role in the main drama of the evening; then, very likely, he performed comic songs or turns in the "olio" which separated the main drama from the farce; and, finally, he cavorted for an additional hour in the afterpiece or farce.

It is difficult for a modern playgoer to visualize the kind of character acting demanded by the repertory of the nineteenth century and developed by the great comedians of that period. It is rarely seen today. The two illustrations which come most readily to mind are foreign actors: Alec Guiness, in such a film as *Kind Hearts and Coronets,* and Fernandel in *The Sheep Has Five Legs.* In these films the leading actor did not play himself; each created several different characters and the comic effect resulted from the uniqueness of the portraits. In separate films, also, Guiness and Fernandel are successful in creating distinct and different characterizations, an example being Guiness's markedly different personalities in *The Swan* and *The Ladykillers.*

The mid-decades of the nineteenth century are illustrious for the surprising number of superlative character comedians who flourished at the time. Heading this illustrious company are four great names: Henry Placide, William E. Burton, John Gilbert, and William Warren. Let us look at the kind of comic acting they practiced.

HENRY PLACIDE

Henry Placide, the first of the great comedians to make his debut, was called "almost a faultless actor," [1] and "the best comedian the United States has yet produced." [2] He had every personal requisite for success —a handsome, expressive face, a supple figure of medium height, a clear, melodious voice, a spirited, vivacious personality, and an alert, inquiring mind which savored all the peculiarities and eccentricities of human nature. Born into a family of actors and acrobats, he became one of the troupe at an early age and subsequently underwent a long and intensive apprenticeship. The results were rare and wonderful: he emerged as an actor whose range of roles was extraordinary. He could play every variety of comic part from broad farce to exquisite high comedy, and was unequalled in three kinds of roles: middle-aged gentlemen, drunken servants, and simple country lads. In addition, his French ancestry and knowledge of the French language gave him an immense advantage in parts requiring a Gallic background. During his twenty years at the Park Theatre in New York he acted more than five hundred roles and was the first portrayer of over two hundred of them.

In all his acting, Placide was the discriminating artist, analyzing his characters and seeking to present their traits and eccentricities with exactness, precision, and rich humor. He never relied on grimace or buffoonery and never distorted a role to gain comic advantage. His power to slough off his own personality and become the character of the play was so great that spectators could not believe they were seeing the same actor play, in succession, the foppish dandy, the stupid country dolt, and the doddering old grandfather. Except for his voice, the purity and clarity of which were always recognizable, Placide's disguises were perfect; so much so that he was never the subject of imitation or impersonation. From role to role there were no uniformities of mannerism or style on which to base an imitation. Placide's achievements in the creation of comic characters earned him the ultimate praise from Edwin Forrest. When that great tragedian was performing in Europe, he was asked to name the best American actor and he unhesitatingly replied, "Henry Placide is unquestionably the best general actor on the American boards, and I doubt whether his equal can be found in England." [3]

WILLIAM E. BURTON

The loyal American fans of William E. Burton, however, would contest this verdict. In the minds of thousands of theatregoers, Placide was great but Burton was "the funniest man who ever lived." [4] The very sound of his voice off stage could send an audience into an uproar, and in the famous drunk scene from *The Toodles* he could hold his spectators convulsed for a full fifty minutes without speaking a line. He could also make them weep, mingling laughter and tears in miraculous combination. No comedian, perhaps, has ever exercised such complete command over the responses of his audience.

Burton, who was English born, had learned his style from the great

British comedian, Liston, and therefore was more broad and exaggerated in his effects than was Placide. A few critics found him unnecessarily coarse at times. All critics and spectators, however, agreed that he was a born comedian who was original in his conceptions, painstaking in building his characters, and masterful at by-play, grimace, and mimetic effect. He had a rather heavy figure, a broad genial face, and a voice of extraordinary flexibility. Some of his funniest effects came from his voice and face. Both were protean: he could vary his tones from the boyish squeak of the terrified adolescent to the roar of the enraged sea captain, while his face was a huge map on which was outlined every degree and kind of comic emotion. Joseph Jefferson, in praising Burton's mastery of facial expression, declares that the comedian's entrance as Van Dunder in a play called *The Dutch Governor* was a picture "so full of genius that it stamped itself indelibly on the mind . . . ," and then Jefferson describes the actor's appearance as follows: "The great stupid face was a blank. The heavy cheeks hung down stolidly on each side of a half-opened mouth; the large, expressionless eyes seemed to look hopelessly for some gleam of intelligence. There he stood, the incarnation of pompous ignorance, with an open letter in his hand. The audience swayed with laughter; for, though he had not said a word, they knew he had just received an important state document and couldn't read it." [5]

Like the other great comedians of his time, Burton was marvelously versatile and creative. He could embody with exquisite humor a sharply conceived character like Shakespeare's Bottom, or he could take a sketchily written part in a modern farce and could so build it, shape it, and embellish it that it became a full-length masterpiece. He never distorted the dramatist's conception, but he always succeeded in adding additional magic which was unmistakably Burtonian. The roles for which he was nationally famous illustrate his versatility. He habitually performed the parts of Timothy Toodles in *The Toodles* and Aminidab Sleek in *The Serious Family* on the same bill, and a spectator, unfamiliar with his genius, could hardly recognize that the person who had acted the jolly, effusive Toodles was, a few moments later, personating the sanctimonious, lugubrious Sleek. Incidentally, these two portrayals were so popular that for years, at Burton's Chambers Street Theatre in New York, Tuesday and Friday nights were regularly set aside for the performance of these plays—and this was in an era, it will be remembered, before the long run had been established.

Burton's other most popular role was that of Captain Cuttle in a stage version of Dickens' *Dombey and Son,* a role which Odell calls "one of the famous things of the stage." [6] However, the great comedian did not confine himself to three roles, great as was the public clamor for a constant repetition of them. He created almost two hundred unforgettable portraits, many of them Shakespearean, and doubtless would have equalled the number of parts played by his great contemporaries had not an untimely death ended his career.

During the years from 1848 to 1856, Burton's Theatre in New York became a nationally famous institution; it was also a training school for an astonishing number of the great comedians of the century. Besides Burton himself, the company boasted Henry Placide, and the following notable performers who will be discussed later: William Rufus Blake, John Brougham, George Holland, Charles Fisher, and Lester Wallack.

Two great comedians who challenged the supremacy of Burton and Placide but who never performed in their company, were John Gilbert and William Warren. Both rank in the top quartet of all-time American comic geniuses.

JOHN GILBERT

John Gilbert, who made his debut five years after the advent of Placide and Burton, was noted for the polish, grace, dignity, and exquisite finish of his style. He was a master technician who modelled his acting after the style of the English genius, Farren, and who became so expert that no matter how painstaking his preparation of a role, the final effect appeared spontaneous and unrehearsed. In his early years he was criticized for being somewhat formal and cold, but in later life he developed a warmth and tenderness which made his portrayal of Old Dornton in *The Road to Ruin* one of his best parts. He portrayed a great number of old men but each was individual and distinct for he was another actor gifted with the supreme power to submerge his own personality and to transform himself into the character conceived by the dramatist. His range was prodigious, and the perfection of his portraiture was the subject of boundless praise. John R. Towse says that his acting of Sir Anthony Absolute "has never been equalled anywhere in the last half century. . . ." [7] William Winter believes that he gave "the best performance of Caliban that ever was seen in America," [8] while Brander Matthews declares, ". . . I have never seen, nor has anyone else in the past half-century, any rendering of Sir Peter Teazle comparable with John Gilbert's." [9] These are only three out of the 1,150 parts he performed during his lifetime and in all of these parts, as William Winter writes, he was "sometimes a great actor . . . always a correct one." [10]

WILLIAM WARREN

William Warren, the final member of the top quartet of comic geniuses, is considered by many critics to have been the greatest of them all. In view of the encomiums I have already cited for Placide, Burton, and Gilbert, it is difficult to contend that another actor could be greater than they. But Warren's claims are strong, and certainly he is a peer of the greatest if, indeed, he does not surpass them.

Warren's career on the stage covered more than fifty years, for he made his debut in 1832 and retired in 1883. The final thirty-six of these years were spent at one theatre, the Boston Museum. Except for a single starring tour in 1864–65, the world had to travel to Boston to see Mr. Warren; he disliked touring and preferred to let others come to him. But even though he remained in one city, in one theatre, and with one stock company, he became a national institution admired equally as much by fellow players as by an adoring public.

Warren was a meticulous student, a penetrating observer, and a genuine lover of his fellow men. He surveyed with a sympathetic eye the thousands of human beings around him, and from them he learned the infinite complexity and drollery of human thought and behavior. Warren drew on his vast storehouse of observation and intuition for each character he played; when finally presented, each creation was "complete, uniform, and fulfilled to its absolute possibilities," [11] and each was suffused with a delicious, genial humor which lacked any trace of sarcasm or satire. Whenever he stepped on the stage—or even before, when his voice was heard off stage—a thrill of joy went through the audience. And this thrill was felt by the players on the stage as well as by the spectators. Mary Shaw, who acted with him many times, declares: "He was so wonderful an actor that simply his standing on the stage seemed to fill and overflow the whole scene . . . I have played with most of the great actors and actresses that have lived during my time, but few of them had the power to affect me personally in the scene, to make me struggle to resist the artistic appeal, which is intended for the audience. But Mr. Warren captured my feelings to such an extent that I found it difficult to hold my place in the scene." [12] H. S. Barnabee, a light opera star who acted with Warren on occasions, pays additional homage when he says: "Talk of your emotional actors! Why, he could and did, nightly, draw tears and laughter in the same breath. To observe his finesse and gradations in marking the many phases of complicated character was a priceless lesson in the art of acting." [13]

Warren's versatility as a portrayer of comic types was practically limitless. He seemed able to create complete and unique portraits out of every part assigned to him. The critics said he was the best Touchstone of his period and incomparable as Dogberry or Polonius or Autolycus or Sir Andrew Aguecheek. He was practically unrivalled in roles from the plays of Sheridan and Goldsmith, and was equally fine in contemporary comic roles such as Triplet, Jesse Rural, and Dr. Pangloss. Another of his strong points was dialect acting—and he was at home in all of them: French, Scotch, Irish, Yorkshire, and Yankee. At the same time, he was said to be unapproachable in farce and low comedy, being able to produce uncontrollable laughter in these parts. A contemporary admirer summarizes his versatility and artistry in these words: "He gave us finished to the finger-tips, to the last intonation, to the last detail of costume, to the last queer turn of dialect, not only an infinite variety of types, but an infinite variety in those types. . . ." [14] During his professional life Warren's powers did not decline: he performed 13,500 times in almost six hundred different roles. Joseph Jefferson said, ". . . it is safe to conclude that this versatile comedian studied and created more parts than any other actor of his day," [15] and Lewis Strang declares, ". . . he was, beyond a reasonable doubt, the greatest comedian that the American Theatre has produced." [16]

Placide, Burton, Gilbert, and Warren form a quartet whose comic genius was without peer. But so vital was the American theatre in their day, and so rich was the array of talent, that this quartet of actors was challenged by nine other comedians whose talent was close to theirs. Of these nine, William J. Florence, William Rufus Blake, and Henry J. Finn belong at the top.

Blake was a portly man with a heavy face and figure, and yet he managed to convey meaning and humor with telling effect. He infused each of his parts with rare spirit, richness of color, and poetic fervor, and was as powerful in roles demanding tender pathos as in those requiring eccentric humor.

William J. (Billy) Florence likewise had versatility and range. He began his career playing serious roles, such as Laertes and MacDuff; then for ten years he specialized in Irish peasant types; finally he broadened his repertory to include most of the roles featured by his great contemporaries. He acted Bob Brierly in *The Ticket of Leave Man* more than 1,500 times, and after creating the role of Bardwell Slote in *The Almighty Dollar,* he played it more than 2,500 times. His portraits were all vivid, consistent, and lifelike—with the actor's own personality entirely effaced. When he died, it was said that he had reigned as a star for forty years without a single failure.

Henry J. Finn, who met an untimely death in 1840, is almost entirely forgotten by historians of the stage, and yet he was considered by many to be "the most versatile comic genius of his day." [17] He began his career as a tragedian and never completely abandoned serious roles. Wemyss reports that as late in his career as 1836 Finn played an engagement which began with the popular comic roles of Lord Ogilby and Paul Pry, continued through such eccentric characters as Dr. Pangloss, Billy Black, Philip Garbois and Beau Chatterley, and ended with—Richard III! However, despite his hankering for tragic roles, it was in the characters of eccentric comedy that Finn was inimitable. His dry, brilliant, sharply etched portrayals led managers and critics to regard him as one of the brightest stars in the theatrical galaxy. Ludlow records that in the role of Philip Garbois, Finn was "pre-eminently superior to any person I have seen attempt it," [18] while Wemyss declares: "his Lord Ogilby . . . his Paul Schack, his Beau Chatterley have never been equalled on the American stage." [19]

Ranking slightly below the overall level of Florence, Blake, and Finn were Charles Fisher, John Sleeper Clarke, John E. Owens, James H. Hackett, William P. Davidge, and Charles Burke. Burke died at the early age of thirty-two, but his grace and wit were remembered for years by his contemporaries. The others all lived to respectable ages and were famous for certain specialties as well as for a worthy versatility. Fisher's sparkle, precision, and courtly grace made him brilliant in such parts as Malvolio, Dandy Dinmont, and Sir Peter Teazle. Owens, who brilliantly carried on the tradition of the Yankee comedian, made a "tangible reality" and a national institution out of Solon Shingle in *The People's Lawyer,* and scored hits as Caleb Plummer in *The Cricket on the Hearth* and as Dr. Pangloss in *The Heir-at-Law.* John Sleeper Clarke, who won a distinguished place on the English stage as well as in the United States, suffused many parts with his own exuberant comic temperament, but was perhaps best known for his role of Major Wellington de Boots in *Everybody's Friend,* which he acted at least 1,000 times in America and many times in England. James H. Hackett, the father of James K. Hackett, was considered the greatest Falstaff of his period as well as one of the best dialect actors of his time. Two of his specialties, which won him renown in America and which were eventually accepted in England, were Yankee roles such as that of Solomon Swap in *Jonathan in England* (Hackett's own adaptation of George Colman's comedy, *Who Wants a Guinea?*) and western frontier heroes such as Colonel Nimrod Wildfire in *The Lion of the West.* William P. Davidge, who was born and trained in England, adopted America as his home and acted here during the last thirty-eight years of his life in a wide variety of comic roles ranging from Sir Toby Belch in *Twelfth Night* to Dick Deadeye in *H.M.S. Pinafore.* He brought to all his roles "a robust humor which could be dry, saturnine, unctuous, or Bacchic at will." [20] Still other names which deserve listing on the roster of gifted character comedians are Daniel E. Setchell, Mark Smith, and James H. Stoddart.

Along with this group of versatile male performers should be mentioned several women: Mrs. Hughes, who usually acted with William E. Burton, Mrs. John Drew, Mrs. G. H. Gilbert, and Mrs. Sarah Ross Wheatley. All of these ladies were known for their brilliant portrayal of such notable comic characters as Mrs. Malaprop, Lady Teazle, Lucretia McTab, and Lady Creamly, and in many ways their art paralleled that of the great male performers.

DION BOUCICAULT

In a somewhat different category, yet still deserving mention in the ranks of the character comedians, was that tireless and multi-talented Irishman, Dion Boucicault. Although he was thirty-three years old when he arrived in the United States in 1853, the "Ubiquitous Boucicault" immediately became a dominating influence on the stage of the United States, and during the remaining thirty-seven years of his life he left his stamp on every department of the American theatre. He died in the United States in 1890.

Born in Dublin in about 1820, he became stage struck at an early age and eventually found his way to London where, says William Winter, he "haunted theatres and wrote plays." [21] In 1841, after serving as an actor in the English provincial theatres, he established a name for himself by producing the highly popular success, *London Assurance*. From then until the year of his death, he never ceased his multifarious activities in the theatre.

One of his principal activities was acting. As a performer he exhibited the same cleverness and skill which he showed in constructing his plays. He did not attempt the varied comic roles of the great comedians like Warren or Burton or Gilbert; rather, he exploited the characters of his own plays, such as Mantalini in his play *Smike,* or Wah-no-tee in *The Octoroon,* or Nana Sahib in *Jessie Brown,* and in these he demonstrated commendable versatility. However, it was as a "lovable Irish" character in his plays based on Irish life that he achieved his greatest success. As William Winter wrote, ". . . his rightful fame is that of an author of romantic Irish plays and an actor of romantic eccentric Irish parts." [22] Three such roles are especially notable: Myles-na-Coppaleen in *The Colleen Bawn,* Daddy O'Dowd in the play of the same name, and Conn, the Shaughraun, in *The Shaughraun.* In all these parts Boucicault mingled tears and laughter, sentiment and shrewdness, in such a whimsical, engaging manner that his audiences were captivated. As Conn, the Shaughraun, Boucicault is said to have "interpreted to the life the generous, hearty, irresponsible, and none too sober wanderer, ever ready to help others but with little of an eye to his concerns." [23]

In all of his acting, Boucicault was primarily the clever technician who could simulate emotion and manipulate the responses of his audience. His long and intimate knowledge of the stage had taught him all the tricks and artifices of the actor's profession; his canny sense of public taste enabled him to utilize his technique at the right times with the desired effects. As a dramatist, he was an imitator and adaptor; it is said that he borrowed the plots of every play he ever wrote. Likewise as an actor he imitated the successful characterizations he saw created by other players and adopted the effects he found useful in his own roles. Thus his portrait of Conn, the Shaughraun, says William Winter, "was, in spirit and drift, an Irish copy of Jefferson's Rip Van Winkle. . . ." [24] But, derivative as his plays and acting may have been, Boucicault always added original, inventive touches of his own which, during most of his life, exactly suited the public taste and won for Boucicault immense popularity. He was always the shrewd opportunist, utilizing and exploiting every whim and fashion and trend of his time.

Boucicault's influence on American acting came not only from his own style of performance but even more so from his other activities in the theatre. Some of his contributions—like the introduction of fireproof scenery, the sponsorship of the first copyright law for the protection of American playwrights, and the innovation of road or combination companies—had little or no effect on the style or technique of acting. But some of Boucicault's other activities exerted considerable influence. For example, he directed innumerable productions and coached hundreds of actors and thus spread his own concepts of effective performance. He promoted the use of box settings which enclosed realistic furnishings, and these settings undoubtedly influenced the style of the actors who appeared in them. But Boucicault's most important contribution to style in acting was the result of his playwriting. For fifty years he supplied the theatres of both America and Great Britain with more than one hundred and thirty of the most popular plays of the century, and these dramas exerted an enormous influence on the actors who performed them.

Boucicault always said that a play was not written—it was rewritten. With him this process occurred in the heat of rehearsal when the actors themselves suggested lines, business, characterizations, and even whole scenes or episodes. In the process of development, the play was shaped to suit the ability of the players and to furnish them a happy vehicle for the display of their talents. In the finished product, plots and incidents were contrived and artificial; sentiments and language were ornate and high-flown; characterizations and psychology were simple and obvious. Yet these plays provided a field day for the actors. The melodramatic situations afforded the player a wonderful opportunity to display passion and vehemence. The picturesque quality of many of the roles offered a chance for vivid characterization. The ornateness of the speeches challenged a performer's skill at reading. In short, in Boucicault's plays the actor discovered "media for the exercise of virtuosité, opportunities for technical display." [25]

Plays of the Boucicault variety inevitably demanded a special skill and a special style of the actor. He couldn't move and speak as he did in ordinary life—because the situations and language were not those of ordinary life. At the same time, he could not assume the classic manner of tragedy because the plays were not tragic or poetic. The actor had to assume a grace or a courtliness or a charm which was exaggerated enough to match the material yet deft enough to hide the exaggeration. His style had to suit the mood and situation of the play and yet be pleasing and convincing in its artificiality. To be sure, many other plays of the period demanded the same style of acting, but the prolific Boucicault must be counted the chief representative of this kind of playwriting. It must not be forgotten that he was a clever, versatile actor and thus deserves mention with the other notable comedians of the nineteenth century; the influence on style of acting exerted by his innumerable plays must also be remembered.

The comedians I have so far discussed were all distinguished for range and versatility. The great reputations they achieved came from their power to transform their own personalities into the likeness of a dramatic character and then to win laughter through projecting the foibles and eccentricities of that character. Unlike the Hopes, Bennys, and Skeltons of today, they did not play themselves or a single character closely related to themselves; they were able to play any comic personality they chose to portray.

Allied with these versatile character comedians during the great decades of the nineteenth century was another group of superlative comic actors who based their fame on the creation of a single part or a single line of parts. They were similar to the comedians of today in that they generally played a single role or line of roles in which they infused the richness of their own personalities; they were unlike their modern counterparts in that the roles they played were within the framework of a drama and not presented as independent, vaudeville-type entertainment. These single-role comedians often challenged the popularity of the versatile comedians; they well deserve the fame they have won in the history of American acting. Prominent among the single role comedians were such talented players as the following:

William B. Wood, whose career began at the end of the eighteenth century and thus antedated the activity of the other great comedians of the nineteenth century. He was famous for his co-managership of the Chestnut Street Theatre, Philadelphia, in its palmiest days, but his admirable playing of a single line of roles, the elegant, artificial, characters of "old" comedy, was equally famous and entitled him to be listed by William Winter as one of the "serene luminaries" of the early American theatre.

John T. Raymond, who so injected his own buoyant personality into the role of Colonel Mulbery Sellers in *The Gilded Age* that he made it internationally famous;

E. A. Sothern, who immortalized the eccentric Lord Dundreary in *Our American Cousin;*

Dan Marble, one of the first and best of the Yankee comedians;

Francis S. Chanfrau, whose dashing portrayal of Mose the Fireboy started a national craze and who played the frontiersman, Kit, the Arkansas traveller, equally well;

James Lewis, who made priceless portraits out of the fussy old men who were his specialty;

Barney Williams, who won the hearts of both British and American audiences with his portrayal of the Irish peasant boy;

George Holland, who was the greatest jokester of his time and who converted every part he played into a vehicle for his own gags and slapstick;

Stuart Robson, whose drolly innocent appearance, squeaky, unpredictable voice, and eccentric movements dominated every role he undertook and titillated audiences for over fifty years;

John Brougham, who had a fair measure of versatility but whose breezy, genial Irish personality infused all his roles and whose fame at making impromptu curtain speeches was as great as his popularity as an actor;

George "Yankee" Hill, Dan Marble, Joshua Silsbee, and Denman Thompson, and a whole host of skillful interpreters of the stage Yankee who carried the fame of Jonathan Ploughboy and other Yankee types to every corner of the country and to England as well, where James H. Hackett's pioneering in similar roles had paved the way for later American comedians.

There were also many skillful actors who specialized in light, romantic comedy. Two of the best of these were Lester Wallack and John Drew. Their charm, dash, and sophistication could easily challenge the mantinee idols of today. All these single role performers were popular and successful. But by far the greatest of them, whose fame surpassed and outlasted the others, was Joseph Jefferson, the immortal Rip Van Winkle.

There are some who might protest the classification of Jefferson as a one role actor, and they will point to the other parts he played before and after he developed his famous characterization of Rip. It is true that he was the original Asa Trenchard in *Our American Cousin* and that he was applauded in such other roles as Caleb Plummer, Dr. Pangloss, and Bob Acres. It is also true that some critics professed to find a distinct creation in each of these portrayals. However, the best of the critics reached a different conclusion. They agreed that Jefferson was a one role comedian, and that every part he played was a variation of his single great creation, Rip Van Winkle. John R. Towse writes, "In parts so diverse as Caleb Plummer, Pangloss, and Bob Acres, the basic individualities were identical. . . . They were all unmistakably the same man in different guises." [26] Henry Austin Clapp calls Rip Van Winkle "the sole and single product" [27] of Jefferson's life, while Lewis Strang declares: "As played by Mr. Jefferson, Bob Acres is not Bob Acres, Caleb Plummer is not Caleb Plummer, Dr. Pangloss is not Dr. Pangloss; but each and every one of them is Rip Van Winkle, absolutely and entirely." [28]

But, what a wonderful creation Rip Van Winkle turned out to be! As finally perfected by Jefferson, this portrait was a masterpiece which warmed the hearts and tickled the risibilities of several generations of playgoers throughout the entire United States. The public did not want him to play a different role; the artistry which Jefferson lavished on this part was considered by the public to be ample recompense for the actor's lack of versatility.

It is not surprising that Joseph Jefferson succeeded so brilliantly in the theatre. He sprang from a long line of successful actors. His great grandfather had gone on the stage under David Garrick's patronage.

His grandfather, the elder Joseph Jefferson, came to the United States in 1795 and made a name for himself. His father, too, was an actor, so it was natural that young Joseph should grow up in the theatre. He made his debut at the age of four, and seventy-one years later, only a year before his death, he gave his final performance as Rip.

Jefferson established himself as a popular comedian very early in his career, but he was not satisfied with the roles he played. He began searching for a character where, as he says in his *Autobiography,* "humor would be so closely allied with pathos that smiles and tears should mingle with each other." [29] He found such a character in Washington Irving's Rip Van Winkle—and he decided to make the character his own even before it was embodied in a play. It was not until 1865, when Jefferson was thirty-six years old, that Dion Boucicault dramatized Irving's story and Jefferson produced it at the Adelphi Theatre in London. The play was shoddy, and the character of Rip was sketchily drawn, but Jefferson's interpretation won hearty approval. Thereafter, for the rest of his life, Jefferson continued to shape and to develop the role of Rip. As he finally played the part, the character was more his own creation than it was the dramatist's. Into the part Jefferson poured all the warmth of his own personality and all the artistry of his many years of acting.

As a man, Jefferson was beloved throughout the whole country for his kindliness, his broad sympathies, his tolerance, his whimsical humor, and his love of the world and the people in it. To him, life was rich and enjoyable; his fellow men, with all their follies, were delightful and lovable; existence was an experience to be savored and enjoyed. These attitudes of the actor, and the captivating personality which embodied them, shone through all of Jefferson's acting and were particularly apparent in his characterization of Rip. This portrayal was notable for ease and naturalness, for the absence of tricks or bombast or the striving for effect. The character had a kindliness, a spirituality, and a humor which were projected so deftly and effortlessly that they seemed inseparable from the actor (and, in reality, they were inseparable). Every moment was filled with expressive action and by-play, and every line was nursed for the tears or laughter inherent in it. Yet the performance had a simplicity and repose which were enchanting. Jefferson's artistry and personal fascination were so consummate that Clara Morris declared he was a "poet of comedy," [30] and Lewis Strang, echoing the unanimous sentiments of his fellow critics, wrote:

"Jefferson's Rip Van Winkle is a wonderful thing, a unique achieve-ment, an astonishing exhibition of virtuosity, a creation impossible to anyone but Joseph Jefferson." [31]

It is an interesting speculation to ask: who was the greater actor—Joseph Jefferson or a performer like William Warren, William Burton, John Gilbert, or Henry Placide? Whose achievement is most note-worthy—the actor who produces a single perfect creation or the versa-tile player who creates a whole gallery of convincing portraits? Per-haps such a question, provocative as it may be, is impertinent and irrelevant. Both kinds of performers can be ranked as first rate and, in actual fact, the crown of greatness has willingly been awarded to many of the actors whose achievements have been limited. And yet a mod-ern critic or playgoer cannot escape the force of the conclusion reached by Henry Austin Clapp when he wrote: "Mr. Jefferson can point . . . to one work of supreme distinction, the sole and single product of his life, the masterpiece of our stage,—the figure of the immortal Rip. Our Warren, like another Rubens, could conduct you through a vast gallery, crowded with noble canvases, of which at least a hundred glow with the beauty and the truth of life, every one bear-ing his firm signature." [32]

In view of the number and brilliance of comic actors during the nineteenth century, one is compelled to echo the remark made by Lawrence Barrett (in other circumstances) when he said that to the playgoer of today "the splendor of this company . . . seems unreal." [33]

Phineas T. Barnum once said that "show business has all phases and grades of dignity from the exhibition of a monkey to the exposition of that highest art in music and the drama. . . ." [34] The "highest art" in show business was represented when Edwin Booth or Charlotte Cushman or William Warren performed in one of the plays of Shake-speare. But as Barnum shrewdly realized, show business also included the exhibition of a monkey—and ten thousand little variety acts, bur-lesque skits, minstrel shows, animal exhibitions, and circus perfor-mances. These forms of "popular theatre" were the common theatrical activities which, like Whitman's leaves of grass, "bathed the globe" during the nineteenth century. And from these vigorous and lusty forms arose a type of performance and a technique of acting which was a stimulating force in the theatre as a whole.

Like television, radio, and the motion pictures of today, the popular theatre of the nineteenth century provided much of the entertainment for the masses. Vaudeville, minstrelsy, burlesque, the circus, and comedies of the Harrigan-Hoyt variety attracted an astonishing number of spectators. Barnum's American Museum, which featured the piously named "Lecture Room" where "concerts" and "variety acts" were presented, drew the tremendous total of 37,560,000 admissions in the years from 1841 to 1865. New York City alone, in 1869, boasted a total of six hundred "concert saloons." In 1846, Christy's Minstrels, having established themselves at Mechanics Hall in New York, began a series of shows which ran continuously for ten years, reaching a total of at least 2,792 performances. In 1869, Olive Logan, speaking before the women's suffrage convention, declared that out of sixteen theatres existing in New York City, fourteen were given over to burlesque or spectacle and only two were offering legitimate drama.

The growth and great drawing power of the popular theatre were due, in the main, to the rapid growth of cities and to the polyglot population which poured into these cities. At the close of the American Revolution, only five urban centers in the nation boasted a population of 8,000 or more. By 1850, there were 141 cities of this size and by the end of the century there were more than five hundred. In 1790, only New York and Philadelphia had populations of 20,000 or more; by 1880, sixty-five cities had reached or surpassed this figure. By 1900, thirty-two per cent of the population of the nation lived in cities —compared to three per cent in 1800.

Into these cities flowed a constantly increasing flood of immigrants. Before 1840, immigrants arrived at the rate of about 60,000 per year. In 1840, the influx was tripled, and in the 1850's it was quadrupled. In every decade thereafter, from 1850 through the 1870's, more than 2,000,000 aliens arrived. In the 1880's, more than 5,000,000 poured in. By 1890, Chicago's foreign born numbered as many as the entire population had totaled ten years earlier. In New York City there were as many Italians as in Naples, as many Germans as in Hamburg, twice as many Irish as in Dublin, and two and a half times as many Jews as in Warsaw.

The cosmopolitan population of American cities created a colorful, carnival-like scene. Dion Boucicault, who arrived in the United States in 1853, described New York City in these words:

It was not a city. It was a theatre. It was a huge fair. Bunting of all nationalities and of no nationality were flaunting over the streets. Poles of liberty accentuated the "rights of man." Bands of music preceded processions of ragged boys bearing flags and tattered banners. Irish was spoken at the wharves, German in the saloons, French in the restaurants.[35]

Such a city, composed of so many nationalities speaking so many languages, could not be expected to support the standard repertory of the English-speaking theatre exclusively. The polyglot crowds failed to understand its language and intentions. Their frustration is illustrated by the riot which broke out in a Rochester, New York, theatre when Edwin Booth, who had been advertized as "Herr" Edwin Booth, began to speak in English and not in German. Patrons who knew only a foreign language could not appreciate long plays in English. But these same patrons flocked to the popular theatre. Spectacle, vaudeville, burlesque, and minstrelsy were received with immense enthusiasm. Such entertainment offered something to please everyone—and it could be understood and enjoyed by everyone.

The cultivated English speaking portion of the population who enjoyed legitimate drama made little effort to alter the taste of the masses or to encourage the production of standard plays. In fact, when the craze for public lectures arose in the 1840's, cultivated people deserted the playhouse and flocked to the lecture rooms. It was considered fashionable as well as educational to hear the great orators and preachers of the day, who could command a larger audience than a celebrated actor. And so the less sophisticated portion of the population and the large foreign speaking elements were left to dictate the taste in dramatic entertainment with the result that the popular theatres grew and flourished and developed a technique of presentation which was distinctive and stimulating.

In the early years of the nineteenth century, vaudeville, burlesque, and minstrelsy were appendages of legitimate drama. A classical play was usually embellished with entr'acte specialties and a farcical afterpiece. For example, a certain performance of *Richelieu* with Edwin Forrest was "enlivened by a 'grand pas de deux' and a 'national descriptive melange' between acts"[36] and ended with a farce entitled *The Double Bedded Room*. As the century advanced, the "specialties" drew away from legitimate drama and emerged as a distinctive type of entertainment housed in theatres of their own.

VAUDEVILLE

The variety show or vaudeville was perhaps the first type to achieve independence. A kind of variety show, revealing most of the elements of vaudeville, is as old as public entertainment itself. Since the beginning of recorded history there have been gatherings where the singer, the reciter, the dancer, and the mimic have performed their bits. For many centuries professional entertainers performed their tricks in inns, beer halls, and public squares. So the entr'acte specialties in the American theatre of the nineteenth century were nothing new. But during the century they broke away from legitimate drama and set up shop in public museums—like Barnum's—and in saloons, beer halls, and concert halls. By the middle of the century they had grown so popular that every city of any size had regular theatres devoted to variety programs. In New York City one house was renamed the "New Theatre of Mirth and Variety" and presented on a single bill such numbers as "Elboleros, Cachuchas, Scotch flings and Strathspeys," plus a selection of "the most astonishing feats of gymnastics and contortions ever presented in this country," and an act described as "the Flying Cord by the unequalled Mr. Ruggles." [37] Clearly this was the type of popular entertainment which was to culminate in the great vaudeville circuits of the early twentieth century.

MINSTREL SHOWS

Vaudeville soon had a powerful competitor in Negro Minstrelsy, a type of entertainment which rose suddenly and took the country by storm. Before 1830 American audiences had seen the forerunners of Negro Minstrelsy. Many actors had blacked up for specific occasions and appeared between the acts of legitimate plays. Very often Negro songs had been sung by circus clowns from the backs of horses. However, it was Thomas D. Rice, in 1830, who began the real vogue for minstrel entertainment when he invented his famous song and jig in imitation of an old Negro named "Jim Crow." It was, to the nineteenth-century audience, an appealing representation, and Rice instantly became a star. He traveled all over the United States and Europe, playing to packed houses wherever he went. Carl Wittke says:

"He was the first blackface performer, who was not only the main actor, but the entire act." [38]

It was not until 1843 that the first complete minstrel show was invented, that is, a show composed entirely of the singing and dancing and "gagging" of a blackface company. The first performance was the inspiration of Dan Emmett and three other actors who styled themselves "The Virginia Minstrels." In costumes that later became traditional, they serenaded the audience with music from a violin, a banjo, a tambourine, and bones.

At about the same time there was organized the "Christy Minstrels," the most famous troupe in the history of blackface entertainment. This organization gave to the show the traditional form for which it became noted: the "first part" with the performers in a semicircle, the interlocutor in the center, and with the endmen with bones and tambourine at the extreme ends; and the "second part" with its stump speech, its "olio" of variety acts, and its "hoe-down" dance at the end.

For many decades minstrelsy was phenomenally successful. Every city had its resident companies, and traveling groups toured the country from Maine to the gold fields of California. In the urban centers the craze was so great that three performances a day—morning, afternoon, and evening—had to be given.

As an indication of the appeal of American minstrel shows, it is interesting to note that in Europe they became almost as popular as they were in the United States. Foreign audiences, entirely unacquainted with American plantation traditions, were strangely moved by the shuffling dances of the blackface artists, by their homely humor, their quaint costumes, and especially their rhythmic, melodious songs—best represented in the haunting music of Stephen Foster. The great novelist, William Makepeace Thackeray, after witnessing a minstrel performance, wrote:

I heard a humorous balladist not long ago, a humorist with wool on his head and an ultra-Ethiopian complexion, who performed a negro ballad that I confess moistened these spectacles of mine in a most unexpected manner. They have gazed at thousands of tragedy queens dying on the stage and expiring to appropriate blank verse, and I have never wanted to wipe them. They have looked, be it said, at many scores of clergymen without being dimmed, and behold, a vagabond with a corked face and a banjo sings a little song, strikes a wild note, which sets the heart thrilling with happy pity.[39]

BURLESQUE

Still another offering of the popular theatre which developed during the nineteenth century and attained great popularity was burlesque. This poor but saucy relative of legitimate drama was originally what its name implies: a take-off or travesty on a serious play. John Poole is said to have started the vogue for it when, in 1811, he produced a burlesque of *Hamlet*. Very soon, however, young ladies, scantily clad and waving shapely limbs, began to invade burlesque. At first the effect upon the audience was shattering. One witness records that the first time a group of dancers appeared on the stage in ballet skirts and tights, "the women in the audience screamed aloud and the greater part left the theatre; the men remained, for the most part, roaring and sobbing with ecstasy. . . ." [40] Pioneers in the introduction and exploitation of "leg art," the art which finally became identified with burlesque, were Mlle. Hutin, who appeared at the Thalia Theatre in New York in 1827; Adah Isaacs Mencken, who starred in *Mazeppa* during the 1860's; and Lydia Thompson, who toured the country with her "British Blonds" in 1868. Miss Thompson is credited with being "the progenitress of American burlesque." However, M. B. Leavitt, an American theatrical manager, gave to this kind of entertainment the typical form it maintained during its prosperous days. He modeled the opening of his program—an act made up of songs, choruses and gags —from the minstrel show. He took the second part—an assorted array of talents and specialties called the "olio"—from vaudeville. The third part, the afterpiece or burlesque, was a development of the minstrel show walk-around: a grand finale by the entire company.

THE CIRCUS

The circus in America was less sensational in its origin and appeal than was burlesque. Still it became a flourishing and well-loved feature of the American popular theatre.

During colonial days little menageries and bands of itinerant acrobats had flourished in the United States. They traveled from town to town, delighting the country folks who never saw any other kind of theatre. In the nineteenth century these little shows began absorbing riding acts from the popular equestrian drama and variety acts from the theatres and museums. Eventually the acrobats and the menageries, with their attendant attractions, began to combine, and finally there emerged the dazzling tent theatricals of Barnum and Bailey's "Greatest Show on Earth."

HARRIGAN AND HOYT

The popular theatre had strong influence in shaping modern musical comedy and revue. But even before these later types emerged it produced a unique and wonderful form of farce—the comedies of Edward Harrigan and Charles Hoyt.

Harrigan and his partner Tony Hart began their theatrical careers as variety artists. They specialized in sketches of city life, presenting humorously and faithfully a wide variety of familiar American characters. In these skits Harrigan acted the male role and Hart impersonated the female, but the authorship of the skits was almost entirely the work of Harrigan. Arthur Hobson Quinn tells us that there is a record of over eighty vaudeville sketches composed by Harrigan between 1870 and 1879. These sketches "take in politics, baseball, life insurance, the army and militia, and deal with the Negro, and the Irish, German, Italian, and other immigrant types." [41]

It was from these vaudeville acts that the full-length plays of Harrigan emerged. The process was a gradual one. In their first form the sketches were popular songs ridiculing some well-known personage or type. The song led to the duet and the duet to the dialogue. Under the inspiration of audience response the dialogue was elaborated and lengthened. New incidents were improvised from performance to performance, and eventually enough material was created for a full length play. Just when the first of these was born is not known, although one of the earliest and most enduring is the comedy *Old Lavender,* first produced in 1877 and expanded in 1878.

Out of the skits on Irish and German immigrant types grew the most famous Harrigan plays—the "Mulligan Guard" series. The first of these, *The Mulligan Guard Ball,* was produced in 1879 and ran for one hundred nights. It was followed with great success by seven or eight other plays all recounting the adventures of a group of Irish and German immigrants, the Mulligans and the Lochmullers, and their Negro and Italian friends. These plays, which were remarkably free from coarseness or lewdness, were glorious mixtures of wild burlesque, lilting songs, dancing and military drills, outrageous puns, breathtaking spectacle, and—above all—knockdown, dragout, slambang farce. They were so popular in their time that, together with other comedies from the facile pen of their author, at least twenty-three of them achieved runs of more than one hundred performances each on Broadway, "phenomenal displays of longevity in those days." [42]

Ned Harrigan and Tony Hart (whom E. J. Kahn, Jr., calls "The Merry Partners") were the perfect team for presenting the plays which Harrigan developed out of his early vaudeville skits. Hart, younger than his partner by ten years, had the round, angelic face of an "Irish Apollo" and could act feminine roles as well as masculine parts with persuasive conviction and compelling charm. Nat C. Goodwin, a fellow comedian, said: "He sang like a nightingale, danced like a fairy, and acted like a master comedian," [43] and Mrs. Fiske thought he had "a smile that would coax the birds off the trees." [44] Harrigan, the older partner, was a "stocky, serene" man with an appealing Irish face and such versatile talents that he successfully wrote his own plays, acted every kind of part in them, produced, financed, and directed them in a theatre he ran himself with a company he recruited and trained himself.

Equally as important as the "Merry Partners" in the success of Harrigan's comedies was the audience which viewed and helped to shape them. This audience was largely composed of the immigrant types represented in the plays. Harrigan drew his inspiration directly from them. He tirelessly haunted the parks, wharves, saloons, and tenements where they congregated, observing their habits, listening to their conversation, taking notes on their eccentricities and even buying the clothes off their backs in order to obtain absolutely authentic costumes for his plays. "I have sought above all to make my plays like pages from actual life," [45] he declared. Late in his career he expressed regret at the passing of these types, saying that if his plays had lost their appeal it was because other waves of immigration had pushed the Mulligans and the Lochmullers out of the picture.

Another colorful figure who contributed to the tradition of the popular theatre in America was Charles Hoyt. His plays were related to the comics of Edward Harrigan because, like the Harrigan plays, they were close to the vaudeville tradition. Songs were interspersed throughout, low comedy "gagging" was plentiful, and the actors were given ample opportunity for comic improvisation. In the first scene of Hoyt's *A Texas Steer,* for example, the action stops while four cowboys sing a quartet. At the end of each act of the play there are gags and tableaux suggested for use in the curtain calls. Hoyt often sat in the audience to note the reactions of his neighbors and to gather ideas for improving his shows. "He capitalized the 'movements' of his day," says Montrose Moses, treating them "with a newspaper deftness which was closely akin to the way contemporaneousness thrusts its way into musical comedy." [46] Indeed, our modern musical comedy is directly descended from the vaudeville-Harrigan-Hoyt tradition.

When one surveys the motley and sprightly offerings of the popular theatre—burlesque, vaudeville, minstrelsy, circus, and the Harrigan-Hoyt comics—two interesting conclusions emerge: (1) These types are intimately related; and (2) in all of them the technique of presentation is similar.

The close relationship of the types is evident. The circus borrowed blackface entertainment from minstrelsy, horseback performances from the equestrian drama, and variety acts from vaudeville. Minstrelsy borrowed its street parade from the circus and its "olio" from vaudeville. In its later development it became almost indistinguishable from vaudeville. Burlesque patterned its show after minstrelsy and introduced song and dance numbers from vaudeville. Vaudeville adopted blackface numbers from minstrelsy, leg shows from burlesque, and acrobatics and animal acts from the circus. In fact, all the types of popular theatre are basically a series of specialties strung together in a characteristic way. Each lays emphasis on a slightly different specialty, but each aims to satisfy the tastes of a polyglot audience by providing novel and varied entertainment which is easily understood.

In each form of popular entertainment the technique of presentation is very similar. The appeal of the actor has to be *immediate* and *direct*. There is no chance for slow build up of atmosphere and revelation of character as in legitimate drama. The appeal, says Caroline Caffin, "is personal and unashamed. It looks its audience straight in the face and says, in effect, 'Look at ME! I am going to astonish you!'

It makes no claim to aloofness or impersonality, but comes right to the footlights and faces the crowd and tells it 'All for your delight WE are . . . here.' " [47]

Moreover, the popular actor aims to achieve a feeling of fellowship with his audience. In the early days of the music hall, when the performers drank beer and swapped stories with the customers, it was easy to establish this relationship. When footlights intervened between spectator and player such friendly contact was virtually destroyed. Still, vaudeville, burlesque, and minstrel performers tried to attain some cameraderie by speaking directly to individuals in the audience, by arguing with the orchestra leader, by relating bits of local gossip, and often by crossing the footlights and parading in the aisles of the theatre.

The most important means of achieving immediate fellowship with an audience is strong, attractive personality. Somehow or other the performer must be able to impress an audience, immediately, with a likable, appealing presence. His ability to do this is equally as important as his skill in any specialty. The popular performer is thus frankly presentational in his method; he appeals to the audience always in his own guise.

Neither the performer or his specialty must ever appear "highbrow." "It is the first law of the cult of vaudeville," says Caffin, "that Highbrow Stuff Never Pays." [48] The spectator in the popular theatre wants to feel at home. He wants the sentiment, the humor, and the language to be familiar to him; he doesn't wish to exert an effort at comprehension or to feel that the entertainment is over his head.

The popular performer must not only be "lowbrow" and "folksy," he must at all times be instantly intelligible. His speech must appear completely unstudied and effortless, and yet must be understood by everyone in the house. The success of his brief number depends on every line striking fire. The popular audience is not interested in poetry or rhetoric; it simply wants to be entertained.

To maintain interest in any individual act and in the program as a whole, speed of performance is essential. Gags must come in rapid fire order. Song and dance numbers must blend smoothly and quickly. The pace of the whole show must be sprightly and exhilarating.

Other prime requisites for the popular performer are *adaptability* and *spontaneity*—the talent for *improvisation*. The sketches in vaudeville, minstrelsy, burlesque, etc., like much of the business in a Harrigan play, were not rigidly set. They were generally intended for spur-of-the-moment elaboration during the inspiration of performance. This was especially true of minstrelsy. Carl Wittke, historian of the black-face art, writes:

. . . a minstrel with a speech of a dozen lines probably never made it twice in exactly the same way,—a good minstrel was always improvising, and adding little comic bits on the spur of the moment while the show was in full progress, quite as much for the amusement of his fellow members in the company as for the audience. The endman's chatter with the inter-locutor usually varied to a greater or less degree from night to night, and many stories and jokes about the local community were introduced with real skill. Some companies actually sent advance agents ahead to pick up bits of local news to be used in their show for the peculiar delight of their special audience.[49]

This type of improvisation was also popular—and necessary—in vaudeville, circus, and burlesque. In the latter, a high degree of skill seemed to be required, for early burlesque was very sketchily pre-pared. The actors were seldom given scripts. Instead, situations were outlined to them and they were expected to create and improvise as they went along. This tradition persisted through the heyday of bur-lesque and still persists in the remnants of burlesque which have sur-vived in the theatre of the twentieth century. In 1965, the sixty-nine year old Steve Mills, a veteran performer appearing in Ann Corio's *This Was Burlesque,* said: "Every audience is a challenge. You find the first thing that hits, then you have to know how to keep it rolling, and you have to know when to stop. Things happen. You ad-lib. You bring it up, keep it revolving." [50]

Thus a successful actor in the popular theatre needed diverse abil-ities. He had to possess an attractive personality and the ability to pro-ject it quickly and directly. He had to establish a feeling of fellowship with his audience and be instantly intelligible—but never labored or highbrow. He had to perform with easy speed and to possess skill at improvisation. The total effect, as Walter Prichard Eaton wrote, had to be one of "unforced, jovial intimacy between audience and stage, of spontaneous fooling, of impromptu jest. . . ." [51]

The American stage was enriched by the training and the oppor-tunities offered by the popular theatre. Thousands of performers, of every level of competence, served their apprenticeship there. Some of them became variety stars who delighted audiences for many years and who never forsook the variety stage. Others graduated to the legitimate theatre and became leading players in the standard drama. Still others appeared in legitimate plays often written especially for them, but always remained the variety artist with all the appeals necessary for that kind of performer.

CHARLOTTE CRABTREE

One of the most famous of the latter group, who epitomized all the skills and endowments of the variety artist, was the sensationally successful Charlotte Crabtree, affectionately known and better remembered as "Lotta." Her career and style of acting will serve as a representative example of the countless performers who were produced by the popular theatre and who exhibited the essential characteristics of the variety artist: personal magnetism, congeniality, deftness, naturalness, articulateness, and skill at improvisation.

Lotta began her dramatic training in California at the age of six when she became the pupil of the notorious Lola Montez, who taught her to dance, to sing ballads, and to ride horseback. Presently the child also learned to play the banjo, and with these skills—plus her captivating looks and personality—she launched a career which was to make her a national favorite. She first became the darling of the California mining camps, which she trouped for ten years under the shrewd and tireless supervision of her mother. In 1864, she left the golden state and began her rapid and complete conquest of the rest of the nation. The reasons for her success, achieved so early and maintained so long, are vividly summarized by Constance Rourke in this description of Lotta's appeal:

If an exacting public wanted diversity, in the small person of Miss Lotta that quality was oddly comprised. She was both sturdy and delicate, full of rowdy caprice and quaintly aloof. Her voice was developing into a flexible soprano with a mezzo range. All her life she was to speak and sing with a smothered fire that seemed at variance with the light content of her words. Her clear tones, which made every syllable carry into the furthest corner of an audience hall, suggested greater force and more ample meaning than anything she had to say. . . . But it was her dancing, well caught within pantomime and impersonation, which aroused the special heady enthusiasm which was to envelop her for years. Jigs, flings, wild polkas, breakdowns, the whole range of soft-shoe dancing. . . . Her dancing was light as gossamer when she wished it to be, or boldly hoydenish.[52]

In 1867, at the age of twenty, she appeared in New York as the star of a play written especially for her by the talented John Brougham. This was a dramatization of Dickens' *Old Curiosity Shop* called *Little Nell and the Marchioness*. It was a great success and ran for six weeks. Later it proved a smash hit whenever it was presented in the United States. Thereafter, and for the rest of her life, Lotta appeared either in burlesque or extravaganza or in light, flimsy vehicles which had been written especially for her and which enabled her to exploit her sprightly charms and captivating skills. The nature of these tailor-made vehicles is evident in the titles of three of them: *Nan the Good for Nothing, Pet of the Petticoats,* and *The Little Detective*.

In acting such comic frivolities, Lotta never attempted a characterization and never tried to conceal her own personality. As John R. Towse observed, she appeared in many parts but "played them all exactly the same way. She never developed or suggested any real dramatic force or adaptability." [53] She was the eternal variety artist, joyously presenting herself to an audience directly and frankly, without artifice or disguise, and cloaking her performance in a youthful innocence which concealed the sometimes raciness of her material. Constance Rourke confirms this conclusion in the statement that "Whatever Lotta became, however often she was to command plays of her own, she remained essentially a variety actress, with the vivacious original turns, the irrepressible humor, the unaccountable mode of the lighter theatre flowing through her chosen parts." [54]

Lotta needed no other appeals. The public adored her just as she was and, until the day she retired in 1891, never tired of her. One critic said: "The charm of Lotta's acting penetrated every heart; she defied convention; she was not measurable by rule or line. The secret of her charm was hidden as the scent of the rose. . . . Lotta was incomparable and inimitable." [55] Even distinguished players of the legitimate drama paid high tribute to Lotta's appeal. The great classic actress, Helena Modjeska, said that her individuality covered all the sins of the commonplace characters she portrayed; that she "infused life" into every part; and that "her realism was simply wonderful." [56] Otis Skinner praised her in these words: "The figure of a child, eyes that held a world of laughter, set in a dimpled roguish face, crowned by a fluff of curling bronze hair, a voice that sang and feet that danced, fingers that tripped nimbly over banjo strings, spirits that never flagged; that was Lotta . . . the embodiment of joy and thoughtlessness." [57]

Lotta epitomizes the endowments and style of the successful variety artist. Many other examples could be cited from every specialty within the realm of the popular theatre. Negro minstrelsy produced such notable performers as Lew Dockstader and the team of James McIntyre and Thomas Heath. Modern burlesque began with the success of Adah Isaacs Mencken and Lydia Thompson, produced comedians like Lew Fields and Joe Weber, and as late as the twentieth century produced a star like Fanny Brice. Vaudeville and the musical comedy stage gave us performers like Eddie Foy and the beautiful Lillian Russell. And so on, ad infinitum.

Many other notable players, later identified with the legitimate stage, received their early training in the popular theatre and testify to its effectiveness as a school for actors. Chauncey Olcott began his career in the ranks of the blackface artist. Francis Wilson was a circus performer and a minstrel before he became a legitimate star. David Warfield was hired by Belasco directly from a Weber and Fields burlesque. Fred Stone, Raymond Hitchcock, De Wolf Hopper, Nat Goodwin, Otis Skinner, and George M. Cohan all played in vaudeville or minstrel shows. Even such great stars as Joseph Jefferson, Edwin Booth, and Edwin Forrest appeared in the ranks of vaudeville, burlesque, or minstrelsy at some time in their careers.

The influence of the technique of the popular theatre was felt in the legitimate theatre quite early. Audiences became accustomed to entertainment which was varied, which moved swiftly, and which appealed to the eye. In the legitimate theatre they became restless during long speeches and wordy dialogue. In 1870 Joseph Jefferson noticed this and remarked about it. Later, when he made his acting version of *The Rivals,* he acknowledged the popular trend by condensing the play and cutting much of the dialogue. Other managers did the same thing. They speeded up the action and the dialogue in their productions and embellished them with eye-filling costumes and scenery. For several decades American plays, in contrast to the British, were notable for the swiftness of their pace. Today even British productions have succumbed to the speeding-up process begun many years ago by the American popular theatre.

After the vogue for burlesque, vaudeville, and minstrelsy passed, their influence was clearly observable in the Broadway revues and musical comedies of the 1920's and 1930's. These productions utilized the old structure and the old techniques. In form they were a series of sketches and specialties, interspersed with songs and spiced with novelty and variety. They were geared to a lightning-like speed and tried to have something happening every instant. The star performers were still expected to be deft, natural, and articulate, as well as skillful at improvisation. During this period influences from the popular theatre were also recognizable in such productions as William Saroyan's *The Time of Your Life,* John Howard Lawson's *Processional,* and the Federal Theatre's *Living Newspaper* because all of them borrowed their techniques largely from vaudeville rather than from legitimate drama. Today the influence of the popular theatre is less discernible in sophisticated musical plays like *South Pacific, My Fair Lady,* and *Hello, Dolly.* Yet the speed, color, and variety of these productions still remind us that they are descendants of an older genre of popular theatre.

The American comic theatre of the nineteenth century was a rich and lusty creation. With its roots deep in the fun loving, polyglot character of America, it achieved a glorious popularity and revealed the magic of theatre to countless thousands of citizens old and new. It also shaped the development of several forms of native drama and created a recognizable technique of acting, the influence of which is still discernible.

[NOTES ON THE SETTING]

The Transition

THE YEARS SURROUNDING THE TURN OF THE CENTURY can rightfully be called a period of transition. The old order of theatrical affairs was passing; the new world of the twentieth century theatre was not yet born. The background, the traditions, the ideals, and the practices which had produced the supreme tragic art of Edwin Booth and the consummate comic achievement of William Warren had weakened and changed until these ideals and practices no longer exerted the inspiration and motivation necessary for creative theatre.

The tempo of life in America had increased and was destined to accelerate at a faster and faster rate as the century advanced. Population continued to multiply and immigrants poured in by the hundreds of thousands. Cities increased in number and size. Rapid transportation reached every village and hamlet in the nation. Industrialization proceeded with giant strides. Inventions of miraculous ingenuity and influence poured from workshops and laboratories. One of these, the motion picture, eventually was to diminish and to supplant much of the activity of the legitimate stage. The automobile began to transform the landscape of every town and countryside and to alter the lives of every citizen, young and old. Social troubles, labor troubles, and political troubles agitated the nation and produced an era of "muckraking" and reform.

In such a changing, complex, burgeoning society, the theatre was not keeping pace—except in one respect which most critics deplored.

Big business invaded show business. Tycoons and speculators began to apply industrial methods to theatrical production. Dramatists wrote plays to appeal to the largest number of customers; productions were turned out on an assembly line basis; the road was organized into a tight monopoly by the infamous Theatrical Syndicate which gained control of the playhouses throughout the nation and dictated which actors should play in which dramas in which cities. Under this system, show business was more prosperous but the overall quality of production was poorer than ever before.

In almost every respect the theatre had become sterile and stereotyped. Playhouses retained the shape and the defects they had exhibited since the eighteenth century. There were thousands of them throughout the United States and promoters continued to build them at a rapid rate. But they were all slightly modified versions of the Restoration playhouse. The proscenium doors and boxes had been eliminated but all other traditional features were there: a picture-frame stage with tiers of boxes and galleries facing it in a horseshoe curve, a lower or "orchestra" floor, poor sight lines, cramped leg space, inadequate lobbies, and poorly ventilated dressing rooms. The inflexible form of stage and auditorium limited directors to a single style of "peep-hole" drama.

The mounting of the play was equally stereotyped. The tradition of flat, two-dimensional scenery consisting of wings, drops, and borders with all décor for both interior and exterior scenes painted on, still lingered in the theatre, particularly in playhouses outside of New York. Such scenery alternated with the carefully realistic settings introduced by Boucicault and perfected by Belasco, in which every object called for in the play was tangible and authentic. If a New York City street scene were needed, real store fronts were erected with actual merchandise in the windows. The street itself was furnished with lamp posts, fire hydrants, sidewalks, garbage cans, gutters, and push carts containing actual vegetables.

The lighting of such settings was sometimes imaginative and suggestive of the mood of the play. Belasco tried to introduce both realism and imagination in the lighting of his productions. In too many plays, however, the illumination was flat, uniform, and uninteresting —as might be expected when its source was a set of footlights in front and a row of border lights overhead, relieved now and then by a spotlight focussed on the leading player.

A survey of the hundred or more plays which reached Broadway every year during this period reveals an astonishing number of flimsy, stereotyped dramas. There were dozens of farce comedies and sentimental comedies; there were melodramas of all kinds, including the domestic melodrama of tears imported from France; there were endless romantic costume plays laid in exotic lands and faraway times. Each one of these popular plays was given as long a run on Broadway as the public would sustain, then it was sent on tour to every village, hamlet and town which boasted a playhouse—and most of them did. When the "road" was exhausted, the play was then released for production by the hundreds of stock companies throughout the nation— companies which now were second rate imitators of Broadway rather than the independent repertory companies they once had been. Now and then a theatre was enlivened by a poetic play or a play of social significance or a play which probed the problems of the individual in a complex society. Also, the plays of Shakespeare or of the old standard repertory were occasionally revived. Julia Marlowe and E. H. Sothern, for example, did their best to create and maintain an interest in Shakespeare. But in the main, the regular dramatic fare of the nation consisted of slick entertainment, easily digested and quickly forgotten. It was the same kind of entertainment which dominates the television screens of today.

With such plays, such scenery, and such playhouses, it was inevitable that much of the acting would be routine and stereotyped. Several schools or styles of acting were popular. There was the Personality School of such sweet and lovely ladies as Maude Adams, Viola Allen, Julia Marlowe, and Ada Rehan. These ladies played in sentimental comedies or historical romances and impressed their audiences with their wholesome charm, their feminine appeal, and their technical competence. There was the Emotionalistic School represented in the acting of Fanny Davenport and Mrs. Leslie Carter. These ladies played the overwrought, hysterical heroines of Victorien Sardou, roles like Fedora and Tosca, and thrilled their audiences by substituting emotional pyrotechniques for acting. There were the actors of the transition, conscientious performers often trained in the classic repertory but now pulled in the direction of the romantic costume drama. In many cases they tried to keep alive the traditions of the classic school but too often the influences of the time led them to specialize in dashing, strenuous roles reminiscent of the heroic school of Forrest and McCullough. There was also the slick, mechanical school, which is found in every period of the theatre, and which is represented by the actor who has mastered the external techniques of speaking, moving, and performing stage business, who can indicate an emotion without ever feeling it or projecting it, and who performs his roles with a competence which is appropriate to the superficial dramas in which he appears. Finally, there was the beginning of the school pioneered by Minnie Maddern Fiske, destined to be not only an influence in the theatrical renaissance of the twentieth century but also a dominant force in the style of acting of the contemporary stage.

VII

COMEDIANS OF THE TRANSITION

THE GREAT TRADITION OF COMIC ACTING, SO BRILLIANTLY ESTAB-lished early in the nineteenth century by such players as Henry Pla-cide, William Wood, and Henry J. Finn and so marvelously enriched later on by geniuses like William Warren, William J. Florence, and Joseph Jefferson, was carried on for a number of years at the end of the century by a corps of younger comedians who were reared in the shadow of their towering predecessors. For a time, the younger group acted the same roles and fulfilled the same ideals. But as the repertory altered and as theatre practice changed to meet the shifting public taste, so did the style and quality of the acting undergo a change.

The comedians of the mid-nineteenth century were challenged by a repertory of unusual complexity and variety. They acted the great comic roles found in Shakespeare and in the traditional comedies of Sheridan, Goldsmith, and Farquhar—playing Bottom, Falstaff, and Dogberry as well as Sir Peter Teazle, Tony Lumpkin, and Bob Acres. In addition, they performed a rich variety of comic roles in the ephem-eral melodramas, farces, and comedies of their own time. Their roles were constantly changing because the production changed almost every night. But they were able to return to these roles at regular intervals because the popular offerings of both the classic and contemporary repertories were repeated several times during a season and in suc-ceeding seasons. This meant that the same audience viewed the same plays year after year and judged the performances of the actors not on the basis of novelty and surprise but on the basis of the quality and effectiveness of the acting. An audience which knew *The Rivals* by heart concentrated its attention not on the developments of the plot but on the skill and inventiveness of the actors who performed Bob Acres and Sir Lucius O'Trigger. An audience which had watched William Warren play the same role a dozen times could judge the variations in his performances and the growth of his characterizations. Such an audience provided an actor with a motive for continuous development. Also, the variety of the repertory challenged the player to increase his versatility and to perfect his techniques. The great comedians of the mid-nineteenth century met these challenges brilliantly.

As the century waned, the repertory changed. Shakespearean comedies and old English comedies were performed less frequently. The farcical afterpiece disappeared. The backbone of the repertory became contemporary comedies—romantic, melodramatic, and sentimental. The cheapening of the repertory was speeded up by the growing commercialism of the theatre. During most of the nineteenth century, theatrical business was controlled by actors and actor-managers. They were interested in financial success, to be sure, but at the same time they loved and respected the art of the drama; they believed it should nourish the heart and the soul of a man and not merely divert and entertain him. Often they sacrificed monetary gain for artistic principle. And so the theatre-going public was nourished and sustained by a consistently rich and healthful dramatic fare. But at the end of the nineteenth century the businessman, whose sole motive was profit, invaded the theatre. He cared nothing for art or public enlightenment: actors were commodities to be peddled to the public; audiences were customers to be exploited for their dollars. William Winter described the situation in these terms: "Fine actors were visible, and here and there splendid things were being done. . . . But actors, and men truly comprehensive of, and sympathetic with, actors no longer controlled the Theatre: that institution had passed almost entirely into the hands of the so-called 'business man'—the speculative huckster and the rampant vulgarian. . . ." [1] The hucksters and vulgarians cared nothing for the great comedies of Shakespeare or Goldsmith or Sheridan. They fed the public any shoddy farce or cheap comedy which could attract an audience. Thus the range and the variety of the roles as well as the depth and complexity of the roles offered to the comedian steadily decreased.

Moreover, the long run continued to gain in popularity. A successful play now held the boards as long as it could attract an audience. The repertory idea, as a general policy, faded and vanished. In general, audiences attended the same play only once, then looked for something new and different at another theatre. Thus an actor was not subjected to the repeated scrutiny of the same patrons but played to a different house each night. If there was a falling off in his performance or an enriching of it, few patrons were able to perceive the change.

Under these conditions it is little wonder that the nature of comic acting changed and that the overall quality of comic acting diminished. Yet the players who met the demands of the new repertory and of the changed conditions were often of the highest caliber and in many cases might have equalled their illustrious predecessors had they been faced with as stern a challenge.

E. M. HOLLAND

One of the best of the group of younger comedians was Edmund Milton Holland (1848–1913), son of the great clown and gagster, George Holland. "E. M.," as the son was generally billed, began his adult career in 1866 just four years before his father died. The two men acted together in Wallack's company during the season of 1867–68, thus illustrating the overlapping relationship of two theatrical eras.

The younger Holland began in humble parts and developed slowly but steadily. For several years, unwilling to trade on his father's popularity and afraid of blemishing so illustrious a theatrical name as Holland, he was known simply as "E. Milton." But when he had achieved a measure of experience and success, he assumed his rightful identity.

In his early career, young Holland played a great variety of roles, many of them parts which the older comedians had made famous. But in his mature years he appeared almost exclusively in the roles provided by contemporary plays and often played one of these roles for an entire season. Examples of the parts in which he excelled are: Pitticus Green in *Hazel Kirke,* Lot Bowman in *Saints and Sinners,* Captain Redwood in *Jim the Penman,* Uncle Gregory in *A Pair of Spectacles,* Colonel Moberly in *Alabama,* and Colonel Carter in *Colonel Carter of Cartersville.* Such roles do not offer either the range nor the complexity of the roles performed by earlier comedians.

The demands placed on an actor in the days of the great character comedians as compared to the demands placed on later comedians is vividly illustrated if we compare the parts played by William Warren in the middle of the century to the parts played by E. M. Holland at the end of the century. During the season of 1850–51, Warren appeared at least 265 times in at least fifty-seven different plays performing at least fifty-eight different roles. His characterizations ranged from the comic singer in two musical spectacles through the roles of Dr. Ollapod in *The Poor Gentlemen* and Mr. Marmaduke Mouser in *Betsy Baker* to Polonius in *Hamlet,* Dogberry in *Much Ado About Nothing,* and Jacques in *As You Like It.* Forty-five years later, in the season of 1895–96, E. M. Holland spent the entire year playing only three roles, two of them characters from contemporary comedies: Hooper in *The Man with a Past,* Jenkins Hanby in *The Social Highwayman,* and Fag in *The Rivals.*

Within the limits of the changed comic repertory, Holland was a gifted player who enriched the roles assigned to him. His thorough apprenticeship, served in the company of accomplished older players, gave him a mastery of comic techniques. He attended to detail in acting a part but did not overelaborate a character. He could be dry and subtle, droll and humorous, but his effects were never labored or strained. He scored his comic "points" sharply and tellingly but did not overdo them or repeat them. Lewis Strang says that "his method was clean-cut and precise. . . . His powers of suggestion were apparently unlimited, and his font of humour unfailing." [2]

Apparently Holland, like the great character comedians who preceded him, could submerge his own personality and create the illusion of a completely different individuality. To accomplish this, he sometimes relied on gait, gesture, and facial expression. He relied even more on assuming the unique psychology of a dramatic character and then allowing action to flow from this identification. William Winter says he was able to "make the *condition* of a personality as positive and effective as the most brilliant stroke of its *action.* . . ." [3] Lewis Strang felt that Holland's ability to efface his own personality was so remarkable that a spectator would be at first puzzled and in the end defeated if he tried to figure out what kind of a man Holland really was, or even what Holland looked like, after seeing him perform a dozen of his best known roles.

Holland's gift as a character comedian inspired several critics to write that he would take the place of such great character actors as William Warren and John Gilbert. He never did. Although he was as successful as any comedian of his time, the roles he played and the audiences he entertained never demanded the greatness of a Warren or a Gilbert, so the performer was never able to prove the extent of his own talent.

MAY IRWIN

May Irwin (1862–1938) is a later representative of the great comediennes who early in the nineteenth century played such roles as Mrs. Malaprop and Mistress Quickly. These comic ladies began their careers in resident stock companies and slowly climbed from the drudgery of playing "utility ladies" to the challenge of acting comic or heavy "old women." Their entire careers were spent in the resident companies, and their comic talents were displayed in the classic and popular plays of the standard repertory. But when May Irwin made her debut, the old theatrical order was changing and her career was typical of the altered traditions.

Although she was born in Canada, Miss Irwin made her debut, in 1875, as a variety artist in Buffalo, New York, where she scored a hit singing duets with her younger sister. Thus encouraged, the two little girls toured the variety houses of such cities as Cleveland, St. Louis, and Cincinnati with a repertory of comic and sentimental songs. One of their most popular numbers was "Sweet Genevieve." Even at this early age—May was 13—she was able to create laughter by her sparkling good nature and her chubby figure. After two years of successful touring, the girls were dazzled by an offer from Tony Pastor to appear in his famous New York variety theatre. They jumped at the offer, and succeeded so well that they remained at Pastor's for seven years. It was here that May developed an expert comic technique by appearing in a rich variety of vaudeville turns, improvised burlesques, dramatic sketches, and musical numbers. Her skills and her appeal eventually attracted the attention of Augustin Daly, then head of one of the most flourishing companies in New York. May became a comic actress in Daly's troupe, where she played such parts as Susan in *A Night Off* and Betsey in *Nancy & Co.* But her love of variety and the greater financial rewards of the variety stage eventually proved too great. After four years with Daly, she returned to her first love and during the remainder of her career, which was a long and successful one, she played farce and burlesque, comedy and vaudeville with a number of companies all over the United States. One of her biggest hits, in which she played her first starring role, was a variety piece by John J. McNally entitled *The Widow Jones*. Another of her contributions was to popularize ragtime, a type of singing she learned from the Negro servants in the hotel where she stayed. She even appeared in an early motion picture, during the course of which she shocked the clergy of the time by reproducing the "kiss episode" from *The Widow Jones*.

Although her career was different from that of an early comedienne like Mrs. Drew, May Irwin's ability to create mirth and laughter was the same endowment which characterized her predecessors. She was a gifted fun-maker, with infectious high spirits and with the ability to enjoy her own humor. She also had a remarkable ability to communicate her sense of fun to her delighted audiences. She was always described as "jolly and stout . . . the image of wholesomeness" [4] or as "a female Falstaff" with a "jolly, rotund figure and with a face that reflects the gaiety of nations . . . the personification of humour and careless mirth. . . ." [5] When she appeared on the stage, every person in the audience sensed her warmth and kindliness and they quickly accepted her as a personal friend. She did not try to transform her individuality and assume the identity of a dramatic character, as did earlier comediennes. Rather, she always exploited her own personality in sketches and roles written expressly for her and thus she is more closely related to the single-role comedians of the mid-nineteenth century who followed the same practice. But Miss Irwin's skills, experience, and natural endowments were great enough to win her a secure place on the American stage for more than thirty-five years, and she is rightfully remembered as a worthy successor to the comic artists of earlier years.

OTHER COMEDIANS OF THE LATER PERIOD

There are many other comedians who might be mentioned here, because the living theatre at the turn of the nineteenth century was prolific and popular. Hundreds of comedies were produced each year in cities and towns from coast to coast and these productions offered employment to hundreds of actors. Most of these were second-rate, run-of-the-mill, and represented the commercialism which dominated the stage of this period. A comedian did not have the stimulus to growth and development which was enjoyed by actors a few decades earlier. Thus, although there were hundreds of performers, there were not many giants. And so a brief mention of a few representative perform-ers is sufficient for the record.

Among the popular comedians who demonstrated both talent and skill were the following.

Nat C. Goodwin (1857–1919) was a light comedian whose first substantial success was gained at Tony Pastor's Theatre and who sub-sequently played comic parts which ranged from Gilbert and Sullivan to William Shakespeare. Throughout his career he retained the appeal and the skills of a vaudeville performer and built a reputation as one of America's favorite comedians—and yet he never ceased to yearn for a career in serious, emotional drama.

Francis Wilson (1854–1935), the first President of Actors Equity Association, made his debut as a song-and-dance artist and divided his subsequent career between comic opera and the legitimate stage. As a comedian he was a great "mugger" who loved to "ham up" a role with as many gags as he could conceive and who would do any-thing for a laugh. Yet he was a thoughtful performer who wrote three books and who declared that the prime requisites for success in acting are personality and sensibility and then said that if one will add to these two qualities "aptitude and enthusiasm, radiant enthusiasm, and then crown all with industry, one will find himself perfectly equipped for the art of acting." [6]

Fritz Williams (1865–1930) made his first appearance on any stage as an infant in the arms of the great William Warren. He saw or per-formed with many of the best comedians of the nineteenth century (his parents were professional actors) and at the height of his career he shared honors with E. M. Holland as a comic star in the 1898 pro-duction of Alexander Bisson's farce, *On and Off*. Williams' best ef-fects were achieved in comic parts which bordered on the eccentric and, although his acting was "remarkable for its brilliancy, vivacity, and unflagging spirit . . . there was very little of the broad sympathy of full-blooded humour in evidence, but a great deal of the biting quality that is inherent in wit." [7]

Sol Smith Russell (1848–1902), bearer of an illustrious name from the annals of early American theatrical history, was a younger comedian who succeeded admirably in certain kinds of roles. His specialty was the awkward, eccentric character with the heart of gold who is found—or supposedly is found—in almost every phase of American life. Russell acted all his characters in much the same style. They each had a pronounced individuality of manner which varied little from role to role. But the awkward absurdity of the style was appealing and so was the quaint pathos which was added to the portrayals. Audiences returned to enjoy Russell's performances so many times that he was able to act a single role in a single play, *Edgewood Folks,* for five years before the public tired of it.

Roland Reed (1856–1901), like Russell, belongs in the group of single-role comedians. He played many of the parts made famous by the earlier company of comedians—such as Dr. Ollapod in *The Poor Gentleman,* Dr. Pangloss in *The Heir-at-Law,* and Bob Acres in *The Rivals*—and he played them in a broad, jolly style with a sure sense of the ridiculous. However, he had little or no gift for impersonation but shaped and adapted each character to fit his own personality. "He won success on the stage," says Lewis Strang, "by remaining distinctly himself. . . . He is never anything but Roland Reed." [8]

William H. Crane (1845–1928) was another popular comedian of the younger group who always played himself no matter what his role. His versatility was limited, but his control of those characters which fitted his own personality was sure and convincing. His humor was broad and genial, without spite or malice, and his open, direct appeal was enhanced by the traits of shrewdness, good sense, and generosity of spirit. Thus he was the perfect embodiment of such characters as David Harum, Colonel M. T. Elevator in *Our Boarding House,* and Senator Hannibal Rivers in *The Senator.* He was characterized in 1901 as "one of the greatest favorites on the American stage." [9]

James A. Herne (1839–1901) was a more versatile actor than Crane and might be listed under a category other than "comedians." He played both serious and romantic parts and was a successful leading man for many years. And yet in the history of American acting he is remembered most vividly for his effective portrayal of comic roles in his own plays. It must be remembered that Herne was a dramatist —and perhaps better remembered as a dramatist than as an actor— because he pioneered in the movement to free American playwriting from the contrivances and artificialities of nineteenth-century melodrama and he helped to establish a true-to-life drama where real characters struggle with real problems. In pursuing his artistic ideals, and in emphasizing character as a basis for dramatic action, he popularized the types of people found in the rural areas of America. Two of his most effective creations are Nathaniel Berry, "Uncle Nat," of *Shore Acres* and Captain Marble of *Sag Harbor*. The dramatist himself played these roles, and played them so well that he created memorable portraits. He made Captain Marble "a perfect representation of gentleness and kindliness, a man, too, bubbling over with humour, and with a heart that inspired kindly sympathy." [10] Uncle Nat was an equally effective portrayal. Although he was closely related to Captain Marble, when the part was played by Herne the character emerged as a man with an individuality of his own. Herne's success in these two comic parts relates him to a long line of American comedians who have portrayed rural types; it also enables one to think of Herne as a successor, in some respects, to the great comedians of earlier years.

VIII

HEIRS OF THE CLASSIC
AND HEROIC SCHOOLS

THE FINAL YEARS OF THE NINETEENTH CENTURY WERE YEARS OF transition and change. The traditions of comic acting were altered by the influences discussed in the previous chapter: the displacement of the old repertory system by the long run, the cheapening of the quality of the plays produced, and the domination of theatrical affairs by "commercial vulgarians." These same influences, in addition to significant other developments, naturally affected the acting of serious drama. The players who can be considered the heirs of Booth, Davenport, Cushman, and Janauschek reflected the changed situation in many ways. A survey of the careers of four representative figures of the transitional period—David Belasco, Richard Mansfield, E. H. Sothern, and Otis Skinner—will reveal and clarify the conflicts and new directions observable in the art of acting at the turn of the century.

DAVID BELASCO

When Edwin Booth played in San Francisco in 1876, his acting was watched with scrupulous care by a keen-eyed, idolatrous young man named David Belasco. There was no spectator, on the stage or off, who felt greater awe for Booth's art; none whose ambition and vision were more inspired by it. Although Booth was completely unaware of his young worshipper with the "clutching eye," he might have been greatly affected to know that here was a man who was to influence the next era of the American theatre, who was, in fact, to be a dominant figure in the period of transition between the great days of the nineteenth century and the new theatre of the twentieth.

Belasco is not generally remembered as an actor. His contributions in the fields of directing, playwriting, and stagecraft are better known. Yet he belongs in the history of American acting because acting was an important part of his early career, and because his later career in directing, playwriting, and stagecraft exerted considerable influence on the styles of performance of his time.

The man who became a leader in the New York theatre at the turn of the century was born in San Francisco in 1853, just a year after Booth had arrived in the city to serve a brilliant apprenticeship. From his early childhood, Belasco was attracted to the theatre. At the age of five, while his parents were residing in Victoria, B. C., he appeared on the stage with Julia Dean and again with Edwin Forrest. When he was eleven he played the Duke of York to Charles Kean's Richard III. At the age of twelve, back in San Francisco, he wrote his first play. Four years later he appeared at Maguire's Opera House as a newsboy in Augustin Daly's *Under the Gaslight*.

Belasco worked laboriously and eagerly at every theatrical job which came his way. He was copyist, call boy, errand boy, and boy-of-all-trades at several theatres. When he was old enough, he traveled up and down the coast as a vagabond player. Between 1871 and 1880 he acted over 170 roles. Unfortunately we know very little about his style of performing during this period.

In 1876 he became assistant stage manager, and later stage manager, at San Francisco's newest theatre, Baldwin's Academy of Music. He continued to hold this position, with a few interruptions, until 1882. It was a job which gave wide scope to his talents. He not only directed the plays which were produced in the theatre, he wrote some of them and adapted many more. Whenever there was an opportunity, he acted in them. During these years he had the opportunity of seeing and studying most of the leading performers of the American stage, players like Forrest, McCullough, Booth, Barrett, and Clara Morris. During this period he also served briefly as a secretary to the active and prolific Dion Boucicault.

Thus qualified in background and experience, Belasco left San Francisco in 1882 to assume his first New York position, that of stage manager of the Madison Square Theatre. The young man from California arrived in New York at a propitious time. The old order was on the verge of dissolution. For the moment, the independent manager, such as Augustin Daly, and the star actor, such as Edwin Booth, still controlled the theatre. By 1902, when Belasco established his own playhouse, the old order had almost entirely vanished. The great stars of the nineteenth century were dead or retired; the independent manager or actor-manager had been replaced by businessmen whose primary interest was making money.

David Belasco was one of the men who assumed a role of leadership in this changing world of the theatre. Almost alone among the "commercial vulgarians," says Winter, he was an artist. He sought to carry on the old tradition of independent management. He tried to maintain the theatre as a temple of art and public service. He contributed to styles in acting, in playwriting, and in stagecraft. He helped to establish the concept of the master director or régisseur. Until the day of his death, in 1931, he continued the active production of plays and during most of his career was acknowledged to be one of the most important figures in American theatrical life.

The kind of plays which Belasco presented exerted considerable influence on the actors who performed them. Belasco himself wrote or re-wrote almost all of the dramas he produced. He was the author of a long list of original plays and the revisor of a great many more. A piece submitted to him by another dramatist was sure to undergo extensive alteration. Every Belasco play seemed to have a distinctive form and substance. Perhaps their most significant characteristic was their suitability for acting. Belasco searched for situations which were effective and dramatic, characters that were vivid and picturesque, dialogue which had snap and sparkle. His method of composition furthered his aim. He gathered ideas, jotted them down on slips of paper, then pinned the slips on a series of screens—each screen representing an act of the play-to-be. The slips—representing ideas, situations, or bits of dialogue—were transferred from screen to screen until the most effective setting was found for them. Then the sequence of situations was acted out by Belasco himself. Every bit of the play was tested in an improvised performance. A secretary sat by and recorded the results. This method resulted in dramas which usually lacked literary merit, but they were perfect vehicles for the actors.

The appeal of Belasco's dramas was directly to the heart. He aimed to arouse and indulge all the popular sentimentalities of the American people. "The theatre of ideas is of secondary consideration to him," says Montrose Moses, ". . . his problem is always how 'to get it across' —into the hearts of his audience." [1] Belasco himself freely admitted this. He wrote: ". . . the complete play is impressive and fulfills its purpose only to the extent that it carries an audience back to its own experiences. If my productions have an appealing quality, it is because I have kept this important fact constantly in mind and have tried, while concealing the mechanism of my scenes, to tug at the hearts of my audience." [2] Such drama inevitably produced a style of acting which was sentimental and appealing—like the performances of the personality school—or it was highly emotionalistic—like the performances of Mrs. Leslie Carter.

Belasco's stage settings, the famous "Belasco realism," also exerted an influence on the style of acting of his productions. He began his career when the scenery for most plays consisted of backdrops, wings, and borders, on which were painted a pretense of reality. Early in his career he began to question the effectiveness of this kind of scenery, for he noted how eagerly an audience responded to real touches and how much these seemed to add to the illusion of the play. In one of his first productions in San Francisco, he experimented with using a flock of real sheep, and in his own drama, *Hearts of Oak,* he introduced a real cat, a real baby, and real food on the table. The public was delighted with all these effects. Belasco continued to supply more and more of them. He determined to bridge the gap between the life he saw around him and the artificial representation of it portrayed on the stage.

At the zenith of his career he came as close to his ideal, perhaps, as it is possible to come. His settings were marvels of solid walls, illusionistic lighting, and authentic properties. "I will allow nothing to be built out of canvas stretched on frames," he said. "Everything must be real." [3] And so the play *Du Barry* displayed furniture and ornaments actually owned and used by Mme. Du Barry. *The Darling of the Gods* used brocades, swords, and trappings imported from Japan. *The Easiest Way* exhibited rugs, furniture, and wall paper which had been removed in toto from a cheap theatrical boarding house in New York City. Such authentic settings influenced a performer to increase the realism of his movements, gestures, delivery, and reactions.

Furthermore, the lighting was designed to heighten the reality of the scenery. Belasco was a pioneer in this field. As early as 1877 he had experimented with locomotive headlights, and had used colored silks as a medium for changing the hue of stage illumination. Later in his New York theatre he maintained a lighting laboratory and spent large sums on experimentation. He did away with footlights because they were unnatural, and he evolved a system of diffused lighting from above which better simulated the light of the sun. For *Rose of the Rancho* he spent a huge sum to create a realistic sunset, and then rejected it because it lacked the quality of a California sunset.

It is interesting to note that Belasco's realism was not always intended for the eye of the spectator. Sometimes its sole purpose was to aid the actor in identifying himself with the mood of the play and with the character he was representing. For example, if the actor were supposed to make his entrance from a stairway, Belasco built the stairway complete, whether the audience could see it or not. He believed it helped the actor get the spirit of his entrance.

In *The Return of Peter Grimm* there was supposed to be a horticultural garden offstage. Although no one in the audience could see it, Belasco created a garden backstage using real fruit trees and bulbs with their scientific names attached to each. In his *The Concert,* the letters which his actors handled were genuine copies of letters by Mozart and other famous composers, although no one in the audience would have known if they had been blank pages.

On occasions, Belasco was criticized for focussing too much attention on setting, lights, and properties, and for distracting attention from the actors and from the play. The evidence seems to show that if this happened now and then, the occurrences were rare and did not truly represent Belasco's aim. His ideal was to produce an environment which, although scrupulously realistic, would strengthen the play and aid the players. When this ideal was realized, the acting inevitably was affected. Realistic settings encouraged realistic performances. By transmitting mood and atmosphere to the audience and to the player as well, the settings heightened the illusion of actuality. Thus atmosphere and scenery were important factors in Belasco's theory of good acting.

Belasco influenced American acting not only through his playwriting and stagecraft, but also through his teaching and training of players. He believed that acting can be taught. It is not, he felt, an art which is entirely God-given; it is the result of certain innate qualities which have been developed through competent training. Belasco's list of the five "all important factors" for good acting includes: ability, imagination, industry, patience, and loyalty. A person with these qualifications should be put through a rigorous course of training, said Belasco. He felt that most young American actors are hopelessly ignorant. They know little about their own art and nothing about the other fields of learning which might aid them on the stage. Since America, unlike France, has no national academy to stimulate acting and to set standards, the young player has little encouragement to develop himself. To remedy this, Belasco advocated training which included elocution, dancing, and fencing. In addition, he recommended that the young actor should learn literature, languages, current history, and composition. Finally, the young actor should be taught to observe—keenly and unceasingly. He should be alert to every living thing around him. "The great storehouse to which all dramatists must go is Life," writes Belasco. "Life must be studied constantly and minutely." [4]

Belasco demonstrated the power of good teaching by himself producing several outstanding performers. He took the novice, Mrs. Leslie Carter, and made her one of America's leading emotionalistic players. He hired David Warfield from a Weber and Fields burlesque show and made him a highly successful character actor. He perceived great potentialities in Blanche Bates and Frances Starr when they were only awkward young girls and through his training they became popular leading actresses. These successful performers are evidence of his faith that acting can be taught.

Still another development in the era of transition is illustrated by the career of David Belasco. During most of the nineteenth century, the actor dominated the world of the theatre. He was often playwright and more often manager. He always had the privilege of interpreting his roles as he saw fit. There was no such thing as a director, in the modern sense of the term. With the advent of such men as Augustin Daly and David Belasco, the régisseur or master director makes his appearance. The actor no longer creates independently. He works along the lines laid down by the director. The actor no longer evolves a style and a manner of performance to which the rest of the play must conform but is told by the director what style to adopt for the good of the play. David Belasco was one of the first of these modern directors or régisseurs. The plays he produced were interpreted through his eyes and his mind. He planned the scenery, the lighting, the costuming; he trained the actors and fitted them, like pieces, into the large mosaic of the play. The actors were not puppets, but neither were they the independent creators which they had been earlier in the century.

In retrospect, it is clear that David Belasco was an influential figure. In several fields he helped bridge the gap between the old order of the nineteenth century and the new theatrical world of the twentieth century. In playwriting, he supplied the romantic, sentimental dramas which, after the demise of the classic repertory, helped to prepare the public for the plays of Ibsen, Shaw, and Chekhov. In the field of directing, he emerged as a régisseur in the modern sense and established practices and procedures which are still followed by directors of today. In scenery and lighting, he helped to destroy the artificial attempts at realism of the nineteenth century and to establish a three-dimensional realism which was a useful link between the old style of mounting a play and the new stagecraft inspired by Adolphe Appia and Gordon Craig. In acting, consistent with his other contributions and influenced by them, he championed a contemporary naturalism which exploited personality and emotion and which is still found, to a degree, on many American stages.

RICHARD MANSFIELD

During the last dozen years of the nineteenth century, it was popular for wags and dramatic critics to declare: "There are good actors, bad actors, and Richard Mansfield." The witticism is revealing because it suggests the controversy and the perplexity which were aroused by the career of one of America's most individual and most exciting actors, Richard Mansfield. During his career on the stage, this actor was lauded and ridiculed, he was adored and hated, he was admired and scorned. Some critics called him the most versatile actor in the world; other critics, equally reputable, declared that he had no versatility at all but submerged every character he played in his own powerful personality and peculiar mannerisms. In retrospect, it is clear that he was not only a controversial performer but a most exciting one.

One essential key to understanding the art of Mansfield was his dominating personality. He was intense, egotistical, and independent to the point of lawlessness. His chosen friends found him a marvel of wit, charm, magnetism, and courtesy. His managers and sometimes his fellow actors found him a demon of temperament and conceit. He was that unique individual who was born to be a star and who *had* to be the star of every situation both on the stage and off or suffer a complete eclipse of personality. For example, as a schoolboy he could lead a footrace but he could not cooperate on a team; as a host he was perfect, but as a guest he was fidgety and uncomfortable; as the star of a production he was the absolute dictator of every detail or he was nothing. John R. Towse declared that Mansfield's outstanding characteristics were "strong individuality, burning ambition, intense egoism, and high artistic instinct." [5]

Mansfield's critics, both friendly and hostile, agreed on one point: that he was an immensely gifted man. He sang beautifully, he danced well, he painted pleasingly, he wrote plays and composed poetry, he was brilliant intellectually, and he was an excellent athlete—all these in addition to his premier position on the American stage. Given these varied talents and his dominating personality, it is little wonder that both Mansfield's acting and his personal life aroused controversy and perplexity as well as admiration and acclaim.

Mansfield's parentage and upbringing were far from ordinary. He was born in Berlin, May 24, 1854, of an English father and a German mother. His father, a London wine merchant by profession, died when Richard was five years old and appears to have had little influence on the life of the boy. But his mother, a noted grand opera singer named Erminia Rudersdorff, profoundly influenced his life and career. She bequeathed to her son artistic temperament and talent; she trained his voice; she developed his sensibilities; she sent him to excellent schools in England and on the continent; she introduced him to the world of art and culture; and finally, she brought him with her to America where, in 1872, she settled in Boston to become a singing teacher. With such a background it was natural for Richard to seek a career in the arts. He first tried painting and, at about the same time, he joined an amateur dramatic group. After five years in America, he went to London but here his painting brought him nothing and to support himself he was forced to become an entertainer. He presented songs and skits at private parties and in public music halls. He eventually secured a role on the stage, his first part being that of Sir Joseph Porter in a touring production of *H.M.S. Pinafore*. He played small roles in other operas and occasionally in plays. When his mother died in 1882, he returned to America where he continued to play inconspicuous roles in various musical and dramatic productions. His great opportunity came when A. M. Palmer offered him a part which J. H. Stoddart had refused, that of Baron Chevrial in a play entitled *A Parisien Romance*. Mansfield, a young man of twenty-eight, created a vivid and startling portrait of a doddering old lecher—a portrait which audiences found both fascinating and horrible. The impersonation was sensationally successful and Mansfield found himself suddenly famous. He continued to play the Baron for several months. Then, with characteristic ego, he launched himself as a star—but was soon forced to return to lesser status. For two years he performed in a variety of productions with moderate success. Then in 1886 he scored another hit as the charming, eccentric prince in a play entitled *Prince Karl*. After this success, Mansfield became his own manager and the star of his own productions. He remained so for the rest of his life.

Mansfield's acting career flourished for the next twenty years. Each season he added a new character to his repertory. He alternated long runs of his popular plays with repertory seasons which featured the most appealing characters from his past successes. During this period he was considered to be America's foremost actor. His prestige and leadership in the United States were comparable to that achieved by Henry Irving in England. Among the roles which won him most renown, in addition to Baron Chevrial and Prince Karl, were Dr. Jekyll and Mr. Hyde, Richard III, Beau Brummell, Shylock, Rev. Arthur Dimmesdale in *The Scarlet Letter,* Captain Bluntschli in *Arms and the Man,* Cyrano de Bergerac, Henry V, Monsieur Beaucaire, Ivan the Terrible, and Peer Gynt. Mansfield's last stage appearance was on March 23, 1907, when he overtaxed himself by playing Peer Gynt at a matinee and Baron Chevrial in the evening. The next day, exhausted from tension and overwork, he was forced to cancel subsequent appearances. Five months later, on August 30, 1907, he died at his home in New London, Connecticut.

Mansfield's vivid personality dominated a body of less than average height but more than average strength. Walter Prichard Eaton describes his physical appearance as follows: "Mansfield's stature was below the normal height, a difficulty which he triumphantly overcame by pose and fire, as well as high heels. He always wore his scant hair cropped, displaying a broad and high forehead. His eyes were brown, his jaw aggressive, his neck large, his shoulders broad, and his whole figure athletic and sturdy." [6]

Eaton also points out, as do all the students of Mansfield's acting, the extraordinary protean nature of his face and body. They could assume, with apparent ease, any shape or appearance or expression he wished to impose upon them. His face in particular was marvelously plastic, and even without the aid of heavy makeup could take on the outline and expression of the character Mansfield was playing.

The unusual flexibility of face and body helped to make Mansfield an expert mimic. In fact, excellence at mimicry became one of his outstanding gifts as a performer and often was mistaken for profound characterization.

Also contributing to Mansfield's success was his magnificent voice. It had richness of quality, flexibility of range, and seemingly limitless reserves of power. Moreover, the actor could use it in long and taxing roles, such as Peer Gynt, without tiring or coarsening it. He always declared that he owed his unusual vocal strength to the method of voice production which his operatic mother had taught him.

In spite of his remarkable voice and body, Mansfield nevertheless was frequently criticized for the way he used them. John R. Towse, always a judicious critic, says that "his manner on stage and off, was apt to be stiff, precise, and angular." [7] Other critics deplored his spasmodic gestures and stiff, jerky walk. Of his voice, Towse wrote: it "was deep, resonant, and musical—few actors have been gifted with a finer organ—but he never learned to take full advantage of it, adopting a falling inflection ending upon the same note at every period, which soon wearied the ear and was especially fatal in the delivery of blank verse." [8] Other critics concurred in this opinion and even William Winter, who was inclined to admire and defend Mansfield's acting on most counts, admitted that he was not "scrupulously heedful . . . in the speaking of blank verse . . . of the niceties of elocution." [9]

In the projection of emotion Mansfield had certain strengths and definite weaknesses. He excelled in portraying the melodramatic horrors of Dr. Jekyll and Mr. Hyde or of Ivan the Terrible. He won universal acclaim for the romantic force and passion he gave to Cyrano de Bergerac. Evidently he could grasp and project the simple, violent, baser emotions which are characteristic of melodrama. However, he was less successful in portraying the more complex emotions of his

Shakespearean characters—Richard III, Henry V, Brutus, and Shylock. Discriminating viewers felt that, with few exceptions, he could not touch either the depths or the heights of great tragic emotion and though he often simulated these emotions there was no "informing soul" behind the simulation. In reviewing Mansfield's Shakespearean performances, Towse continually complains of the shallowness and lack of sincerity which Mansfield manifested in scenes of passion. "The loftier heights of tragic emotion he could not scale," Towse declares flatly.[10] In this connection it is significant to note that Mansfield's list of Shakespearean characters is limited and that, ambitious and egotistical as he was, he never attempted such roles as Hamlet, Othello, or King Lear.

Mansfield's success at transformation—that is, at suppressing his own individuality and projecting the illusion of a created personality —depended on the role he was playing and upon the spectator who was observing him. In such eccentric, bizarre characterizations as Baron Chevrial or Dr. Jekyll and Mr. Hyde, the actor created convincing portraits for most spectators. In picturesque, off-beat, romantic young men such as Prince Karl, Monsieur Beaucaire, or Cyrano he was equally successful. Also, he was universally praised for Captain Bluntschli in Shaw's *Arms and the Man* because Mansfield was able to identify himself perfectly with the "stolid imperturbability," the "deliberate speech," and the "quizzical manner" of the character.[11]

Evidently whenever there was an element of the superficially eccentric, the out-of-the-ordinary, or the bizarre in a character, Mansfield's extraordinary powers of mimicry came into play and he was able to construct an artfully convincing portrait for all his audience. However, when he played Richard III or Henry V or even Shylock—out-of-the-ordinary as these characters are—the discriminating viewer felt that Mansfield failed to identify himself with the character and, instead, substituted too much of the Mansfield personality and too many of the Mansfield mannerisms. Opinion, of course, differed. There were those who marvelled at his versatility and felt that he created in each role a unique and sharply differentiated character. Others felt that his strong individuality infused and dominated every role so that his only convincing creations were those where the actor's personal eccentricities fitted the eccentricities of the dramatic character.

But the outstanding success of Mansfield's acting, on which everyone agreed, came from a certain "electric" quality. His acting "gave off sparks, it was strangely exciting," says Eaton.[12] Spectators were absorbed and their attention was riveted. There was never a dull moment no matter how awkward the movements of the actor or how monotonous his utterance. A personal force and magnetism, akin to the hypnotic power of Clara Morris in her prime, vivified all his performances and made Mansfield the most talked-about actor of his time. Towse declared that "Few actors could be more interesting and attractive than he when at his best, still fewer more exasperating when he was at his worst," [13] and William Winter summarized his qualities in these words: "He was one of the most extraordinary, versatile, and, above all, interesting actors that have ever graced our stage." [14]

Mansfield had a passionate dedication to his career and to the art of the theatre. His major productions were lavishly mounted and prepared with scrupulous attention to every detail. And each detail was supervised by the intense, high-strung star whose explosions, when things went wrong, were the terror of managers and fellow performers. Once the production was prepared, however, and once the actor was ready to perform, he lost himself in the role he was playing. An incident which occurred in 1894 during his production of *Scenes and Incidents from the Life of Napoleon Bonaparte* illustrates his power of absorption and concentration. Shortly before the curtain rose, Mansfield had exploded in fury when a stage hand had accidently dropped a broom against his dressing room door. But during the performance, when Mansfield was waiting in the wings to begin the crucial scene at Waterloo, a supernumerary stumbled over a stack of rifles and sent them clattering to the floor. The cast was petrified, expecting a titanic outburst. But Mansfield did not move or blink an eye. He appeared not even to have heard the noise—so absorbed was he in the thoughts and feelings of his imaginary situation.

In many ways, Mansfield represented and hastened the transition from one theatrical era to another. He was close to the tradition of repertory; he produced and acted fine plays (including Shakespeare) in the grand manner; and he, the star performer, was the dominating force and the center of attraction in all his productions. At the same time, Mansfield anticipated the changed theatre of the twentieth century and made his contributions to the new order: he acted far fewer roles than his great predecessors, and his seasons of repertory were secondary to the long runs of his hit plays; he produced two plays of

G. B. Shaw and performed them in a manner which suited their satiric, modern content; he was the first to produce Ibsen's *Peer Gynt* in the United States and contributed to the growing recognition of the great Norwegian.

Can Mansfield be grouped with such notable performers as Booth, Davenport, Barrett, and Murdoch? In a sense, he represents the vanishing tradition of which they were the great representatives. But his background and achievement do not measure up to theirs. He did not undergo the long, varied, and intense apprenticeship which gave Booth and Davenport experience in hundreds of roles representing every form of spoken drama from broad farce to high tragedy. During Mansfield's apprenticeship he acted only twenty-six different parts, many of them minor roles in operettas. After his first major achievement as Baron Chevrial in 1884, his career continued for twenty-two years and during this period he acted twenty-seven additional roles— slightly more than one per year. This record contrasts sharply with the achievements of a Booth or a Davenport. For example, in his prime Edwin Booth's active repertory included twenty-five of the greatest roles in poetic drama, to say nothing of the numberless other roles he had acted or could act.

Of the twenty-seven roles which Mansfield performed after 1884, only four were Shakespearean characters: Richard III, Henry V, Marcus Brutus, and Shylock. These cannot be called the most profound or complex of Shakespeare's creations. Neither can Mansfield's embodiment of them be called his most successful performances. The versatile tragedians of an earlier period performed these four roles plus a score of others, including the most demanding parts in all of dramatic literature: Hamlet, Macbeth, Othello, King Lear, Coriolanus, Sir Edward Mortimer, Richelieu, etc. In these complex, demanding roles the versatile tragedians achieved their greatest triumphs and they continued to act these roles until the end of their careers.

Mansfield, of course, was a product of his times. As has been noted, the taste for the great roles of the poetic drama was vanishing; the varied repertory of the old stock companies was giving way to the long runs of popular successes; the emphasis on plays concerned with contemporary problems or manners was creating a restrained, unpoetic style of acting. Richard Mansfield was pulled in two directions—toward the vanishing traditions of the old century and toward the emerging practices of the new. With his strong individuality and marked dramatic talents, he contributed to the traditions of both centuries.

E. H. SOTHERN

Edward Hugh Sothern, another representative of the transitional period, did not move toward the theatre of Shaw and Ibsen during the early years of the twentieth century as did Richard Mansfield. Instead, he returned to the traditions of an earlier period by establishing himself, first, as a leading representative of contemporary comedy, then as an exponent of romantic drama, and finally as a tragedian and a Shakespearean specialist. His career falls into three distinct phases.

The first phase in Sothern's development was his apprenticeship in comedy. Born in New Orleans on December 6, 1859, the son of the comedian who immortalized the character of Lord Dundreary, he was hopefully but unsuccessfully trained for a career in painting. After this ambition was abandoned, Sothern gravitated to the theatre and, at the age of 19, made his stage debut in the company of his famous father. His first appearance, in a one-line part, was a dismal failure, but with the persistence, energy, and earnestness which marked his whole career, he plugged along in minor roles and slowly acquired skill and poise. After seven years of apprenticeship, he became leading man at Daniel Frohman's Lyceum Theatre in New York. Here he established himself as a light comedian of charm and adroitness who was justly described as a player "of unusual finesse, of much subtilty, of splendid sincerity, of great personal charm. . . ." [15] His typical roles in this period were Jack Hammerton in *The Highest Bidder* and Lord Chumley in a play of that name.

Still under the aegis of Frohman, with whom he remained for fourteen years, Sothern next began to appear in the dashing, romantic roles of cloak-and-sword drama. He possessed all the necessary physical endowments for success in such roles. Although he was only average in height, he had a manly, handsome face, fine brown eyes, a lithe, expressive body, and an overall air of distinction. He became the near-perfect embodiment of such heroes as François Villon, D'Artagnon, and the Prisoner of Zenda. Walter Prichard Eaton nostalgically writes that "Those who saw Sothern act in . . . *The Prisoner of Zenda,* will most fondly remember him as the dashing, charming, alluring symbol of that pseudo-romance which had such a brief but beautiful Indian summer before the realistic new century set in. Better than any other player on either continent, Sothern embodied its humor and gaiety, its chivalric love, its delicate grace, its wistfulness." [16] At this point in his career, William Winter summarized Sothern's artistic achievement as "the development and practical perfection of a distinct, authoritative, crisp style, not unique, but neat, expert in mechanism, and felicitous in assumption of nonchalant, lackadaisical demeanor." [17]

Even at this stage of Sothern's career, successful as it was, judicious critics noted a certain lack of emotional sweep, a faultiness in clarity and cadence of delivery, and a deficiency in spiritual and intellectual grasp. These were flaws which were to keep Sothern from the highest achievement in the third stage of his career.

The third stage began late in 1899 when Sothern appeared as the hero of Hauptmann's poetic tragedy *The Sunken Bell*. It was not a great performance, but it astonished the public by its excellence and, even more, by the fact that so different a role should be undertaken by an actor who previously had been identified exclusively with parts in light comedy and romance. Sothern's followers noted that the actor's elocution had improved and his emotional responses were stronger and truer.

The "new" Sothern, who first emerged in *The Sunken Bell,* was fully revealed in 1900 when the actor performed Hamlet for the first time. During the rest of his career he devoted himself with dogged perseverance and earnest studiousness to developing himself as a tragedian and as a specialist in Shakespearean drama. Before he retired in 1927 he had achieved his goals. He was considered to be the best tragedian since the great days of the nineteenth century and, together with his partner and wife, Julia Marlowe, the leading Shakespearean actor in America.

Sothern played a large number of Shakespearean roles. They included: Romeo, Hamlet, Macbeth, Antony, Shylock, Malvolio, Petruchio, and Benedict. To all of his performances the actor brought earnest studiousness, honest artistic standards, a never-ending zeal for self-improvement, and great capacity for hard work. The results were uniformly sound and praiseworthy. With rare exceptions, however, the critics agreed that his performances could not be called great.

The excellence of Sothern's acting could be found in the care with which he analyzed his characters and the skill with which he executed

Viola Allen in a scene from Caine's *The Eternal City.*
From the Theatre Collection, University of California
Library at Berkeley.

Julia Marlowe.
Photograph by Falk.

Maude Adams in 1904. From the
Theatre Collection, University of California Library at Berkeley.

(*right*) Henry Placide. From the Harvard Theatre Collection.

Ada Rehan as Beatrice in *Much Ado about Nothing*. Photograph by Dupont.

(*right*) Joseph Jefferson as Rip Van Winkle. From the Ross Theatre Collection, University of California Library at Berkeley.

(left) Dion Boucicault as Myles-na-Coppaleen in his own play, *The Colleen Bawn*. From the Harvard Theatre Collection.

A scene from Thompson and Ryer's *The Old Homestead*. Photograph by Houseworth.

(left) Thomas D. Rice as Jim Crow. From the Harvard Theatre Collection.

Lotta Crabtree.
Photograph by Sarony.

(left) Lydia **Thompson** as Robinson Crusoe. A British beauty, she introduced burlesque to the American stage.

E. H. Sothern and Julia Marlowe
as Romeo and Juliet.

Richard Mansfield.
Photograph by Elite.

Otis Skinner as Hajj in *Kismet*. From the collection of Cornelia Otis Skinner.

William Gillette as Sherlock Holmes. Photograph by White.

Minnie Maddern Fiske in her prime.

Mrs. Fiske as Tess in Stoddard's adaptation of *Tess of the D'Urbervilles.*

his conceptions. He was a patient and thorough student and, with each year on the stage, he became a surer technician. In his early appearances he was awkward and mannered and his voice lacked both power and flexibility. But as his career advanced, he grew in confidence and in the ability to execute his effects with vigor and precision. His voice and delivery, too, steadily improved in the direction of control, power, and variety of utterance. When he performed the roles of Romeo, Hamlet, and Malvolio in London, Arthur Symons was so impressed that he wrote a pamphlet entitled *Great Acting in English,* in which he declared that the only great performances of Shakespeare to be found anywhere in the English speaking world were the performances of E. H. Sothern and Julia Marlowe. Symons said that Sothern's Romeo "has an exquisite passion, young and extravagant as a lover's, and is alive." [18] Symons called Sothern's Hamlet "majestical" and exclaimed, "How magnificently he interprets, in the crucifixion of his own soul, the main riddles of the universe!" [19] And finally, Symons' highest praise went to Sothern's portrayal of Malvolio. "It is an elaborate travesty," wrote Symons, "done in a disguise like the solemn dandy's head of Disraeli." Sothern "acts with his eyelids, which move while all the rest of his face is motionless; with his pursed, reticent mouth, with his prim and pompous gestures; with that self-consciousness which brings all Malvolio's troubles upon him. It is a fantastic, tragically comic thing, done with rare calculation, and it has its formal, almost cruel share in the immense gaiety of the piece." [20]

Such fulsome praise was not echoed by the critics who knew Sothern best. After studying his performances for many years, they agreed that Malvolio was his finest Shakespearean portrayal, but they found deficiencies in his acting of the great tragic roles. For all his excellences, they agreed that Sothern lacked "the great ground-swell of passionate emotion," [21] the magic of supreme poetic utterance, and the penetrating spiritual insight which produces truly great acting. William Winter summarizes the general consensus when he writes:

. . . while it cannot justly be said that this actor has provided any splendid, inspiring example, or made upon the theatre and the public mind an impression destined to endure, it can justly be declared that he has exhibited energy and zeal, a high order of talent, much force of character, and that, as a whole, he has exerted a beneficent influence. He . . . largely dominates the dramatic field in America, partly because of his abilities, and partly because of the dearth, which seems to increase, of dramatic genius and artistic competition. The sum-total of his achievement is substantial and admirable, and he has richly deserved the public gratitude and esteem.[22]

OTIS SKINNER

In 1939, Otis Skinner, then eighty-one years old, published a book entitled *The Last Tragedian*. Readers unacquainted with the volume assumed that it was an autobiography. It was not. The book is a tribute to Edwin Booth. However, if one surveys the career of Otis Skinner, the author, one is inclined to say that he and not Booth should be considered "the last tragedian," or at least the last of the old guard. Skinner outlived Booth by almost fifty years. Skinner did not possess the consummate genius of the older actor, but Skinner was an outstanding performer who played classic roles well into the twentieth century. Trained in the old traditions, possessed of a versatility akin to that of his great predecessors, he was a man who helped to link the contemporary stage with the theatre of the previous century. If he was not *the* last, certainly he was *one* of the last of the versatile performers of the old school.

Otis Skinner served a rich and vigorous apprenticeship. Born in 1858, the son of a Universalist clergyman, he made his professional debut in 1877 as a member of the resident stock company of the Philadelphia Museum. During his first season he acted ninety-two characters of every age, color, and description. "There was no kind of part I did not play," he writes, "even sex was no bar, for I was sometimes clapped into skirts for nigger wenches and coarse old hags. I scowled as villains, stormed as heavy fathers, dashed about in light comedy, squirmed in character parts, grimaced in comics, and tottered as the Pantaloon in pantomime." [23]

Skinner continued this kind of apprenticeship for several more years, acting with many of the ablest veterans of the nineteenth century. He was a member of the Walnut Street Theatre, Philadelphia, for a season. He supported Edwin Booth for ten weeks. He played "seconds" in Lawrence Barrett's company for three years. He acted with John McCullough, Fanny Janauschek, and Mary Anderson on various occasions. He joined Augustin Daly's famous troupe and for five years played with such performers as Mrs. Gilbert, May Irwin, John Drew, and Ada Rehan. For two seasons he was Helena Modjeska's leading man, acting the roles of Henry VIII, Orlando, Shylock, Macbeth, and Sir Edward Mortimer. In the season of 1895–96, he filled an emergency engagement in Chicago where he played Hamlet for two weeks. His success on this occasion was triumphant. During his appearances, "The house held audiences that had not been duplicated since Edwin Booth and Lawrence Barrett were the stars." [24]

As a result of such extensive experience, Skinner acquired a knowledge and technique of acting which served him admirably for all of his life. He never ceased to be grateful for this apprenticeship. Writing many years later, after the old order had vanished, he expressed his appreciation in these words:

I am glad I was able to be in . . . before the old system quite passed away; glad that my novitiate was one of hard knocks that compelled me to swallow my technique in great gulps; glad of the vast experience that gave me every sort of character—in two years I had played over 140 parts; glad of that compulsion of quick study and performance which renders the body supple and the mind obedient; and glad that my dramatic kindergarten was placed among men and women filled with the knowledge of their trade, and with honor for their calling—residents of a true Bohemia since changed for an estate of greater respectability and social recognition and less art.[25]

The success which Otis Skinner achieved, and which was sustained through a career lasting almost sixty years, was based not only on thorough training but on ample endowments of body, voice, and mind. He had a well knit, athletic build which enabled him to wear Elizabethan tights or Roman togas or, indeed, any manner of costume with handsome effect. His face was strong, masculine, and appealing; his voice was resonant and flexible; his temperament was magnetic. He was a scholarly man, too, even though his formal education had been slight. Amy Leslie called him a person "of deep poetic thought" with a "fine hardy brain," [26] and this description must be reliable because the several books which came from his pen show perception, sensitivity, and scholarly competence.

With such endowments, there is little wonder that Otis Skinner was an ideal romantic hero. He played many such parts, acting them with convincing dash and authentic appeal. But he was more than a matinee idol. He was also a skillful comedian, an able delineator of character roles, and a fine tragedian. In surveying his accomplishments, Lewis

Strang exclaims, "Here is versatility to an unusual degree, and versatility, moreover, that has been tested, that is real and genuine." [27]

During the early years of his career, Skinner played the varied and ever changing roles which were characteristic of the versatile actors of the nineteenth century. But the influences of an era of transition overtook him. At the height of his career he succumbed to the long run. He played Colonel Bridau in *The Honor of the Family* for two and a half years; he played Hajj in *Kismet* for three years. He succumbed also to the changed public taste in drama. Instead of roles in Shakespeare or in "old comedy" or in Restoration tragedy—the roles in which he had learned his art—he played mostly in quaint, sentimental comedies or in romantic costume dramas. The list of these is long but among the most popular, in addition to *Kismet* and *The Honor of the Family,* were such favorites as *His Grace de Grammont, Prince Otto, Mister Antonio,* and *Blood and Sand.* Unlike Richard Mansfield, who recognized the growing importance of Ibsen and Shaw, Skinner remained an exponent of the kind of drama which has already been described as "that pseudo-romance which had such a brief but beautiful Indian summer before the realistic new century set in." [28]

Whether Skinner acted his romantic costume parts or the roles of Shylock, Falstaff, Charles Surface, and Petruccio—to which he occasionally returned—in all his acting he demonstrated the skill and authority of his "classic" nineteenth century training. He knew how to make an effective entrance; he knew how to listen and still hold attention; he knew how to control his efforts for the maximum effect in crucial scenes; he knew how to keep a cool head while arousing tears and thrills in his audience; he recognized that "it is a collaboration between actor and audience that makes for cohesion and unity" [29] and he developed this collaboration for maximum response; finally, he knew the range and versatility of the human voice and he used his voice to communicate the heartbreak of tragedy, the rapier sting of satire, and the healthful mirth of comedy. Writing in 1900, Lewis Strang praised Skinner for his versatility, for his magnetic appeal, and for his artistic honesty, but he criticised the actor because he felt that Skinner lacked strong dramatic instinct. "His art is not intuitive," wrote Strang, "and the effects he produces are the results of hard study and painstaking effort." [30] Thirty years later, John Mason Brown analyzed Skinner's acting and found it mature and impressive with few of the weaknesses Strang had observed. Brown wrote: "It is a veteran's method, sure in its devices, conscious of its 'points' and certain in making them. . . . It is character acting enlarged beyond the ordinary; bold, romantic, mellow but high-tensioned. It admits no moments of loafing and is never more active than when someone else is speaking. . . . See his fine Falstaff . . . and you understand just what 'the great tradition' can mean in poise, in manner and authority. . . ." [31]

During an era of transition, Skinner carried on many of the great traditions of nineteenth century acting. In his autobiography, written in 1924, he declares with justifiable pride: "In taking an inventory of my professional experience, I find that I have played in all 325 parts; have appeared in sixteen plays of Shakespeare, acting therein, at various times, thirty-eight parts, and I have produced under my direction thirty-three plays." [32] Skinner lived until 1942 and continued to prove the effectiveness of his training and his style of acting even when they were used in the new theatre of the twentieth century.

ROMANTIC HEROES

The romantic costume plays, which formed so large a part of the later repertory of Otis Skinner, were attractive to many other players. Actors who might have developed varied skills under different circumstances became specialists in romance and confined themselves largely to one kind of role. There have always been romantic heroes on the American stage and love for the kind of play in which they appear. The late nineteenth and early twentieth centuries are notable for the unusual popularity of this kind of drama, and the players who developed a style of acting appropriate to the romantic costume plays are first cousins—albeit more suave and sophisticated cousins—of Edwin Forrest and the members of the heroic muscular school.

An outstanding example of an actor who specialized in romantic roles was James O'Neill (1847–1920), father of Eugene O'Neill. He began his career as a versatile player who acted many parts and who showed promise of becoming a worthy successor to Booth, Davenport, and Barrett. But presently he was cast as the Count of Monte Cristo in the famous play of the same name by Alexandre Dumas. His fate was sealed. His success in the part was so great and the monetary returns were so enormous that he continued to play the role year after year. He occasionally tried other parts but, like a drunkard to his bottle, he kept returning to Monte Cristo. Gradually his ambition for self-development declined; his versatility withered away, and he became solely identified with one role. At the end of his life he regretted the abasing of his talents and the atrophy of his reputation, but it was too late. As an actor, he is remembered solely as the dashing, romantic hero of *Monte Cristo*.

William Faversham (1868–1940) was called in his prime "a matinee girl's ideal" and the "hero of a thousand matinees." He deserved the titles because he was a handsome fellow, tall, muscular, vigorous, and healthy, who kept himself in superb physical condition by careful diet and strenuous exercise. Although he was born in London and served a brief apprenticeship on the stage there, he came to the United States in 1887 and built his career in this country, eventually becoming an American citizen. He played many roles during his lifetime including such Shakespearean heroes as Romeo and Marc Antony. However, he won his greatest popularity as the vigorous, masculine, romantic hero of such plays as *Under the Red Robe, Lord and Lady Algy, The Squaw Man,* and *The Prince and the Pauper*. Lewis Strang says he was "at his best in characters requiring buoyancy and vivacity of spirits and rapid, energetic action—action, moreover, that is open, and above board without subtilty or ingenuousness." [33] His last role, however, was an ironic contrast to the handsome heroes he had embodied so well in the early years of the twentieth century: he ended his career by playing Jeeter Lester in that shabby modern play, *Tobacco Road*.

James K. Hackett (1869–1926), son of the fine comedian James H. Hackett, was another matinee idol who provided Faversham with keen competition in romantic roles. Like Faversham, he was tall, handsome, and athletic. He excelled in swimming and fencing and was proud of his reputation as a football player at New York City College. He made his stage debut in 1892 and soon thereafter was playing Shakespearean roles for Augustin Daly. He later joined Daniel Frohman's company where he became the leading romantic actor, causing palpitation of the heart in thousands of ladies who watched him as *The Prisoner of Zenda* or as *Rupert of Hentzlau*. In these roles his shapely, muscular legs were a noticeable asset. One critic wrote that "Mr. Hackett's brilliant, quivering, scintillant legs in 'Don Caesar' are really the best thing he has ever done." [34] Toward the end of his career, after many years of performing in romantic costume drama, he returned to Shakespearean roles but found that the "picturesque artificiality" of his romantic style limited his accomplishment in the great roles of Macbeth or Othello.

John B. Mason (1857–1919) belongs in a somewhat different group from O'Neill, Faversham, and Hackett. Like them, he excelled in romantic roles but he was even more successful in the performance of classic and modern comedy. His career is typical of many actors of the transition. Before the turn of the century he was the leading man at the Boston Museum. He joined the company in 1879 while William Warren was still active, and during his first few seasons there played romantic juveniles and light comedy parts. Also he was given considerable experience in old comedies such as *The School for Scandal,* the revival of which was a feature of each season at the Boston Museum. When he became leading man of the company in 1888, he was cast for such romantic roles as Captain Vere in *Bells of Haslemere,* Lt. Kerchival West in *Shenandoah,* Eliot Grey in *Rosedale,* and Lord Travers in *Hazel Kirke.* He brought to these parts so much "grace, dash, . . . masculine charm . . . sincerity and . . . mastery of technique" that he lent "conviction and force to the wildest melodrama." [35]

After Mason left the Museum company in 1890, his star went into partial eclipse. But in 1898 he re-established his reputation as a superior actor by making an outstanding success of the uncongenial role of Horatio Drake in Viola Allen's famous production of *The Christian.* Following this achievement, he became the leading man of Daniel Frohman's Lyceum Theatre Stock Company. Here he made the transition to roles in the comedies of Arthur Wing Pinero and Henry Arthur Jones and won the accolade from Lewis Strang of being "the finest modern comedy actor in the country." Strang contends that in the roles of modern comedy Mason "displayed an art so delicate, so subtle, so natural, so human, that it has seemed the realism of nature instead of the realism of art." [36]

Mason can be counted among the romantic heroes of the transitional period because he mastered such roles early in his career. He can also be counted among the comedians of the twentieth century because when the vogue for the romantic drama passed, he cultivated his other talents and won a new reputation as a skillful performer in modern comedy.

There are many other popular players who earned reputations as romantic heroes. The list is too long for detailed discussion. However, one additional name—that of William Gillette (1855–1937)—deserves mention because he specialized in a particular kind of romantic role, he was the author of several enormously popular plays, and he propounded a particular theory of the art of acting.

Gillette, who was the son of a United States Senator and a friend of Mark Twain, ran away from home in order to pursue his dramatic ambitions. After a short apprenticeship in the stock company of Ben De Bar, he made his New York debut, 1877, in a two-line role in *The Gilded Age*. He trained himself carefully and developed steadily as an actor. He was aided by good looks and a compelling personality. One description called him "tall, slender, studious looking . . . a man of wit, charm and great vanity." [37] In 1881, he appeared in the first play from his own pen, a character study called *The Professor,* and made a decided hit. Thereafter he wrote or adapted or collaborated in the writing of some twenty plays, of which the most famous and popular are *Secret Service* and *Sherlock Holmes*. Both of these are colorful, suspenseful melodramas, and in both of them Gillette played the firm-jawed, resourceful, imperturbable hero. Instead of performing his heroics with cape and sword as O'Neill, Faversham, and Hackett usually did, Gillette used a pistol, a magnifying glass, and native cunning. His manner was so effortless, and his crisp, staccato delivery of lines seemed to be so spontaneous, that he projected "the illusion of great naturalness." [38] He created such a vividly convincing image of the fictitious character, Sherlock Holmes, and he so impressed this image on American and English audiences, that for several generations of playgoers Gillette *was* Sherlock Holmes. Even today when elderly playgoers visualize the imaginary detective they unconsciously recall the firm jaw, the hawk nose, the keen eye, and the authoritative manner of William Gillette.

In all of his roles Gillette exploited his own strong personality. In fact, he chose only those parts which perfectly suited his own personality. He believed that successful acting is the projection of the actor's own individuality through the medium of a dramatic character. Gillette declares: "In all the history of the stage no performer has yet been able to simulate or make use of a personality not his own. . . . The actors of recent times who have been universally acknowledged to be great have invariably been so because of their successful use of their own strong and compelling personalities in the roles which they made famous." [39] Gillette was aware that many of his fellow actors disagreed with him, but he nevertheless held strongly to his belief in the importance of personality in performance.

Gillette was also an advocate of the "Illusions of the First Time in Acting." The increasing realism of the plays of his time, and of his own plays, their "closeness to life" as Gillette termed it, demanded that the performer abandon the exaggerated gesture, the unnatural stride, and the elocutionary delivery which, Gillette implied, suited some plays of the nineteenth century. Instead, the performer must cultivate verisimilitude and produce the illusion of actual life. Each time the actor performed a role, said Gillette, he must listen as though hearing the lines for the first time and respond as though formulating his replies for the first time. In every bit of action and stage business he must create the impression of spontaneity. Finally, the spirit of the whole play must be so alive and fresh that:

Each successive audience before which it is given must feel—not think or reason about, but *feel*—that it is witnessing, not one of a thousand weary repetitions, but a life episode that is being lived just across the magic barrier of the footlights. That is to say, the whole must have that indescribable life-spirit or effect which produces the Illusion of Happening for the First Time." [40]

In all his activities in the theatre—in playwriting, acting, and theorizing—Gillette helped to reshape the acting of the nineteenth century and advance it toward the psychological naturalism of the twentieth. He also used his own strong, manly personality to create vivid portraits of a special kind of romantic hero.

IX

MRS. MINNIE MADDERN FISKE

MINNIE MADDERN FISKE'S ROLE AS A PIONEER IN THE AMERICAN theatre is often overlooked. Although she is rarely given credit for being an innovator, her career marks a clean break with the traditions of the nineteenth century and the emergence of those ideals which dominate the stage of our own time. She was a champion of the works of Henrik Ibsen and encouraged plays which, like his, discussed modern problems in a truthful, realistic manner. She deprecated the star system and tried to develop a company of players in which the individual was subordinate to the ensemble, and in which all elements of the production served the design of the dramatist. She advocated a simple, natural style of acting based upon psychological truthfulness and freedom from theatrical trickery. Above all, she demanded that the intellect of an actor control his emotions and direct both his conception and his performance. Clara Morris represented the triumph of emotion over intellect. Mrs. Fiske, in sharp contrast, addressed the minds of her spectators before she tried to touch their hearts. She was the most intellectual actress of her day, and played a significant part in shaping the stage history of the twentieth century.

It is important to remember that Mrs. Fiske did not emerge at the end of one era and, through a brilliant new theory and practice, convert her contemporaries and inaugurate an entirely new era of acting. Mrs. Fiske's career extended from 1870 until 1931, and thus she served her theatrical apprenticeship and reached stardom during a period when many other styles of acting were vigorous and flourishing. Her contemporaries in the late nineteenth century and the early years of the twentieth were classical performers like Helena Modjeska, who acted until 1907, or emotionalistic actresses like Mrs. Leslie Carter, who acted until 1929, or players of the personality school like Maude Adams and Julia Marlowe, who acted until 1918 and 1924, or actors of the transition, like Sothern, Skinner, and Gillette, whose careers extended well into the twentieth century. Mrs. Fiske's theory and practice in the theatre were not typical of the generally accepted theory and practice during most of her career. Not until her last years and in the years which followed did her style and her methods become a dominant influence.

A few characteristics sharply differentiate her school from those which preceded it and which were or are contemporary with it:

1. Emphasis on psychological truthfulness in the portrayal of a character;
2. Concentration on inner feeling with simplified, repressed external action;
3. Cultivation of a simple, true-to-contemporary-life manner of moving and speaking;
4. Fidelity to the design of the play with all performers and effects subordinate to the over-all purpose of the dramatist.

The follower of this school believes that his head should guide his heart in preparing a role. He aims to grasp the psychological truth which motivates the dramatist's character and to build his portrayal according to the logic of this psychological truth. In contrast, the emotionalistic actress grasped her characters intuitively and subordinated psychological truthfulness to emotional display, while the player of the personality school achieved psychological truthfulness only if the logic of the dramatic character fit his or her own personal psychology. The player of the modern school is closest in method to the performer of the classic school who also sought to grasp his roles intellectually and to understand the motives which shaped the actions of a dramatic character but who worked without the assistance of modern psychological insights.

Emphasis on psychological truthfulness in the portrayal of a role leads the performer of the modern school to concentrate on inner feeling; the expression of this inner feeling takes the form of a simplified, restrained external action. In contrast, the player of the classical school, acting the great tragic roles of the standard drama of the nineteenth century and performing them in large, dimly lighted theatres, used broad movements, bold gestures, and strong facial expression. The emotionalistic actress, performing in sentimental melodrama, surrendered herself to her passions and cultivated extravagant overt display. But the player of the modern school usually performs realistic plays dealing with social problems or contemporary manners, and in these plays a restrained, suggestive style is used, the effectiveness of which is made possible by the small, artfully lighted theatres in which he performs. Even when he acts a Shakespearean role, the modern player tends to eschew both exhibitionism and broad, bold action, relying, instead, as in all his performances, on the cumulative force of subtle, simple effects consistently built up during the whole course of the performance.

His concentration on inner feeling and his restrained expression of this feeling often leads to a neglect of adequate elocution. His speech is not cadenced and poeticized to fit blank verse or declamatory prose; it is the speech of everyday life with its broken rhythms and more limited, less varied range. In fact, the performer of the modern school is sometimes criticized for his slovenly, unintelligible speech and is urged to cultivate greater clarity and precision of delivery.

The ideals of contemporary stagecraft have helped to shape another characteristic of the style of the modern player. The star of the play is no longer the main element of the production but only one of the many elements, all of which must blend into a harmonious whole. At certain periods in the history of American acting a leading player has been able to carry a production despite shoddy scenery, shabby costumes, and a careless third-rate supporting company. But the ideal of the modern school is a production where every element of acting and stagecraft are uniformly excellent and all are coordinated to fulfill the overall design of the dramatist. Thus, the leading player of the modern stage must be part of the ensemble. He or she cannot dazzle like a comet in the night sky—unless the play calls for such a comet. The dazzle of the portrayal must fit into the constellation conceived by the dramatist, and the performance must shine or flicker or fade according to the demands of the play. The ideal of harmonious ensemble acting blended with the other elements of a production to achieve a vivid embodiment of the dramatist's conception is not a new ideal, to be sure. It has been respected and observed, at times, by players and managers of every school of acting. However, it is only in the modern school that this ideal has been universally accepted and has become a dominant force in American dramatic production.

Many influences, both direct and indirect, have been responsible for the establishment of the modern school of psychological naturalism in the United States. The most powerful foreign influence came from Russia where, at the turn of the century, the Moscow Art Theatre began applying the theories of Stanislavsky and Meyerhold in the production of a new kind of play by Anton Chekhov and other realistic dramatists. The Russian example, and particularly Stanislavsky's system of training actors, became a major force in the classrooms and theatres of this country later in the century. However, before the theories of the Moscow Art Theatre gained currency in America, Minnie Maddern Fiske was teaching similar principles and applying them in her productions. She began her adult career as an actress in 1882, her ideals and methods reached maturity as early as 1897, and she organized her Manhattan Theatre Company in 1904 as a repertory company to demonstrate her theories of acting and play production. The Moscow Art Theatre was not founded until 1898, and the first Stanislavsky-trained player to perform in the United States, Alla Nazimova, did not appear in this country until 1905. So Mrs. Fiske can rightfully be called a pioneer in the establishment of the modern school of psychological naturalism.

Minnie Maddern was the daughter of theatrical parents who began her career as a babe in arms. Throughout her infancy and youth she was in steady demand as a child actress and thus had acquired extensive experience by the time she made her adult debut in 1882 at the Park Theatre, New York. The part she played on this occasion was that of Chip in a comedy-melodrama called *Fogg's Ferry*. Her backers had hoped she would become another Maggie Mitchell or Lotta Crabtree, but in this she disappointed them. She could neither sing nor dance, but she nevertheless exerted a youthful charm which won favorable comment. *Music & Drama,* for May 20, 1882, said: "Magnetic she certainly is; for everybody was pleased with her, although she did nothing extraordinarily pleasing," while the New York *Mirror* declared: "She possesses a native grace, freshness, and a quaint mischievous sense of humor all her own. . . . There is no art about Minnie Maddern. She is perfectly natural. The ebullition of animal spirits, the charm of youth; these are the materials she employs. . . . She is a ray of dancing sunshine." [1] Other comments on her early appearances mention her wealth of bright red hair—which gave distinction to an otherwise plain face—her slight figure, and her clear, dry voice, "predominantly a head voice," which was considered staccato and unmusical by many listeners.

These early reviews presage many of the comments made on Mrs. Fiske's mature style. When she became a star she continued to be praised for the strong attractiveness of her personality and for the simple naturalness of her manner. In the course of the years, she did not become physically beautiful, nor did her voice develop outstanding richness and range, but she did cultivate her mind and perfect her technique. It became customary to regard her as the most intellectual actress on the American stage.

Evidently Mrs. Fiske was intellectual and analytical by nature. Her approach to any role was careful and studious. Before acting a character, she tried to understand both his mind and his heart, and to know the reason or impulse which prompted his words and actions. Lewis Strang says: "She goes straight to the source of all vital action and all enduring achievement—the infinite power of mind. Mentally she comprehends . . . the full scope of the drama, and the fact that she does comprehend so much makes possible the conviction, the positive appeal, the truth, and the suggestive power manifest in her acting." [2]

Some actors grasp a character instinctively or by intuitive leaps. Mrs. Fiske dissected her characters element by element, scrutinized each component, then assembled the bits as one assembles a mosaic. For the finished creation, she included only those elements which fulfilled the overall design. Anything confusing or superfluous was eliminated. When her character emerged, each detail counted; every gesture and tone had significance. She developed a gift for revealing her characters in deft, subtle strokes. The New York *News,* in reviewing her performance in Ibsen's *Doll's House,* said:

One of the marked features of her acting is the care she gives to detail. She is not given to bold, sketchy portrayals. . . . If she makes an entrance in street costume, she suggests her mood by the manner in which she doffs her gloves, wrap, and bonnet. . . . Her characters are not commonplace or lackadaisical because of these details: they are strongly drawn, intensely interesting and well sustained; the detail introduced by her furnishes the proper tone effect and enhances the vividness of the picture.

Mrs. Fiske's acting was not intuitive and impulsive, like Clara Morris's. Whereas the portrayer of Alixe and Miss Multon depended upon the stimulus of an audience and the inspiration of the moment to evoke startling effects, the impersonator of Becky Sharp and Salvation Nell planned every gesture and inflection of her role with painstaking care. Her acting appeared spontaneous and natural but Lewis Strang discovered, after watching her act the same role several nights in succession, that her effects were "as fixed, as determined, and as certain as the perfect engine, smooth running and positive in its action. . . ." [4] Mrs. Fiske confirmed this impression in a conversation with Alexander Woollcott when she declared, "Any one may achieve on some rare occasion an outburst of genuine feeling, a gesture of imperishable beauty, a ringing accent of truth; but your scientific actor knows how he did it. He can repeat it again and again and again. He can be depended on." [5]

Clara Morris was a triumphant "first nighter"; the excitement and challenge of an opening inspired her best efforts. Mrs. Fiske, on the other hand, was a wretched "first nighter"; she was not at her best until her effects had been perfected in numerous performances. Both Miss Morris and Mrs. Fiske declared that they believed in maintaining a cool-headed control no matter how impassioned the scene, but Miss Morris's acting indicated that she valued the passion more than the control, while Mrs. Fiske's acting illustrated her own dictum that an actor must first of all "have the mechanism of his character at his fingertips" and after that he should try to "fill it in with soul." [6] She also said, "The eternal and immeasurable accident of the theatre which you call genius, that is a matter of soul. But with every genius I have seen—Janauschek, Duse, Irving, Terry—there was always the last word in technical proficiency." [7]

Of course Mrs. Fiske's technique did not suddenly emerge, full blown, like Venus rising from the waves. The deftness of her artistry was the result of long practice and experience. The actress grew and developed as the years went by, apparently reaching her prime in her performance as Tess of the D'Urbervilles. The following review from the Boston *Transcript* for March 5, 1897, is typical of the high praise she received for Tess: "Her mental capacity to analyze a character to its core has never been more evident. Her temperamental capacity to embody and reveal it has gained new force. . . . The execution was worthy of the conception. Her play of feature, in significance, power, and swiftness of transition, is comparable to La Duse's herself. Her voice reflects the mood of the moment. . . . Her gestures reveal and emphasize. She knows the worth of repose, reserve, silence. She has attained a human verity that makes the stock theatrical devices pale and hollow."

Mrs. Fiske's greatest asset, her intellectual strength, was also a weakness, for it opened her to the charge of "coldness." It was said that she was all head and no heart. Her characters were presented with incisive acumen and skill but, according to many of her critics, she omitted the warm, human appeal which Clara Morris was able to project so effectively. The reviewer of the New York *Transcript* declared that she could analyze and dissect but could not synthesize or vivify. On the other hand, many observers asserted that she could be deeply human and passionate whenever the occasion justified it, while Alan Dale of the New York *World* felt that her "chill, intellectual" interpretations had a fascination which far exceeded the appeal of an ordinary "human" interpretation. Mrs. Fiske herself was sensitive to the criticism that she was too cold and analytical. At a press interview in 1901, she said: "Don't emphasize my mentality, please. If my intellectual proclivities are hurled at the public much more they will begin to believe that I have no feeling to spur emotional expression, although I sometimes think I overstudy a part, that I analyze too much." [8]

Mrs. Fiske's temperament and artistic method created a style of acting which was quiet and repressed, yet, at its best it was charged with vital intensity. The actress avoided noise, display, and theatrical trickery. She suggested rather than exhibited the emotions of her characters and often gained powerful effects by so doing. Strang says she was marvelous at exhibiting "the inherent force of suppression," [9] while the Milwaukee *Sentinel* declared: "Her most powerful effects are gained by the suggestion of intense repressed force. She is one of the few who can project not only words, but thoughts over the footlights and make the audience grasp a mental process without the aid of a spoken line." [10] Alexander Woollcott, who considered Mrs. Fiske's portrayal of Lona in Ibsen's *The Pillars of Society* to be the finest acting he had ever seen, described her performance as "the outgiving of a dynamic being, an inspirational, communicable emanation, a transcendent expression of the spirit." [11]

One of Mrs. Fiske's most successful scenes in *Salvation Nell* was a scene lasting ten minutes during which she sat on the floor, almost motionless, holding her drunken lover's head in her lap without uttering a word. Even though hurried activity was going on around her, she riveted the attention of the audience on her own silent agony. After watching this scene in performance, the distinguished actress-singer, Mary Garden, is said to have exclaimed, "Ah, to be able to *do nothing* like that!" [12] George Arliss, a fellow actor, said: "Her great moments come in flashes—in silences, in exclamations, or in brief utterances." [13]

Apparently all observers were not as acute as Mr. Arliss or as the reviewer of the Milwaukee *Sentinel.* Some of them complained that Mrs. Fiske repressed so much that an average spectator could not follow her. Because she omitted the customary gestures, movements, and expressions, the spectators couldn't divine what the actress was up to. Most of them were accustomed to acting in which a player had an easily recognizable way of expressing the cardinal emotions. The trouble with the "new school" of Mrs. Fiske, according to its critics, was that the player concentrated on feeling correctly and deeply the emotions belonging to a situation and then trusted to the "happy chance of nature" to put the desired expression on his face. The Boston *Herald* accused Mrs. Fiske of doing this. In the issue of July 22, 1896, occurs the following criticism:

Those who remember Minnie Maddern in that dire failure, "Hester Crewe," recall moments when she walked to and fro, expecting the audience to see the working of her mind, which they did not understand at all. That was simply because she refused to train her face and to make certain that the emotion she wished to express was there. She was content, instead, to feel certain that she was experiencing the right feeling and would doubtless have considered it the loss of, or the stupidity of, the public that could not understand.

Mrs. Fiske was further criticized for the unintelligibility of her delivery. Early in her career, she developed a rapid tempo and a clipped enunciation which baffled many listeners. They complained that she crowded her words together, dropped the terminal sounds, and rushed headlong through her speeches without regard to clarity or emphasis. Charles M. Bregg asserted, "it isn't artistic to speak in quick, staccato passages which completely obscure the sounds of words," and then he declares: "As if to add to this amazing defect, Mrs. Fiske has recently acquired the habit of talking with her back to the audience." [14]

Such irritation over Mrs. Fiske's delivery * was not shared by Alfred Ayres. He, of all people, admired fine elocution and bewailed its disappearance from the American stage, yet he found Mrs. Fiske's delivery to be entirely admirable. He claimed it was her chief asset and had won her foremost rank among American actresses. Her elocution, he said, was happily free of the sing-song, the chanting, and the "conjuring with tones" that marred the speaking of so many players. "The distinctive characteristic of her elocution," he wrote, "is its simplicity, its exceeding naturalness, its freedom from any apparent effort to be effective. With her the thought and nothing but the thought determines." [15]

It is interesting to note that in the latter part of her career, Mrs. Fiske began to insist on the importance of voice and speech in the practice of acting. In one of her conversations with Alexander Woollcott, published in 1917, she declared that her first admonition to an inspiring actor would be this: "Dear child . . . consider your voice. It is the beginning and the end of acting. Train that until it responds to your thought and purpose with absolute precision. Go at once . . . to some master of the voice, and, if need be, spend a whole year with him studying the art of speech. Learn it now, and practice it all your days in the theatre." [16] When Woollcott questioned this dictum and asked about the value of imagination in acting, Mrs. Fiske told him it is

* In 1910, Franklin P. Adams wrote some amusing verses that accurately characterized Mrs. Fiske's voice and manner of speaking. They read, in part:

> Staccato, hurried, nervous, brisk,
>   Cascading, intermittent, choppy.
> The brittle voice of Mrs. Fiske
>   Shall serve me now as copy.
>
> Time was, when first that voice I heard,
>   Despite my close and tense endeavor,
> When many an important word
>   Was lost and gone forever
> Though unlike the others at the play,
> I never whispered: "Wha'd she say?"
>
> Some words she runs togetherso;
>   Some others are distinctly stated
> Somecometoofast and s o m e   t o o   s l o w
>   And some are syncopated,
> And yet no voice—I am sincere—
> Exists that I prefer to hear.

only by means of a perfectly trained voice that an actor can communicate the inspiration of his imagination. She then somewhat qualified her original assertion by explaining that "If I put the voice first, it is a little because that is something he can easily develop . . . he is likely to forget its importance and if we put it first, he will remember it longer." [17] Mrs. Fiske also admitted that her early style of elocution, "staccato . . . nervous . . . intermittent, choppy," was no part of her theory of acting but was "simply slovenliness," after which she confessed that: "For years I had no appreciation whatever of the importance of careful speech. Only of recent years, after some preliminary lessons given to me by Victor Maurel, have I learned to use my voice." [18] Evidently, then, Mrs. Fiske improved her manner of delivering lines in the later years of her career, and yet her elocution continued to be a subject of debate and analysis among her critics.

One trait of Mrs. Fiske's acting, on which all observers agreed, was its naturalness. In her very first roles she was praised for being simple, charming, and *true to life*. During all of her subsequent career she was admired for the "unstudied" realism of her style. Clara Morris had been praised for naturalness, too, but hers was a different kind from Mrs. Fiske's. Miss Morris displayed raw emotionalism, untouched by poetic elevation. Her strong physical displays heightened the effect of the late nineteenth century French drama, a drama which seemed realistic compared to the earlier melodrama of Victor Hugo, Sheridan Knowles, and Bulwer-Lytton, but which appeared sensational and artificial beside the plays of Henrik Ibsen. Mrs. Fiske acted the realistic plays of Ibsen in a simple, repressed style, and this manner seemed far more true to life than that of Clara Morris or any other actress of the time.

An outstanding example of the Fiske realism, both in acting and staging was found in her production of *Salvation Nell*. This play, produced in 1908, depicted a Salvation Army lass working among the barrooms and tenements of the New York slums. The sordid side of life was revealed so faithfully and daringly in the acting, situations, and setting, that the country was shocked. A Chicago newspaper expressed the general reaction in these terms: "Here is a frankness that sets aside the conventional code of theatrical propriety in characterizing fallen women and drunken brutes; audacity that makes a veritable panorama of debauchery and poverty."

The realism of Mrs. Fiske's acting was based on ideals which are distinctly modern. The plays she produced had to pass the test of truthfulness and reality. Of every situation she asked the questions: "Is it true? Do people do this?" She said she could not interpret a character or read a line unless both were convincing and life-like. "I've tried to play 'Frou-Frou,' " she once told a reporter, "but unsuccessfully, because in analysis the fabric of the character failed; I felt as if I were speaking lies." [19] George Arliss tells us that her constant warning to her fellow actors was, "Keep it true—keep it true." [20]

In preparing a role, Mrs. Fiske first of all analyzed her part thoroughly and discovered the psychological and emotional make-up of the character. She then worked slowly and carefully to identify herself imaginatively with the personality she had conceived. Concerning her method she once said: "For months before I attempt even to rehearse a part, and many weeks before I begin to study the words assigned to me to say, I am imagining myself to be the character to be assumed. Eating, reading, walking up and down the stairs even, I am Becky or Tess as the case may be." [21] On one occasion, in preparing the role of Hedda Gabler, she locked her cousin, Emily Stevens, out in the cold while she recreated a scene between Hedda and Lovborg, and later, when Emily expressed astonishment over the fact that the scene was not in the play—having been imaginatively conjured up by Mrs. Fiske, the older actress answered: "Ibsen shows us only the last hours. To portray them I must know everything that has gone before. . . . I must know all that Hedda ever was. When I do, the role will play itself." [22] On another occasion she said that modern acting, such as hers, aimed "to penetrate deeper and deeper into human consciousness." [23]

Whether Mrs. Fiske ever succeeded in penetrating into the human consciousness of her characters and creating the illusion of separate personalities, is a matter of sharp dispute. For each observer who said she did, another observer declares she did not. Many reviews praise her for displaying versatility in a wide range of parts, while just as many claim she was always herself and never acted any role but that of Minnie Maddern Fiske. John R. Towse wrote: "In all her 'creations' she has presented her own identity without any substantial modification of speech, gesture, look, or manner." [24] On the other hand, Walter Prichard Eaton said "her sympathy with every part she plays seems so great" that in each different role he felt "strongly the sense of true impersonation." [25] The truth of the matter seems to be that Mrs.

Fiske's vivid personality and individual style were apparent in all her creations. She did act a variety of roles and each one of them was built around a different conception, and yet in her embodiment of these different conceptions her own personality and style were always apparent. Those spectators who grasped the differing conceptions felt that Mrs. Fiske was versatile; those who observed only the style of rendering the conceptions claimed that her roles were undifferentiated. Probably neither observer was entirely right and neither was entirely wrong. Mrs. Fiske herself came close to explaining the puzzle when she said, "Indeed, the greatest actors have, in a sense, always played themselves. When I remember Duse . . . I cannot think of her variations. I think only of the essential thing, the style, the quality, that was Duse." [26]

Mrs. Fiske exerted strong influence on the stage, not only as an actress, but also as a manager and a stage director. As a manager she fought the theatrical syndicate, encouraging other actors and managers to be independent, and helped to loosen the stranglehold of the syndicate's monopoly. As a stage director she adopted many of the practices of the modern régisseur. She tried to develop expert ensemble playing in which small parts were as well acted as the large parts, and in which each actor served the overall design of the play. She believed in giving special attention to the weaker sections of the play so that the whole drama would be strengthened. She announced that the aim of a production should be "perfect harmony . . . one on a par with the performance of a well balanced orchestra." [27] As the leading actress she did not care whether her own part had two lines or many hundreds, and she willingly subordinated herself when she felt that a scene demanded it. George Arliss reports that when he acted with her in the cast of *Leah Kleschna,* "Our greatest difficulty . . . was to prevent her effacing herself." [28] In order to realize better her artistic ideal of expert ensemble playing, Mrs. Fiske organized her Manhattan Company as a permanent troupe, and in its heyday the company was declared, somewhat extravagantly, to be "in every respect equal to the ensemble of the Comédie-Française." [29]

In directing her actors, Mrs. Fiske worked tirelessly to develop their awareness of psychological truth. She demanded that her players have a reason for every movement they made and for every speech they uttered. In rehearsals she carefully explained the circumstances of each scene, the state of mind of each character, and then the company worked out the business which seemed logical and appropriate for the scene. Once the action and the details were decided on, they were rehearsed until they fitted perfectly into the smooth flow of the drama. Mrs. Fiske's advice to her company was: "Take plenty of time. Don't hurry. Tremendous situations, wonderful emotions, great events do not rush. They are like the mills of the Gods, grinding slowly but exceedingly small." [30] That Mrs. Fiske practiced what she preached is indicated by the testimony of Beatrice Sturges who, after watching her direct a rehearsal, wrote: "Nothing is too small for the eye and the attention of Mrs. Fiske—whether it be the gesture of an actor, a detail in stage setting or lighting, a tone of voice, or a strain of music—and it is her watchful care and artistic sense that have made her company a model one to see." [31] Mrs. Fiske even worried about how the ushers in the front of the house performed their tasks. The morning after a strenuous opening night in Kansas City, a newspaper reporter visited the Shubert Theatre and was astonished to find Mrs. Fiske busy drilling a squad of ushers. In answer to his startled question she replied, ". . . I find that I can neglect nothing. I have to give much thought to the details of establishing the correct relationship between the stage and the auditorium." [32]

Mrs. Fiske's artistic ideals and her style of acting were necessary correlaries of the kind of plays she preferred to produce. Her tastes and convictions led her to one kind of drama and, in turn, the successful staging of this genre inevitably influenced her methods and her style. While Clara Morris, Fanny Davenport, and Mrs. Leslie Carter were titillating their audiences with the emotional dramas of such playwrights as Sardou, Dumas, Feuillet, Daly, and Belasco, Mrs. Fiske was introducing the United States to Ibsen's *Doll's House, Hedda Gabler, Pillars of Soceity, Rosmersholm,* etc., and praising these plays not only for their substance and truth but also for their drawing power. "Our finest plays," she said, "have always, with one exception, been the ones that made the most money." [33] At the same time, Mrs. Fiske was searching for plays which portrayed the lives and problems of ordinary American citizens. In her speech to the Harvard Ethical Society in 1905 she indicated her dramatic preferences when she said: "Today we live in a practical age. . . . From great general principles the drama is coming down to specific incidents in life, and there are arising masters of the craft who can make the details of existence, even the homely or sinister details, suggestive and instructive. From grand reaches and highly colored and heroic figures, we have been brought to the basis of everyday problems. . . . I confess that my own interest is more definitely enlisted by the modern drama." [34] Some years later, in a speech prepared for the Society of American Dramatists and Composers, she reiterated her beliefs when she said: "I am one with the modern American theatre in its fresh themes from our daily lives, freshly treated." [35] Mrs. Fiske's search for dramas of this kind was rewarded only occasionally when she found such plays as *Salvation Nell* by Edward Sheldon, or *Mrs. Bumstead-Leigh,* by Harry James Smith. At other times she was forced to act in foreign importations like Sardou's *Divorçons* or Meilhac and Halevy's *Frou-Frou,* while two of her most successful vehicles were the plays based on Hardy's *Tess of the D'Urbervilles* and Thackeray's *Vanity Fair.* Still, her preference for the dramas of Ibsen, and for their American counterparts, was strong, and this preference had a profound influence on the style of her productions and her own style of acting. These, in turn, had a significant influence on the American theatre of the twentieth century.

While she was alive, critics found it hard to estimate the stature of Mrs. Fiske. Some declared that she was a great actress who could vivify a dramatization of the telephone directory, while others believed that her achievements were in no way extraordinary. The very diversity of opinion she created indicates the vividness of her personality, and, perhaps, the originality of her methods. The least that can be said of her is that she was an accomplished actress with a strong personality who occasionally achieved moments of greatness; that she illustrated in both her acting and directing many ideals and techniques which are still dominant; and that, as a player, manager, and régisseur, she was a pioneer who helped to establish a modern style of acting which has exerted considerable influence on the stage history of our time. Many of the players who have followed her, and whose performances can be seen today on the stages, in the movie houses, and on the television screens of the nation, are largely inheritors and adaptors of a style of acting perfected many years ago by Mrs. Fiske.

[NOTS O N A NEW SETTING]

The Twentieth Century

IN GENERAL, THE AMERICAN THEATRE AT THE ONSET OF the twentieth century was sterile, stereotyped, and commercialized, despite the efforts of such a pioneer as Mrs. Fiske. It clung to traditions and practices which had produced great theatre in the nineteenth century but which failed to provide inspiration and creativity for the twentieth. The time had come for rejuvenation and change. Every other aspect of American life was feeling the burgeoning influences of the new century. Now the legitimate theatre was to undergo a renaissance in playwriting, architecture, stagecraft, acting, and public enthusiasm. It was to be transformed into a revitalized force in American life. But it was also, alas, to meet such competition from the motion picture—and eventually from radio and television—that its new enthusiasm and creativity were to flower for a brief period only.

The influences which transformed the American theatre in the early years of the twentieth century were varied, and they came both from Europe and from the United States itself. The most powerful of these influences emanated from four great European dramatists: Henrik Ibsen, August Strindberg, Anton Chekhov, and George Bernard Shaw. These giants revolutionized the writing of plays. They discarded every stale convention of nineteenth-century dramaturgy and opened up unexplored fields of subject matter and technique. They taught their contemporaries new ways to construct a play, new truthfulness in character portrayal, new realism in action and dialogue, and new approaches to the problems of modern society. They freed their fellow dramatists from the clichés of melodrama and sentimentality, and introduced a whole new world of formerly forbidden subject matter dealing with social, economic, and moral problems. Their influence penetrated every nation of the western world and had profound effect upon American playwriting.

These pioneer playwrights—Ibsen, Strindberg, Chekhov, and Shaw —were writing startling new realistic plays long before there were directors and audiences to appreciate them. If the influence of these dramatists was to be felt, their plays had to be produced and understood. In every country, there was a response to this need. Starting in Paris with the Théâtre Libre of André Antoine, the idea of free theatres to introduce new playwrights and to experiment with new methods of production spread from country to country like a chain reaction.

Antoine opened his theatre in the spring of 1887 and for ten years presented to private audiences the revolutionary new works of dramatists who could not get a hearing elsewhere. It is interesting to note that while Antoine was introducing the problem plays of Ibsen, Strindberg, and Tolstoi to French audiences, the biggest hits on the American stage were those marvelously contrived and wholly artificial melodramas, *Hazel Kirke* and *Shenandoah*.

Other countries soon followed the lead of André Antoine. In Germany, the Freie Buhne, under the direction of Otto Brahm, opened with a performance of Ibsen's then-shocking drama, *Ghosts,* and within a month produced the first play of Gerhart Hauptmann, the dramatist who was to dominate German playwriting for a generation. In London, J. T. Grien launched the Independent Theatre Society with a production of *Ghosts* and soon thereafter presented a play entitled *Widowers' Houses* by a new playwright named George Bernard Shaw. In Moscow, seven years later, Constantin Stanislavsky and Vladimir Nemirovich-Danchenko founded the Moscow Art Theatre, which nurtured the playwriting of Tolstoi, Chekhov, and Gorky, and which evolved a method of acting soon to exert a noticeable influence on American performers. At about the same time, the Irish Literary Theatre was founded by William Butler Yeats and Lady Gregory for the purpose of inspiring the writing of Irish poetic drama. The results of the movement were the establishment of the Abbey Theatre Company and the encouragement of several gifted Irish playwrights.

The impulse toward revitalization of the theatre next reshaped the architecture of the playhouse and the art of stagecraft. Toward the end of the nineteenth century, Richard Wagner built his first festival theatre in Bayreuth, which rejected the pit, boxes, and galleries of the Restoration theatre and, instead, placed all the seats on a single floor which sloped up sharply from the stage. Shortly after the turn of the century, Max Littmann, Europe's leading theatre architect, copied this plan for the Munich Art Theatre. From these two buildings spread the influences which eventually transformed the playhouses of Germany and America—and other western nations—into auditoriums which, as Sheldon Cheney writes, were "so democratic that practically every spectator could see the stage." [1]

The revolution in stagecraft was even more startling. It was fomented principally by two men: Gordon Craig, an Englishman, and Adolphe Appia, a Swiss. They rejected not only the two-dimensional reality of nineteenth-century scenery and lighting, but also the detailed, authentic realism of David Belasco. Instead they advocated a noble simplicity which related the three-dimensional actor to the surrounding three-dimensional scenery by means of "living light," light which changed from moment to moment as the mood and action of the play changed from scene to scene. Neither Appia nor Craig believed that the setting should be an end in itself, designed to create a spectacle and to delight the eye of the spectator. They believed, instead, that the scenery and lighting were means to an end: through simplification, suggestion, and synthesis they helped to reveal the truth and beauty of the drama. The "New Stagecraft," as the movement founded by Appia and Craig was called—inspired innovations in lighting, stage machinery, and every aspect of scene design. The movement also inspired a brilliant corps of American designers—Norman Bel Geddes, Robert Edmund Jones, Cleon Throckmorton, Lee Simonson, Donald Oenslager, and Jo Mielziner—who were to give to the American theatre the finest stagecraft it has ever enjoyed.

The influences emanating from Europe were important in revitalizing the theatre in the United States. But also many American men and women were reacting independently to the need for change and reform and were making independent contributions. Mrs. Fiske evolved a theory and style of acting which paralleled the Stanislavsky method and which antedated it by several years. A group of wealthy New Yorkers established and financed the New Theatre in New York City in the hopes that it would become a national repertory company. The project failed, but it contributed to the movement toward reform and rejuvenation.

Many other American influences shaped and stimulated the theatrical renaissance. In 1910, the Drama League of America was founded with the aim of establishing study groups all over the nation where citizens could develop an appreciation for good drama and through which they could exert pressure for better plays and productions. The universities, led by Professor George Pierce Baker of Harvard, began to accept the study of theatre arts as a discipline in their curricula. Professor Baker's class in playwriting, English 47, encouraged the work of such dramatists as Eugene O'Neill, S. N. Behrman, Sidney Howard, Philip Barry, and Percy MacKaye, while Professor Baker's 47 Workshop, which produced the student-written plays, provided training and inspiration for a host of American theatrical leaders including Winthrop Ames, Sam Hume, Irving Pichel, Theresa Helburn, John Mason Brown, Kenneth Macgowan, Osgood Perkins, Lee Simonson, and many others. Percy MacKaye, the son of Steele MacKaye, led the movement to establish civic theatres throughout the nation where large numbers of citizens could join together in creative theatrical enterprises. MacKaye's fervent essays on the subject of community drama, as well as the impressive pageant plays which he wrote and produced, stimulated activity in many communities. But even more successful was the movement to establish Little Theatres throughout the nation. In Europe the "free" threatres provided a show place for the work of the new dramatists whose plays were rejected by the censors and the commercial producers. In America, the Little Theatres became the outlet for these plays, and they also provided a laboratory and training ground for directors, actors, designers, and technicians of all kinds. The Little Theatre movement, begun in 1912 in Boston, Chicago, and New York, spread with astonishing rapidity and soon blanketed the nation with earnest, energetic producing units. In the 1920's Kenneth Macgowan found that there were literally thousands of active Little Theatres in the country. Four of the earliest of these, all launched in 1915, deserve special mention because they made unusual contributions to the theatrical renaissance in America.

Stuart Walker's Portmanteau Theatre toured the country for several years bringing new plays imaginatively mounted to thousands of children and adults. The Neighborhood Playhouse, of New York City, organized the community of the lower East Side into a theatrical group that produced dozens of plays, dance festivals, revues, concerts, and even motion pictures—and continues to exert an influence on the American theatre through the surviving Neighborhood School of the Theatre. The Washington Square Players of New York, during the four years of its active life, introduced such new dramatists as Philip Moeller and Zoe Atkins; gave the designer, Lee Simonson, his first opportunity; provided training and experience for such talented players as Roland Young, Katharine Cornell, Frank Conroy, and Glenn Hunter; and furnished the inspiration for the establishment, in 1919, of one of America's primary producing organizations, the famed Theatre Guild.

Perhaps best remembered of these four influential organizations is the Provincetown Players. This group gained immortality by giving Eugene O'Neill his first hearing and by nurturing him until he was firmly established as America's most important playwright. The organization—representing young writers and artists who were stirred by the intellectual ferment of the early twentieth century—was founded in Provincetown, Massachusets, but after two seasons there moved to Macdougal Street in Greenwich Village. Here the group helped to train and inspire a large number of talented people. Among the individuals who claimed membership in the organization were Floyd Dell, Edna St. Vincent Millay, Lawrence Langer, Jasper Deeter, Walter Houston, Cleon Throckmorton, and many others. However, Eugene O'Neill, America's first playwright of worldwide importance—remains the greatest name associated with the Provincetown Players.

In addition to the organized groups in towns and cities, there were individual pioneers—sometimes inspired by the example of the groups and sometimes completely independent—whose names stand out as leaders in the theatrical renaissance. Sam Hume is one of these. A native Californian, he studied with Gordon Craig in Italy, then returned to the United States to help introduce the New Stagecraft to America and to introduce, also, Craig's radical new ideas on the purpose and possibilities of theatrical art. Another pioneer was Sheldon Cheney, also a Californian, who founded the magazine *Theatre Arts* in 1916 and made it the leading theatrical publication for many years, one which helped to raise the artistic and intellectual standards of the entire American theatre. Still other representative pioneers were Frederic McConnell, who built the Cleveland Playhouse into a great noncommercial theatre, and Gilmor Brown, who guided the Pasadena Community Playhouse to prosperity and to worldwide recognition.

For a few brief years the American theatrical renaissance bloomed and flourished. The influences from abroad and the groups and individuals at home combined to revitalize and reshape every aspect of the living theatre. When the renaissance had spent its force, all the outmoded traditions and practices of the nineteenth century had been swept away, and in their place were new inspiration, new ideals, new concepts, and a new technology. Playwrights now probed every problem of the individual and society, creating new form and structure for their works and experimenting with every kind of technique which might truthfully and dramatically communicate their ideas. Architects redesigned the playhouse giving it new beauty, new comfort, and a flexibility of shape which enabled directors to experiment with many different modes of presentation. Designers invented new machines and techniques, and with them created visual beauty which aided the director and strengthened the impact of the play. Audiences were awakened to the significance of drama as a means of interpreting modern life, and which could, at the same time, provide both entertainment and satisfying aesthetic experience.

Even more powerful influences in re-shaping the total world of the theatre in the twentieth century were the motion picture, radio, and television—those mechanical marvels so typical of the inventive genius of the new century. The early twentieth century not only saw the living stage revitalized, it saw the creation of a fabulous new kind of popular theatre.

ORIGIN AND DEVELOPMENT OF THE MOTION PICTURE

On April 14, 1894, in a phonograph parlor located at 1155 Broadway, New York City, occurred an event which had a profound effect upon the theatre and, indeed, upon the world in general. On that date Thomas A. Edison's "kinetoscope" was first offered to public view. It was a peephole box containing a spool of pictures photographed on George Eastman's new flexible film. When a spectator dropped a coin in a slot, turned a crank, and glued his eyes to the peephole, the spool of pictures revolved and created the illusion of motion. Thus the first moving pictures came to America and opened a fabulous new era in public entertainment.

Edison's invention was the culmination of a series of discoveries which had begun centuries before. As far back as the time of ancient Egypt, men had noticed the phenomenon of the persistence of vision, that is, the phenomenon of the "after image." They discovered that if a series of pictures is passed before the eye, the image of one picture lingers on the retina of the eye and seems to merge with the image of the succeeding picture. If the pictures represent a sequence of motion and if they pass before the eye at a considerable speed, the illusion of continuous motion is created. Centuries after this phenomenon was first noted, Leonardo da Vinci discovered the principle of the "camera obscura" and, following this, curious men in several countries tinkered with machines which combined a series of photographs with a device for rotating them to create the illusion of motion. In the nineteenth century several such devices were invented. In England, in 1833, one of these devices was called "The Wheel of Life." It comprised a hollow cylinder with pictures pasted inside which could be viewed through slits in the upper part of the cylinder. As the device revolved, the viewers saw a succession of images which seemed to be in motion. Other inventions of a similar nature were called, variously, an "auto-scope," a "motorscope," a "vibroscope," etc., but were regarded as toys rather than steps in the evolution of an important invention.

Pioneers in many parts of the world contributed improvements to the existing devices. The final step in the creation of the motion picture is generally credited to Thomas A. Edison who, in an effort to provide a visual accompaniment to his phonograph, experimented with pictures recorded in spirals on a cylinder. These first efforts were unsatisfactory, but when flexible photographic film was placed on the market by George Eastman, Edison found the material he needed and proceeded to build his first peephole moving picture machine, the kinetoscope. Later, the principle of the magic lantern was applied to the peephole pictures of the kinetoscope and when Thomas Armat's successful projector was finally combined with Edison's kinetoscope, a new machine, the vitascope, was born. It was capable of projecting a series of photographs or moving pictures to a whole group of people assembled as an audience. The vitascope made its appearance just two years after the debut of the kinetoscope and entranced an audience which had assembled to see a vaudeville show at Koster and Bial's Music Hall in New York City.

With the invention of the kinetoscope and the vitascope, the dazzling, incredible career of motion pictures was launched. Here was a new form of popular theatre with a kind of magic and a style of acting destined to win the devotion of millions of people—and destined, also, to inflict an almost mortal injury on the legitimate stage. Here was a new medium of mass entertainment capable of attracting audiences on a scale undreamed of in the nineteenth century and destined to flourish prodigiously for fifty years—until it received from a younger competitor, television, the same kind of grievous injury the legitimate stage had suffered. But before the movies faced the competition of television, they achieved a success and an artistic individuality which added richly to the history of American acting.

During the nineteenth century, as we have seen, the popular theatre consisted of the sprightly, motley offerings of vaudeville, burlesque, minstrelsy, circus, and related entertainments. They developed in the fast growing cities of America and were nourished by the polyglot populations who, speaking a babel of tongues, were unable to understand clearly or to appreciate fully the offerings of legitimate drama. Such audiences nevertheless needed the relaxation and recreation which theatre can give. Vaudeville and its fellow entertainments reached, at the most, a modest ten to twenty per cent of the population. A less expensive, more available, and even more understandable form of theatre was needed for the remaining eighty per cent. The motion picture came as a boon and a salvation to this gigantic group.

Once invented, vitascope booths began to appear in penny arcades throughout the nation. They stimulated curiosity, they attracted attention, and soon they became so popular that the other attractions of the arcade were abandoned and the whole establishment was turned into a vitascope parlor. The booths or parlors were located in the most congested areas of the big cities and were open continuously from early morning until late at night. For the small sum of ten cents anyone could purchase admission and could lose himself in the marvel of pictures which moved—and which soon began to tell stories, to report news events, and to depict the exotic beauties of foreign lands. These pictures on the screen did not require a knowledge of the English language in order to be understood. They were silent and communicated their meaning through visual representation which everyone could grasp. If occasionally there was a subtitle in English it did not detract from the visual enjoyment and might even be an advantage because it could be used by the growing immigrant population as a simple aid to learning the language. The admission price of ten cents was not excessive but, to make the appeal of the movies even wider, this price was soon dropped to five cents.

In 1905, John P. Harris and Harry Davis remodeled a storeroom in McKeesport, Pennsylvania, installed ninety-two seats and a piano, and announced their theatre as a "nickelodeon," admission to which was only five cents. Their first attraction was *The Great Train Robbery,* produced in 1903 by an Edison cameraman, and later credited with establishing the art of narration on the screen. So popular was the nickelodeon and so fascinating was a story picture like *The Great Train Robbery* that similar movie houses showing similar thrillers sprang up everywhere. Within four years there were at least 8,000 nickelodeons in the United States.

One influential factor in the shaping of film fare has already been implied: the majority of the audience was polyglot, poorly educated, and working-class. Another, equally influential factor was the canny, small businessman promoter, who perceived the possibilities of the new medium and who devoted his life to establishing and building the motion picture industry. In general, the stars, managers, and directors of the stage were not interested. Leaders in the fields of art and entertainment, captains of finance, and the educated classes in general all ignored the new invention. Most of them thought it was cheap and tawdry, unworthy of their attention. They saw it as a passing fad which offered no real threat to the established theatre and no real opportunity for financial exploitation. As late as 1915, Daniel Frohman, a leading producer of legitimate plays, declared: "As for the motion picture being a menace to the theatre . . . that is manifestly impossible. . . . As long as civilization endures, the stage will form one of its chief sources of amusement. . . ." [2]

The men who perceived the potential of the movies and who risked their careers to exploit it were a strange but remarkable group. For example, one of them was a cowboy, Thomas Tally, whose imagination was so aroused when he saw his first motion picture that he sold his horse and invested the money in a vitascope booth. He pioneered in building public confidence and educating his audiences to the wonders of the motion picture. Even more influential were men like Carl

Laemmle, Adolph Zukor, Marcus Loew, and William Fox, who forsook their positions in business to gamble on careers in the motion picture. Carl Laemmle, for example, was a Bavarian immigrant who worked many years in a Wisconsin clothing store, scrimping and hoarding in order to amass enough money to start his own establishment. When he had made his stake, he traveled to Chicago in search of a suitable location. In the course of roaming the city, he ran across one of the new vitascope booths. Fascinated, he watched a steady queue of customers come and go in what seemed a never-ending stream. When he inquired into the finances of the operation, he discovered that a man could make as much money from the movies in one month as he had been able to save during twenty years of labor in the clothing business. He immediately abandoned his plan to open a store and, instead, began a career which made him a leader in the motion picture industry.

The movie industry, from the very start of its career, grew and flourished without the leadership of people experienced in the ways of the legitimate theatre. A few of the early actors, directors, and producers had some stage experience but, in general, the founders of the movie industry were true pioneers. They came without preconceived notions or past experience in the field of entertainment and they worked with a brand new medium. Also, it should be pointed out, their aim was a practical one, namely, to make as much money as possible by giving the public the kind of entertainment that pleased it most. Such conditions for development offered decided advantages—and serious disadvantages. Producers and directors were not hampered by a commitment to traditional ideas and practices but often they were uncommitted to artistic ideals either.

POPULARITY OF SILENT MOVIES

There quickly developed an enormous demand for motion pictures. Millions of ordinary people, hungry for entertainment and escape, flocked to the films. Vitascope booths flourished and became nickelodeons. Nickelodeons multiplied and became movie theatres. Movie theatres waxed rich and became Palaces of the Cinema. In 1914, the Strand Theatre in New York, boasting 3,300 seats and an orchestra of thirty pieces, opened its doors and welcomed an audience of 40,000 during a single week. At the same time, D. W. Griffith's masterpiece, *The Birth of a Nation,* was sweeping the country, playing to audiences which paid as much as two dollars for admission. Between 1915 and 1929, this picture earned $18,000,000 and many subsequent films were similarly lucrative. By 1916, there were 28,000 movie theatres in the United States.

During the early years of the motion picture, the legitimate theatre continued to hold an audience and so did vaudeville, burlesque, and the circus. But as more and more movie palaces opened, and as film idols like Douglas Fairbanks, Mary Pickford, and Charles Chaplin produced better and better films, the living theatre started to feel the competition. Instead of growing with the nation, it began to decline and shrink—but it was unaware of how great the shrinkage was destined to be.

RADIO AND TALKING PICTURES

In the early 1920's, the motion picture industry experienced its first serious competition. Radio broadcasting became widespread and popular. There had been broadcasting as early as 1909 when a pioneer station in San Jose, California, station SJN, began to transmit regular programs of spoken announcements and phonograph music. However, it was not until after 1920 that broadcasting began to flourish on a grand scale. It grew fantastically and soon blanketed the nation with a network of stations transmitting an infinite variety of programs in hectic, round-the-clock fashion. It is estimated that by 1939, there were at least 43,000,000 radio sets in operation.

In the mid-1920's, the movies began to feel this competition. Film fans deserted the neighborhood cinema in order to listen to their favorite broadcasts. In alarm, the movies offered door prizes, vaudeville acts, live orchestras, and all manner of enticements. But the public remained at home, enchanted with the free entertainment offered in its own living rooms. Then Warner Brothers, one of the major film producers in Hollywood, introduced talking pictures in the fall of 1927, and the film industry quickly recovered its audience.

Talking pictures became enormously popular. They also dealt the coup de grace to vaudeville, which had been declining for some time, and caused further shrinkage in the legitimate theatre. The drawing power of talking pictures continued well into the years of the great depression. Even during this time of financial panic, when other forms of entertainment collapsed, the motion pictures continued to attract customers. Eventually the movies felt the effect of the depression—but not for long. Toward the end of the 1930's, war in Europe and the preparation for war by the United States created a new boom in Hollywood. With movie production suspended in most foreign countries, the demand for American films increased. With almost every citizen employed in the armed forces or in war production everyone had money and everyone, servicemen and civilians alike, felt the need for entertainment. American movies prospered fantastically, turning out over four hundred films per year—some of them in color, an innovation which had appeared in the late 1930's. In 1947, motion pictures attracted an estimated weekly audience of 90,000,000 people.

TELEVISION

The movie boom ended with the advent of television—and motion pictures began to suffer the same fate it had dealt the legitimate theatre. Experimentation with television, which had begun before the Second World War, was suspended during the conflict, but as early as 1945— with the war barely ended—television sets began to appear in the United States. By 1948, there were forty-eight T.V. stations in twenty-five cities sending programs to more than 700,000 receiving sets. A year later, there were seventy stations and 2,000,000 sets in operation —and the numbers continued to increase by leaps and bounds. By 1958, the sending stations totaled 512 and the receiving sets, 50,-000,000. A year later the television industry claimed that eighty-five per cent of the people of the United States were watching television.

The impact on the movies of this tremendous growth was cataclysmic. Spectators by the millions deserted the cinema and stayed home to watch "the big eye." Customers who for years had regularly attended the movies once or twice a week stopped abruptly. From an estimated weekly attendance of 90,000,000 in 1947, the figure dropped to 28,000,000 in 1957. In 1947, gross receipts had been $1,565,000,000; in 1956, they shrank to $1,185,100,000. In 1945 there had been 20,355 movie theatres in the United States. Ten years later, 6,000 of them had closed. In panic, film producers tried to stem the tide. They introduced wide screens, three-dimensional effects, stereophonic sound systems, and epic spectacles—in the hope of luring customers back to the movie houses. But the enticement of free motion pictures—however old or distorted on a T.V. screen—and the lure of occasional "live" programs—however cheap or heavily burdened with commercials—were far too great to be resisted. The shrinkage of movie audiences went on and continues to do so. Patronage decreases year by year and so does the number of films produced in Hollywood. In 1941, the number reached an all-time high of 497. In 1959 only 224 films were made.

Television had a different effect upon radio. It altered the kind of programs produced and virtually destroyed the national networks, but it did not eliminate the medium. Instead, the coming of national television gave a tremendous boost to local radio stations specializing in recorded music, in local news and sports, and particularly local advertising. In 1962, home viewers were likely to watch the national network television programs but they listened to the local, independent radio station. Since 1948, the first big year for television, the number of AM and FM radio stations has more than doubled. Now there are over 3,000 of them broadcasting programs to at least 90,000,000 home receiving sets and 40,000,000 car sets.

THE DECLINE OF THE LEGITIMATE PROFESSIONAL THEATRE

The early years of the twentieth century were years of international ferment and rejuvenation for the living stage. For a time, as was noted above, the American theatre was more vital and creative than it had been in many decades. Then, in the midst of prosperity came competition, and shortly thereafter came nation-wide financial depression. During the 1920's the popularity of the motion pictures and radio caused the closing of hundreds of theatres and stock companies throughout the nation, although the Broadway stage continued to prosper. At the end of the decade, the financial panic and ensuing depression speeded the decline which had already begun. Many more theatres closed, production on Broadway shrank alarmingly, and hundreds of actors were thrown out of work. The legitimate, professional theatre suffered a reversal of fortune from which it has never recovered.

The disastrous years of the 1930's were relieved by several significant developments in dramatic affairs, the two most important of which were the establishment of the Federal Theatre by the national government and the organization of the Group Theatre by a band of dedicated young actors and directors.

The first of these developments, the Federal Theatre, provides an unusual chapter in the annals of the American stage. It is the only example of a Federal program devoted solely to the theatre. The project was not motivated by concern for the arts but, rather, by concern for the unemployed artists of the theatre. It was launched in 1935 as a division of the gigantic make-work program of the Works Progress Administration, and was an ambitious undertaking which aimed to give employment to as many theatre workers as possible. The nation was organized into regions and producing units were established in each region. Within a year there were active groups operating in thirty-one states and the District of Columbia, employing more than 12,000 actors, directors, writers, technicians, and theatre people of all kinds. The undertaking was harried by many troubles: red-tape, confusion, quarreling, hurt feelings, and charges of subversion. Yet the project, under the overall direction of Mrs. Hallie Flanagan, managed to grow and flourish and to accomplish its major objective. During the four years of its existence, before it was abolished by Congress on the charge of subversion, it provided employment and creative opportunities for thousands of theatrical workers. Among its productions were not only hundreds of regular stage plays but also pageants, ballets, musical comedies, operas, puppet shows, radio plays, vaudeville, revues, and even a circus. No definable style of acting developed from all this activity, but hundreds of performers were enabled to practice their art and develop their technique through the opportunities offered by the project. At least two of these actors, Orson Welles and John Houseman, used their start in the Federal Theatre to launch their own Mercury Theatre which, for a time, provided some original and exciting productions.

Another significant development of the 1930's, the establishment of the Group Theatre, exerted far more influence on American acting than did the Federal Theatre. In fact, the Group Theatre and its individual members became the principal promoters of the Stanislavsky method of acting in the United States.

The idea of gathering together a company of young actors and directors who could help each other to achieve artistic maturity within a common set of ideals was the brain child of Harold Clurman, an apprentice actor and a play-reader for the Theatre Guild. He propounded his ideas to his fellow workers so persuasively that by the summer of 1931 he had gathered a group of twenty-eight actors and three directors to form a summer colony at Brookfield Center, Connecticut. The colony drew its principal inspiration from the ideals of Stanislavsky and the Moscow Art Theatre, ideals which had been introduced to the United States by the writings of Stanislavsky, by the visit of the Moscow Art Theatre in 1923, and by two noted teachers of the Stanislavsky method, Richard Boleslavsky and Maria Ouspenskaya. The influence which the Stanislavsky-inspired Group Theatre was later to exert on the American stage is indicated by the names found on its original roster. The directors included, besides Clurman himself, Lee Strasberg and Cheryl Crawford. The actors included Elia Kazan, Stella Adler, Clifford Odets, Franchot Tone, Morris Carnovsky, and J. Edward Bromberg. Most of them later became noted exponents or teachers of "Method" acting.

After a summer of study, self-analysis, and rehearsal at Brookfield Center, the Group opened its first production in New York City in September, 1931. The play was Paul Green's *The House of Connelly* and it achieved a run of ninety-one performances after receiving excellent reviews. Then followed three more productions, two of which were failures and one, a moderate success. The financial position of the Group was precarious until it presented Sidney Kingsley's *Men in White,* which proved to be a smashing success. From then until the end of the decade, the Group continued to produce plays and to achieve success in a variety of ways. It discovered that Clifford Odets, one of its apprentice actors, was a gifted playwright and helped him launch his career. It gave a hearing to other serious young playwrights like Paul Green, Irwin Shaw, and William Saroyan. It provided the training which made first-rate actors or directors out of several of its people. And it spread the gospel of Stanislavsky's principles until his method became a major force in American acting. Although the Group ceased its operations in 1941, after ten years of activity, its influence is still felt in the teaching and directing of such men as Kazan, Strasberg, and Clurman.

During the great depression and despite the contributions of the Federal Theatre and the Group Theatre, all the inherent weaknesses and ills of the professional stage were exposed and magnified and the competition from movies and radio was intensified. The effect, which has continued to the present day, is vividly illustrated by the sharp decline in the number of plays produced on Broadway. In the season of 1927–28, there were 280 new productions staged. Twelve years later this number had shrunk to eighty. By 1948–49, it was down to seventy, and by 1963–64 it was only fifty-seven, including musicals and revivals of the classics.

Competition from the mechanical media of entertainment is the main reason for this decline, but there are other important causes which stem from long-standing weaknesses. One of these is the concentration for many decades of professional theatre activity in New York City. Instead of many centers of drama drawing inspiration and nourishment from the varied regions of the United States, there has been, during much of our history, only one center to which all theatre workers have had to gravitate. Plays and performances have had to meet the tastes of a single metropolitan audience and if they did they were then sent on tour to cities all over the United States. Theatrical activity thus has had a narrow base so that when the New York stage suffered so did all the other stages in the nation.

The peculiar economics of professional play production is a factor which discourages experimentation and expansion in New York City and elsewhere. There is little or no public subsidy for professional theatre activity such as there is for playgrounds, beaches, zoos, and baseball parks. Private investors must risk their money to produce a play on Broadway, and they are usually chary of doing so when the chance for profit is small. The cost of staging a play, renting a playhouse, and meeting the demands of the fragmentized theatrical unions is so staggering that only smash hits can return a profit. The play with a moderate appeal which might enjoy a moderate run cannot hope to pay its way. Thus, fewer and fewer professional plays are presented.

Broadway playwrights complain that the fate of their work is in the hands of a few supercilious professional critics. Playgoers themselves are not allowed to judge the merits of a production but must accept the verdict of a dozen men who arbitrarily mete out life or death sentences to each theatrical offering. Is it any wonder, asks the playwright, that professional play production is a discouraging enterprise?

The professional actor has for many years faced an equally unpromising situation. Only Hollywood or New York has offered him much chance for employment and often an appearance on Broadway has been the best entree to Hollywood. Thus many players have flocked to Broadway where they have found no stock companies or repertory companies to give them experience. Only a handful of plays which promise to be smash hits have been in production. If the novice were lucky enough to secure a part in one of these, he has found himself performing a single small part in a single play for many months or even years. If he wished to get broadening experience he has had to join an acting class or find some other substitute for active participation in living theatre. The obstacles to the achievement of versatility and distinction in acting have been formidable.

The melancholy state of the professional theatre is undeniable. Yet hopeful developments are observable and these offer real promise for the future. For example, because the cost of presenting a play on Broadway is so extortionate, producers who wish to try out experimental or unorthodox plays or who have meager budgets now present these plays *off* Broadway in little theatres or makeshift theatres of various kinds where often rents and production costs are relatively low. In the season of 1956–57, there were 75 productions of this type. In the season of 1962–63, the number had grown to 117, if productions of the ANTA Matinee Theatre, the Equity Library Theatre, etc., are included. Many of these Off Broadway productions have offered the kind of original, exciting experimentation which is so necessary if the theatre is to grow and advance, and Off Broadway can point with pride to the development of such creative talents as Edward Albee, Arthur Kopit, and Jose Quintero—to name only three. But, alas, the disease of higher and higher costs has begun to afflict Off Broadway activity as well. Stella Holt, a persistent producer of Off Broadway shows, reports that a production which she staged for $500 in 1953 would today cost her $15,000. "Such economics are murderous," she adds.[3] As a result of these increasing costs, some Off Broadway productions have fled to attics and coffeehouses and to the remotest areas of greater New York, thus creating the phenomenon of "Off Off Broadway" activity.

The continuing growth of summer theatres is another encouraging situation of the present day. Such theatres are firmly established on the east and west coasts and in many cities and vacation colonies in between. Besides offering summer employment to established actors, they provide experience for hundreds of novice players and a stage where new plays can be tested in actual production. They range in emphasis from musical comedy to Shakespeare and offer astonishing variety both in scope and quality. Some of these summer theatres are attempting year-around operations and a few of them are succeeding.

A third hopeful development and one of the most exciting is the revival of interest in community-sponsored repertory theatres. In the early years of the twentieth century, the community theatre movement produced such notable centers as the Dallas Theatre, the Pasadena Playhouse, and the Cleveland Playhouse. The latter, setting a pace for the rest of the nation, "has been overflowing with good productions" for fifty years.[4] After the initial outburst of enthusiasm which produced these playhouses, interest in community theatre declined. It has been vigorously revived in the past few years by the establishment and growth of repertory theatres in widely separated sections of the country. *Life* magazine for February 28, 1964, reports that "Community theatre is growing so explosively that it is almost impossible to tell where Broadway . . . ends and Main Street begins. New drama groups are popping up all over, in superbly equipped theatres as well as makeshift ones. More and more of these companies are using professional actors and directors." On the east coast can be found such repertory theatres as the Charles Playhouse of Boston, the Arena Stage of Washington, D.C., with a handsome total of 11,000 subscribers, the McCarter Theatre of Princeton University, and the much publicized repertory theatre of New York's Lincoln Center. The middle west can boast of not only the famous old Cleveland Playhouse, but of Milwaukee's Fred Miller Theatre; of the Association of Producing Artists, which moved from New York to the University of Michigan; and of Minneapolis' Tyrone Guthrie Theatre which, like some of the other repertory theatres, serves both as a community theatre and also as a laboratory in dramatic art for graduate students of the University of Minnesota. The southern section of the country shows vigorous interest with such centers as Memphis' Front Street Theatre, Houston's Alley Theatre, Oklahoma City's Mummer's Theatre, and Dallas' Theatre Center Group, while the west coast is proud of the Seattle Center Playhouse, the Theatre Group at U.C.L.A., and San Francisco's famous Actors' Workshop.

This list is by no means exhaustive because there are dozens of other repertory groups which are thriving or beginning to thrive or hoping to thrive. The Ford Foundation has been the angel for many of them, having donated $7,000,000 to various repertory theatres in the four years between 1960 and 1964. Help also has come from other foundations and donors, from local governmental agencies, and from loyal subscribers. With adequate support and with the enthusiastic participation of both professional and non-professional artists, the repertory theatres have been so successful that a report in *Time* magazine for February 14, 1964, declares: "Broadway shows are having difficulty finding understudies . . . almost every serious young actor who can walk or crawl has gone off to a repertory company." Certainly here is a development which offers hope that the old, old dream of an American theatre decentralized from Broadway, dispersed over the length and breadth of the land, and drawing inspiration and character from the proudly different regions of the country may, at long last, be on the verge of reality.

Equally encouraging, and often intimately associated with the repertory companies, are the college and university theatres of the nation. Beginning with the pioneer course instituted by George Pierce Baker at Harvard, curricula in theatre have been established in more than three hundred institutions throughout the nation. They offer courses in dramatic history and literature, in playwriting, acting, and every art and craft of the theatre. They encourage the production of new and original plays and they keep alive the classic drama of all nations. Every year they stage hundreds of productions of all kinds which often combine the best professional talent, engaged as "artists in residence," with the most promising university students. Such productions give inspiration and practical experience to neophyte actors and technicians and they introduce dramatic literature to thousands of students and townspeople. They are often housed in the newest and finest theatres of the land. Centers of the performing arts, with a playhouse or playhouses as the heart and center of the complex, are rising on an astonishing number of campuses. For example, the University of California at Berkeley, which has never in its long history had a playhouse or a theatre building, is now spending $7,000,000 for an edifice which will contain a large theatre seating two thousand and a smaller one of great flexibility seating five hundred. Included in the complex are workshops, rehearsal rooms, dressing rooms, storage rooms, broadcast studios, offices, and all the other adjuncts of a major theatrical center. The newest and most experimental features of playhouse architecture are represented in the Berkeley complex, and the same can be said for the numerous other college and university theatres being built all over the nation. In these theatres, also, the newest and most experimental techniques of play production are being tried and tested. In view of this outpouring of enthusiasm, creative energy, and money on the campuses of the United States, many observers believe that the major responsibility for preserving and adding to the great cultural heritage of dramatic art rests jointly with the regional repertory companies and with the colleges and universities of the nation.

X

THE ACTOR IN THE
NEW THEATRE

The events and developments which re-shaped the American theatre of the twentieth century had a striking effect upon the actor and upon his manner of performance. That most revolutionary development, the motion picture, produced a unique style of acting, particularly in silent films, as well as a group of gifted performers who perfected and illustrated the possibilities of the cinematic style.

STYLE OF ACTING IN EARLY MOVIES

In early silent films, two distinct kinds of presentation are evident. One represents the transplanting of stage techniques to the screen. Films of this kind are simply stage plays photographed, like the 1964 production of *Hamlet,* starring Richard Burton, which was photographed on the stage of the Lunt-Fontanne Theatre in New York, then shown in movie houses throughout the nation. An earlier example, less sophisticated but more illustrative of the photographed stage play, is the classic film *Queen Elizabeth,* a four-reel tragedy starring Sarah Bernhardt which was made in France and first shown in the United States in 1912. Throughout this film the camera remains in one position—as though it were a spectator facing a proscenium arch—and all the performers move in and out of the frame. Entrances are made from the back or sides of the setting, and then the actor moves to the center of the picture—just as he would move to the center of the stage in legitimate drama. When a scene terminates, there is no fade-out, no dissolve, and no blending with the ensuing action; the scene simply ends, as though a curtain has been dropped. The camera angle never changes and, of course, there are no closeups. Subtitles are freely used and there is much lip movement as the actor stands and recites his lines, unheard by the audience. The scenes are all interiors and the actors are crowded into the setting, grouped always within a single frame. Movement is subdued, much of the performance is static, and when gestures are made they seem artificial and stagy. *Queen Elizabeth* is simply a stage play recorded on film, without imagination and without awareness of the possibilities of the new medium. This style of presentation disappeared when the pioneers of the motion picture began to discover how to use their cameras and how to direct their actors in performances which pleased the eye and stirred the heart of the spectator.

In the first movies which developed in the direction of true cinematic art, pantomime is the principal means of communication. It is crude, exaggerated, and obvious. If a character wishes to tell another character that he is about to leave a room, he points at himself, then at the door, then at himself again. Eventually he strides to the door, measures its outline, examines its knob, then swings it open with a flourish. No one in the audience, however dim his wit or however poor his command of the English language, can mistake the intention of such an action. But crude pantomime of this sort did not persist. Slowly but surely movie makers discovered the uses of pantomime for comic or emotional effects rather than for simple communication of ideas. As they learned their craft, they found that the intimacy of the camera allowed for pantomime which was even more subtle than stage pantomime. They also discovered the immense advantage of a camera which follows the action rather than remaining stationary. In so early a film as *The Great Train Robbery,* produced in 1903, one can see the beginnings of those techniques which are unique to the motion picture and have no connection with stage plays. In this film, the camera changes position constantly, following the action through a wide variety of indoor and outdoor scenes. The characters of the story do not make entrances into a peephole setting; the camera finds them and follows them into action. Scenes often fade out or blend with succeeding scenes. The whole story is clearly told through visual action and there is no need for subtitles. The movement and gestures of the characters often seem exaggerated but they are subtler than the pantomime in many earlier films.

The motion pictures and the enthusiastic men who produced them progressed and developed with astonishing rapidity. Several of the young directors who began working with the new medium turned out to be men of talent and imagination. By the time that one of these, D. W. Griffith, produced *The Birth of a Nation* in 1912, cinematic art had already discovered its real potential and had established its basic techniques. This film demonstrated magnificent use of devices unique to the motion picture, such as montage, the closeup, fade-outs and dissolves, angle shots, and many other techniques. These, with improvements and refinements, became the basis for the subsequent development of motion pictures.

The style of acting which evolved in motion pictures was shaped by the conditions of motion picture production. These conditions, markedly different from those which surround the performance of the stage actor, create the significant differences between acting for the screen and acting for the stage. Style in motion picture acting can be understood only if these differences are perceived. It should be remembered that stage and screen performers have much in common. The same endowments of body and mind, personality and sensitivity, are important to both—although they may be used in different ways. Many of the same techniques of assimilating character and projecting emotion are used by both—but in different degrees and for different effects. The fact that stage technique is not alien to the movies is shown by the numerous players who learn their art on the legitimate stage and then perform successfully in the motion pictures. Yet there are some significant differences in acting for the stage and acting for the screen which are clearly revealed if we compare the conditions which surround the stage actor with those which surrounded the actor in the silent films before the introduction of sound.

The stage actor performs in a theatre before a live audience; the screen actor performs in a studio or out of doors before a camera and a director. This is an obvious and easily recognized difference—but the consequences are tremendous. A stage actor is confined in space and can be viewed by any one spectator from only a limited range of angles. He must project his voice, his facial expressions, and his movements to the entire audience, from the business executive in the first row of the orchestra, to the student in the last row of the gallery. He must orient his acting in one direction and he must enlarge it so that words, expressions, and movements will carry a considerable distance. If he is performing in a playhouse seating two or three thousand people, his effects must be exaggerated if they are to be effective. In contrast, the film actor is not confined to a single space but may roam the world at will—with the camera following him from any distance and at any angle. The film actor *must not* project his gestures or expressions; the camera will do it for him because it can catch and enlarge the smallest movement or the most subtle change of expression. The camera, with its omnipotent eye, can search out tiny details or minute objects and give them enormous significance. Thus the screen actor can perform with maximum realism; no action or reaction need be faked or simulated. Furthermore, he must perform with restraint and complete naturalness for any exaggeration or artificiality will be enormously enlarged by the camera.

The presence of a live audience has great influence on the stage actor. It stimulates him to develop his personal magnetism and to find a way of projecting it to the spectators. It challenges him, night after night, to establish a rapport with the ever-changing audience he faces. Personal appeal and sensitivity are vital elements in the success of his art. The screen actor, on the other hand, faces only his director and the camera. He performs in isolation for one man and a machine. His personal magnetism can rarely be projected to an audience as a living influence. It may be captured, in part, on film, but more likely it is an effect created by the director through montage and skillful editing, and enhanced by colorful publicity. The stage actor varies his performances to win the response of varying audiences; he is a free agent while the curtain is up and performs his role as his training and inspiration dictate. If the director of the play dislikes the performance, he must wait until the play is over before giving instructions. The film actor has no such freedom. He is almost a puppet in the hands of the director and must shape every movement and expression and gesture to suit the demands of his single spectator. As Mortimer Adler writes, "the actors are technicians to be used by the director for the sake of the work being made. It is his art, not theirs, which must dominate." [1]

The director's artistic dominance is established in many ways. A motion picture is not photographed as a continuous whole but is made in bits and pieces. Final scenes may be shot early and opening scenes may be photographed late, with the intervening scenes recorded in a jumbled sequence which only the director may understand. The actor may know the script as a whole but may be unaware of the position or purpose of individual scenes. He is thus completely dependent on the word of his director and must follow, often blindly, the suggestions given to him.

In the final editing or piecing together of the film, the director, again, is the controlling artist. He can create any effect he desires by joining scenes together in certain sequences. He can make an actor appear effective and powerful or awkward and dull. Many stars of the cinema have been created through ingenious directing and editing; many successful careers have been sustained by artful cutting. The style or effectiveness of any movie actor owes much to the director; it is often, in fact, the creation of the director and not the performer.

The standard method of making films in bits and pieces has another effect on the technique of the performer. He must be able to summon a mood or an emotion instantly, sustain it a few moments for a particular scene, then shift to an unrelated emotion for a succeeding scene. The stage actor, following a coherent script, can develop his emotion logically and gradually as the play develops. He can "warm up" to the big scenes and fit them into a unified pattern of response. In contrast, the movie actor must perform on demand, without warm-up, and in a jumbled sequence which follows no emotional logic. Thus he must be an expert at instant emotional response—or at least the director and editor of the film must arrange the scenes so that the actor *appears* to be projecting the desired emotions.

The differing conditions of performance faced by stage and screen actors produce another result which is both obvious and significant. The stage actor, repeating his performance *in toto* night after night for differing audiences will vary noticeably in style and effectiveness. Some nights his inspiration and vitality will be high; on other nights he may feel tired and depressed. Even on the nights when his inspiration and energy are equally high, his performances will differ because he cannot hope to reproduce, night after night, precisely the same tones, gestures, expressions, and effects. As Lawrence Barrett remarked many years ago, the stage actor is forever carving "statues of snow."

The situation of the screen actor is completely different. He performs only for a director and a camera, and he repeats a scene over and over again. Innumerable shots are taken from which the director finally chooses one which he feels represents the best performance of the particular scene. When this performance is included in the finished picture, it is fixed and unchangeable—a statue in marble—which will remain exactly the same as long as the physical substance of the film endures. The viewing public sees and studies only the unchanging, best single performance of any screen actor in any film.

The biggest difference between silent films and the stage is, of course, the silence. On the stage, voice and delivery are of paramount importance; they are major tools of the actor's art. Without them, half the actor's effectiveness is lost. In the silent film, however, the actor has no voice; delivery is of no consequence. The movie actor's appeal is purely visual. He must rely upon his facial expressions, his gestures, and his movements to communicate the narration as well as the thought and emotion which accompany it. The camera provides such an intimate view of the performer and is so capable of enlarging even fleeting expressions that no exaggeration is needed. In fact, precisely the opposite—subtlety and suppression—are desirable. As Iris Barry writes, "There is an intimacy between the cinema audience and the film actor as great as between any two persons talking face to face." [2]

The absence of sound and the need for subtle but expressive pantomime created an admirable style of acting in the silent movies. It ranged from the hilarious slapstick of the Keystone comedies, through the graceful acrobatics of Douglas Fairbanks, to the expressive art of Charles Chaplin. The best way to study the acting of the silent films is to survey the style and achievements of a few outstanding performers. Four pioneers who deserve mention for their notable contributions to film acting are Mary Pickford, Douglas Fairbanks, William S. Hart, and Charles Chaplin.

Mary Pickford, who earned the title not only of "America's Sweetheart" but "the World's Sweetheart," has been identified with motion pictures for a large part of their history. Born Gladys Mary Smith in Toronto, Canada, in 1893, she was attracted to the stage at an early age. When she was only five years old she made her debut with the Valentine Stock Company of Toronto and after four years of apprenticeship reached stardom—this at the age of nine—in a play called *The Fatal Wedding*. She continued to play leading roles both in Canada and the United States in such formidable favorites as *East Lynne* and *Uncle Tom's Cabin*. Then, in 1907, David Belasco engaged her to create the part of Betty Warren in his production of *The Warrens of Virginia.* At the same time he persuaded her to drop the label of Gladys Smith and adopt a name which had more glamor and appeal.

During all these early years, Miss Pickford, née Smith, enchanted her audience with her elfin, appealing charm. She was a petite youngster with huge, expressive eyes and a mass of golden curls. She could be lively and tomboyish; she could be wistful and tremulous. Her sensitivity to changing moods and her ability to portray them in an unaffected, poignant fashion won the hearts of her theatre audiences— just as they captivated her movie audiences a short time later.

Soon after *The Warrens of Virginia,* Miss Pickford made her first motion picture under the direction of D. W. Griffith at the Biograph Studio—and her career as America's Sweetheart was launched. She returned to the legitimate stage once, to perform a leading role for David Belasco, but after that she concentrated on film acting and achieved a success which may never be duplicated in motion pictures. In three years her salary rose from $40 per week to $2,000 per week plus fifty per cent of the profits of her films. In 1916, when the Mary Pickford Film Corporation was organized, her salary again jumped— to $10,000 per week plus fifty per cent of the net profits. At the time, it was said that she "was receiving the largest salary ever paid to any woman in the world." [3]

During this period, Miss Pickford made films in rapid succession and each film increased her popularity. Such pictures as *Tess of the Storm Country, The Little Princess, The Poor Little Rich Girl, Rebecca of Sunnybrook Farm,* and *The Little American* won overwhelming acclaim for the actress and endeared her to millions of people throughout the entire world. In all these films she played essentially the same character and used the same appeals which had proved successful on the stage. She was always the wholesome child, alternately hoydenish and wistful, who won love and created happiness wherever she went. Like Maude Adams in her prime, Miss Pickford gave her audiences a clean, sweet sense of hope and enjoyment. She fulfilled their dreams of goodness and success. As Elinor Hughes wrote in 1932, she acts "in the sort of plays that appeal to young and old alike —the Cinderella theme predominating, to be sure, but filled with humor, pathos, and plenty of excitement." [4]

To project her appeal, Miss Pickford adapted the style of performing which she had learned on the stage to the requirements of the camera—and quickly became a master of film acting. Her sensitive, expressive face and eyes perfectly mirrored the emotions of the moment. Her movements and gestures, shy and natural as a child's, communicated meaning without the need of subtitles. In her early films —as in most early films—her pantomime was sometimes obvious and exaggerated, but, as the film art developed, Miss Pickford's pantomime became increasingly refined and subtle.

In the early 1920's, after playing children's roles all of her life, Miss Pickford decided to experiment with adult roles to see if her public would accept them. She produced a series of films which included *Rosita, Dorothy Vernon of Haddon Hall,* and *Little Lord Fauntleroy,* in the last of which she played both the mother and the son. These films fell far short of the popularity of her former pictures, so she returned to little girl roles—but only temporarily. Late in the 1920's, talking pictures made their debut and took the country by storm. Miss Pickford decided to cut off her curls, to abandon children's roles for good, and to make her talking debut in the adult role of *Coquette*—a play made famous on the stage by Helen Hayes. The picture won Miss Pickford an Academy Award as the best motion picture actress of the year 1928–29, but it did not attract the popular following which Miss Pickford had come to expect. Following *Coquette* she made a few more films and then quietly retired from the screen to devote herself to civic and business enterprises and to the management of the large fortune she had accumulated. She is still a powerful figure in Hollywood but is best remembered as the sensitive child with the golden curls who mastered the techniques of film acting when the medium was new and who was able to project so appealing an image that she became "the World's Sweetheart."

Closely associated with Mary Pickford in the public mind is another pioneer film idol, Douglas Fairbanks. For fifteen years, from 1920 to 1935, he was the husband of "the World's Sweetheart" and during these years the two celebrities represented the dream marriage of filmdom. They were the unofficial King and Queen of Hollywood, and their mansion, Pickfair, was visited by notable men and women from all over the world. Like Mary Pickford, Douglas Fairbanks earned his distinction by creating a film personality and a style of acting which were unique and inimitable.

Fairbanks, born in Denver, Colorado, in 1883, won a reputation on the stage before he experimented with film acting. An active, restless, exuberant boy, he was educated at Jarvis Military Academy and the East Denver High School, then attended college at the Colorado School of Mines. He also took dramatic lessons from a local teacher who introduced him to the actor Frederick Warde. Encouraged by Warde, Fairbanks abandoned his college education and traveled to the east coast. In the fall of 1900, at the age of seventeen, he made his debut with a road company in Richmond, Virginia, performing the role of a lackey in a play entitled *The Duke's Jester.* A few minor parts followed, and then the restless young man left the stage to try his luck at various odd jobs and to take a vagabond tour of Europe. He returned to the stage in 1902, joining Minnie Dupree's company in *The Rose of Plymouth Town.* He continued to act, with increasing popularity and success, and he developed an exuberant, athletic manner of performance which Miss Dupree described, unflatteringly, as "a bad case of St. Vitus dance." But the public liked his happy athleticism and by 1909 he was playing a starring part for William A. Brady in a play called *A Gentleman from Mississippi.* The play and its star were so successful that they enjoyed a run of two years. During the period from 1910 to 1915, Fairbanks was "an established Broadway success, never exciting great critical acclaim but sure of his public and himself." [5]

In 1915, the Hollywood producers persuaded more than sixty popular actors and actresses to leave their Broadway billets and join the rapidly growing movie colony in Hollywood. Few of them remained for long, but Douglas Fairbanks, who was lured with a salary of $2,000 per week, proved to be a smash hit. His high spirits and exuberant athleticism "brought to the camera an instinctive, natural grace that proved to be the best of silent movie acting," says Arthur Knight. "Within the year, he was among the most popular of all screen players, ranking with Charles Chaplin, Mary Pickford, and William S. Hart; within the decade his buoyant, healthy personality and flashing grin had become familiar—and loved—throughout the world." [6]

During the first six years of his movie career, Fairbanks played the part of a healthy, optimistic young American who overcame obstacles with a leap and a grin, who exposed the evils of sham and pretense, and who preached the gospel of confidence and success at a time when America needed just such a tonic. The optimism of films like

The Americano (1916), *He Comes Up Smiling* (1918), and *Knickerbocker Buckeroo* (1919) was reinforced by a series of eight inspirational books written by Fairbanks and bearing such titles as *Laugh and Live, Making Life Worthwhile, Profiting by Experience,* and *Whistle and Hoe—Sing as We Go.* Fairbanks emerged as a popular hero, says Alistair Cooke, who "stood for the film industry's total respectability . . . a positive ideal worthy of any small fry's devoted emulation." [7]

Fairbanks' early films and the style of acting he demonstrated in them did more than entertain and inspire. They showed the visual rhythm and pictorial effectiveness which distinguished the motion picture from the legitimate stage. Louis Delluc, a French critic who stumbled onto the early Fairbanks films long after they were withdrawn from general circulation, hailed them as "something not of the theatre, something which is simple, direct, sincere, with a vital rhythm . . . in fact a true moving picture." [8]

In 1920, Fairbanks produced his first costume picture, *The Mark of Zorro,* and scored an even greater success than he had with his red-blooded-young-American films. The exotic settings, the romantic costumes, and the deeds of daring found in this film were perfectly suited to Fairbanks' temperament and style. He enjoyed the milieu so enormously that henceforth, with the exception of a film called *The Nut* (produced in 1921), he devoted himself exclusively to costume pictures and will be forever remembered as the dashing hero of such spectacular romances as *The Three Musketeers, Robin Hood, The Thief of Bagdad,* and *The Black Pirate.* In these films, so vividly remembered by all moviegoers and especially by spectators who were children when they first saw them, Fairbanks was not only the star actor; he assisted with the writing; he outlined the action; he set the tone, the pace, and the style of the entire production. Everything about the picture, says Knight, "was designed to follow the almost balletic trajectory of his own lithe figure and broad-gestured acting." [9]

There has never been any style of acting quite like Fairbanks'. Heroes galore have graced the stage; heroes who could wield a sword, ride a horse, and rescue a maiden with dash and style. But Fairbanks exceeded them all in grace, inventiveness, and dazzling dexterity. He was a superb athlete with a body so marvelously trained that it responded to any demand instantly and beautifully. His acrobatics had an effortless, instinctive grace which reminded many spectators of ballet rather than athletics. His physical feats delighted the viewer with their rhythm and fluidity—and also with their ingenuity. The most unexpected and inventive exploits were continuously developing in a Fairbanks film. Everything from a simple entrance to a daring escape was performed in so clever and surprising a fashion that the spectator was forever gasping in astonishment and pleasure. Says Alistair Cooke:

Fairbanks' glory, the mystery of his visual fascination, is that he could throw all the textbook tricks on the makeshift apparatus of life. He appears to the moviegoer to be a sort of Ariel, leaping where he has a mind without any of the natural checks of gravity. . . . To Fairbanks the limb of a tree suggests a hocks-off; a narrow lane with high walls is a risky, but workable, set of parallel bars; a spear is a pole to vault with . . . it is that virtuoso use of the landscape as a natural gymnasium whose equipment is invisible to the ordinary man, the use of his own body as a crazy but disciplined bow on something that turns into a handy fiddle, that made him an enchanting image. . . .[10]

Enhancing his superb athleticism was Fairbanks' captivating grin, always ready to disarm and delight, and his radiant personality, always a happy concomitant of his physical dexterity. The glow of Fairbanks' exuberant optimism and wholesomeness was strongly projected from the silent celluloid to the hearts of all his spectators, and the world seemed brave and new because it had such a person in it. As his old friend and associate, Charles Chaplin, has said, "The spirit of his pictures, their optimism and infallibility, were very much to the American taste, and indeed to the taste of the whole world. He had extraordinary magnetism and charm and a genuine boyish enthusiasm which he conveyed to the public." [11]

Fairbanks' spell remained potent and his popularity dazzling until the advent of talking pictures. Then, although he made a few successful talking films, his star began to decline. He continued to write, to direct, and occasionally to act, and he continued to live the same vigorous, athletic life he had always enjoyed. His death in 1939 was a shock to the world. It came without warning while he slept, and removed him from the screen before decrepitude could destroy his image as the wholesome, unconquerable hero of a thousand wonderful adventures.

A third idol of the silent films was the original Western Hero of the movies, William S. Hart. He never achieved the same world celebrity as Mary Pickford or Douglas Fairbanks but he earned immense popularity and established a style of acting which exerted an influence on dozens of his fellow performers.

Although his pre-cinema career has been forgotten, it is interesting to know that Hart was a successful stage actor for twenty-five years before he appeared on the screen and during much of that period he was a popular leading man. Born in Newburgh, New York, in 1872, he made his stage debut seventeen years later and soon was performing important roles in Shakespearean repertory with Lawrence Barrett. Subsequently he acted with Helena Modjeska, playing such parts as Duval to her Camille, Benedick to her Beatrice, and Marc Antony to her Cleopatra. He was the original Messala in the first stage version of *Ben Hur,* he made a notable character of Cash Hawkins in *The Squaw Man,* and beginning in 1907 he played the title role of *The Virginian* for two years. It was not until 1914 that he joined the exodus to Hollywood, by which time he had already perfected the character of the strong, silent hero in western romances. He continued to play these roles in the movies and although he had numerous competitors, he quickly outdistanced them to become the model of the firm-jawed, clear-eyed, square-dealing, hard-riding, straight-shooting western hero. The image he created has influenced western heroes ever since. Also, his suppressed style of under-playing his roles set a new fashion in movie acting. When Hart began his film career many actors continued to use broad gestures and exaggerated movement and facial expression before the camera. Hart perceived the power-to-enlarge inherent in the camera and he demanded the right to underplay his roles, that is, to suppress the over-emphatic pantomime used by other players. His first film made for the Triangle Corporation was a great disappointment to the producers. They told Hart that his acting would be considered wooden, that he did not exaggerate enough, and that the public would feel that he wasn't acting at all. The Triangle people, fearful of losing money, sold Hart's first film to another releasing organization. The film proved to be a great success and Hart's style of acting was vindicated. On the basis of this experience, it is said that Hart "was one of the first, if not the first, to prove that screen acting should be natural, and not a series of exaggerated movements." [12]

The actor of the silent screen who did most to establish cinema as an art and who perfected a comic character which won the hearts of the whole world is Charles Spencer Chaplin—the immortal "Charlie" of the toothbrush mustache, the baggy pants, the jaunty derby hat, and the willowy cane. He became the foremost artist of the silent screen and firmly established his claim as one of the greatest comedians of all time.

Although generally considered to be an American actor because almost his entire film career has been pursued in the United States, Chaplin is English by birth and has never changed his citizenship. He was born in London in 1889 of theatrical parents, and made his stage debut at the age of five when, on the spur of the moment, he substituted for his mother in a variety act because her voice had failed her. "That night," says Chaplin, "was my first appearance on the stage and my mother's last." [13]

At the age of twelve and a half, Chaplin began regular stage appearances when he successfully acted the role of a newsboy in a play entitled *Jim, the Romance of a Cockney*. His first American appearance was with a traveling English company in a variety sketch entitled *The Wow-wows*. Evidently Chaplin's comic talents attracted notice because, when he returned to the United States in the fall of 1912 on his second visit, the Keystone Film Company offered him $150 per week. After completing his engagement in vaudeville, Chaplin accepted the offer and traveled to Hollywood to begin a film career which was to be meteoric. Within two years his salary jumped to $10,000 a week plus a yearly bonus of $150,000. The comedies he produced in a single year were sold by his studio to the British empire for $670,000—and the British distributors, in turn, made a handsome profit on the deal. This sensational rise to fame and fortune illustrates not only Chaplin's genius as a comedian but also the explosive popularity of the movies in the early years of the twentieth century.

The character of Charlie the Tramp, which Chaplin was to immortalize, appeared in the second movie he made, a ten minute film without plot and without distinction except for the character which Chaplin introduced on the spur of the moment. Chaplin had been standing by in Mack Sennett's studio watching the filming of a comedy when Sennett suddenly ordered him to put on a comic make-up and introduce a few gags into the scene. Chaplin records that "I had no idea what make-up to put on. . . . However, on the way to the wardrobe I thought I would dress in baggy pants, big shoes, a cane and a derby hat. I wanted everything a contradiction: the pants baggy, the coat tight, the hat small and the shoes large. . . . I had no idea of the character. But the moment I dressed, the clothes and the make-up made me feel the person I was. I began to know him, and by the time I walked onto the stage he was fully born." [14] Chaplin was not aware of the enormous potential of the character he had created—suddenly and full-grown—but he was soon to discover its possibilities, and he was to spend his life elaborating the character and adding depth and dimension to the first rough sketch.

Once created, the character of Charlie the Tramp, began to weave an irresistible spell. Audiences took an instant liking to the funny little man who, as Robert Payne observes, "does all the absurd and wonderful things which people do when they think they are alone and not being watched." [15] At first the antics of the little clown—his ingenious battles with an exasperating world—were enjoyed as pure slapstick. Spectators both young and old roared with laughter at Charlie's inventive clowning and did not bother to analyze its unusual appeal. It was much later that critics recognized in Charlie the Tramp, an epitome of the human condition in all its ridiculous poignancy and pathetic bravery. The little man in the baggy trousers wears a tragi-comic mask which is somehow the mask of all of us.

During his first year in the movies, Chaplin made thirty-five films for the Keystone Company. He then accepted an offer from the Essanay Studios and during the following fourteen months produced an average of one picture per month. His fame grew by leaps and bounds and, as it did so, his films increased in length and elaborateness. In 1917 he signed a contract with First National Pictures and through them he released such classics as *Shoulder Arms, The Kid,* and *The Pilgrim.* A year later he became an independent producer and soon thereafter joined Mary Pickford, Douglas Fairbanks, and D. W. Griffith to establish the United Artists Corporation, a company founded to distribute the productions of the "Big Four."

As the years passed, and as both Chaplin and the public developed a fuller appreciation of the Tramp, more and more was expected of each film, and so fewer and fewer pictures issued from the Chaplin Studio. Instead of slap-dash filming of almost impromptu scripts, now each picture became an elaborate and carefully worked-out production. Each one represented the creative genius of a single individual—Charles Chaplin. He wrote his own scenarios; he composed the musical accompaniment; he produced the film; he directed the film; and of course he performed the leading role. He became a perfectionist who agonized over every detail of a production and shot thousands of feet of film before he obtained the effects he wanted. In *Modern Times,* for example, he exposed 215,000 feet of film to get the 8,000 feet which were finally used in the picture.

The character of the little tramp who now appears in these carefully wrought films is a fully and marvelously developed portrait— unforgettable in such pictures as *The Gold Rush, City Lights,* and *Modern Times.* The Tramp appears, thinly disguised, as *The Great Dictator* in 1940—another unforgettable film. In *Monsieur Verdoux* (1947), the Tramp wears a disguise so sophisticated as to make the character almost unrecognizable. This film disappointed the public and enraged many critics yet it is considered by some to be a masterpiece. In Chaplin's latest films, *Limelight* (1953) and *The King in New York* (1957), the classic character of the little tramp is almost entirely abandoned.

Chaplin was not immune to the crisis in Hollywood caused by the introduction of talking motion pictures. Hollywood capitulated to the new Frankenstein of sound but for many years Chaplin refused to do so. He had discovered and exploited the immense advantages of the silent film and had demonstrated the artistic capabilities of true cinema. He felt that to adopt spoken dialogue was to destroy the uniqueness of motion pictures and to make them merely a mechanical imitation of the stage. He was willing to introduce synchronized music and special sound effects and demonstrated how such additions could enhance a silent picture without destroying its essential character. A classic example of his ingenious use of sound is the whistle scene in *City Lights.* In this sequence, Charlie's frantic little whistles, when he tries to conceal the fact that he has swallowed a policeman's whistle, is an uproarious addition to the pantomime of the scene. It was not until the end of his picture-making career that Chaplin finally surrendered to the overwhelming demand for spoken dialogue and introduced it into his last films.

The perfection of Chaplin's comic style is difficult to describe—but it can be studied by anyone who takes the time to attend a re-run of his films. He is a master of pantomime from the tiniest gesture to the wildest slapstick, and from the most fleeting expression to the most violent pandemonium. Moreover, every one of his movements, gestures, and expressions has meaning and conveys with exquisite timing and clarity the precise emotion or idea Chaplin has in mind. Belly-laughs or tears, pathos or satire—Chaplin communicates them all without clumsiness or strain and with magnificent humor. The range of his inventiveness is limitless. His manipulation of people and things is endlessly surprising but always comically logical for the given situation. And all of this superb clowning seems to result from the natural reactions of a dramatic character which has universal human appeal. Charlie, the tramp, is a tragi-comic Everyman forever portraying the human dilemma in a crazy world. Chaplin's supreme achievement is to join a marvelous technique of performance to a significant, enduring character. The uniqueness and importance of his creation is ably summarized by Robert Payne when he writes:

In time Chaplin will be forgotten, but Charlie will remain. He will have a place in the cosmography of the imagination which every generation maps afresh, but in every thousand years only a few new legends are permitted to enter. He will live in the world inhabited by Alexander the Great, Napoleon, and the Borgias, with Robin Hood, King Arthur and the Wandering Jew as his companions; Punch, Pierrot and Harlequin will be his accomplices in mischief. . . . It is even possible that his place is at the very centre of the fabulous island, since of all the heroes he is most like ourselves once we have removed our false beards, ear-trumpets and magnifying spectacles and show ourselves more naked than we care to be. . . . The elements have been so mixed in him that the recreative activities of latter-day actors will hardly be able to change him. For all the foreseeable future he will walk down the brightly lit roads of the mind, swinging his cane and dexterously picking up cigarette butts, flaunting his absurdly human dignity in the face of the world's importunity, a pirate nailing his flag to the mast, but instead of crossed bones and a skull the flag shows a pair of battered boots and a polished derby, those signs of human dignity and waywardness.[16]

Many other capable performers contributed to the growth of the movies and to the development of film acting. Often these players—like Chaplin, Hart, Pickford, and Fairbanks—served an apprenticeship in the legitimate theatre before turning to the screen. But as the movie industry grew, many new performers were trained and developed within the film studios themselves and became stars without any experience on the legitimate stage.

ACTING IN TALKING PICTURES

The introduction of the talkies in 1927 caused a major revolution in the film industry. Production became vastly more complicated and expensive; acting now demanded voice as well as looks and pantomime. For a while, the new dimension of sound arrested the development of cinema technique, and movies again resembled photographed stage plays—just as they had done in their earliest infancy. Instead of communication through rhythm, pantomime, and significant movement of the body, communication now depended on the spoken word. In place of a roving camera which achieved its effects through free and fluid movement, there was substituted a static machine which recorded set conversations. Much of this conversation was affected and unnatural. Movie actors, anxious to maintain their jobs, flocked to teachers of elocution and often acquired an "elegant" delivery which was stilted and unconvincing. It took time for actors to realize that if they had reasonably pleasant and flexible voices they need only to follow the usual patterns of conversation and to use the natural tones of normal speech to produce acceptable delivery. Projection of volume and exaggeration of articulation—so necessary for effectiveness in large legitimate theatres—were wholly unnecessary before a microphone which magnified every tone and every syllable. Directors also needed time and experience to realize that the techniques they had learned in silent films were still valid—and that a good movie still depended on visual excitement. Sounds and spoken words, they discovered, were merely additional means of reinforcing the dramatic impact of the pictures, and were to be used as counterpoint is used in music—to repeat and vary, to expand and emphasize the thought and emotion of the scenario.

Many actors and directors of the silent screen made the transition to sound with notable success. Directors like Lewis Milestone and Cecil B. DeMille, who were veterans of the old order, became skillful users of film-with-sound. Players like Greta Garbo and Zazu Pitts startled their fans when they opened their mouths but proved to be equally capable—and sometimes more effective—as talking stars than as silent performers. Some popular players failed to make the adjustment because their voices were squeaky or monotonous or incompatible with the image they had created in the silent films. The romantic hero, John Gilbert, is a notable casualty of the era of sound. Yet, after much stress and strain and after several false starts, Hollywood mastered the use of sound and learned that the basic differences between film acting and stage acting—which had long been accepted in silent pictures—were unchanged. The camera was still free and mobile, unconfined to an area enclosed by a proscenium arch. The film actor was still subject to the relentlessly intimate scrutiny of this camera, which recorded every nuance and enlarged every expression, discouraging exaggeration or artificiality and encouraging a subtle simplicity and realism to match the natural world which surounded the actor. In addition, the film actor still performed without a live audience; he was subject only to the imperious dictates of the camera and the director and was asked to perform a role not as a unified whole but, as in silent films, in bits and pieces which made emotional sense only when the tiny individual scenes were properly pieced together. The necessity to speak did not alter the player's working conditions. Speech was an additional tool which, when properly used, enhanced the art of cinema without destroying its unique character.

Many players utilized the new opportunities of talking pictures to achieve performances of genuine artistry. The noted teacher of legitimate stars and artistic director of the Actors' Studio in New York, Lee Strasberg, declares that "with the rise of sound movies, the role of the individual actor increased. Greta Garbo, Emil Jannings, Harry Baur, Bette Davis, Paul Muni, Luise Rainer, Spencer Tracy, Sylvia Sidney, Humphrey Bogart, Katharine Hepburn, Sir Lawrence Olivier, Marlon Brando and others created authentic acting performances which could have held their own on the stage."[17]

In the new era of sound, actors began to move freely from stage to screen and back again. Players who mastered one set of techniques found they could ajust to the other set without great difficulty because the traditional skills and endowments of the actor were required in both. The legitimate stage once more became a training ground for movie performers and provided Hollywood with many experienced actors. In turn, the movie producers began regularly to send their players back to the living stage for refreshment and stimulus. The roster of performers who list or have listed themselves truthfully as stars of both stage and screen is a long one and includes such notable names as Lionel, Ethel, and John Barrymore, Helen Hayes, Frederic March, Tallulah Bankhead, Shirley Booth, Marlon Brando, Ruth

Chatterton, Lillian and Dorothy Gish, Katharine Hepburn, Ed Wynn, and many others.

ACTING IN RADIO AND TELEVISION

For a time, radio—another mechanical marvel of the twentieth century—developed a unique but limited technique of performance which was different from either the legitimate stage or the motion picture. The silent film was visual entertainment and communicated thought and emotion through sight alone. Radio relies wholly upon sound and requires a type of performance based exclusively on the power and expressiveness of the human voice. In a radio play, no movement, gesture, or physical expression can be seen. They exist only in the mind of the listener. They are created by him imaginatively from the sounds he hears. The radio gives him many clues and suggestions: doors are slammed, papers rattled, shots fired, and lips smacked—but the human voice is the principal medium of communication. In the early 1920's, the marvelous flexibility and infinite variability of the human voice were recognized and cultivated once more. Actors discovered anew that emotion could be stirred, attitudes and states of mind could be revealed by nuances of tone and variation in vocal quality. Comedians returned to the verbal gags which had been a mainstay of vaudeville but had died with the movies. Performers who excelled in vocal expressiveness, either comic or serious, became stars of radio and commanded a popularity as great as the following of the film idols. To be sure, radio never duplicated the pageantry, the spectacle, or the visual excitement of the films—but it had an inherent advantage which the movies never offered. It was free and it was mobile. A broadcast could be listened to—without charge—in one's home or one's car, in public or in private, on land or at sea. The sales slogan of those who manufactured receiving sets soon changed from "A Radio in Every Home" to "A Radio in Every Room," and presently the ubiquitous device was found in every automobile and almost every purse and pocket.

But the heyday of radio acting was brief. As soon as television invaded the living room, radio acting all but disappeared. The national radio network programs which had commanded an audience of millions were transferred to television. Soap operas, comic serials, and adaptations of standard plays deserted radio, and the hundreds of performers who had learned to act with voice alone while remaining stationary before a microphone now had to adjust to the techniques of television, that is to say, to the techniques of the talking picture. The radio performers who remain today and who are employed by the hundreds of local radio stations, which appeared after the demise of the national networks, can hardly be called actors. They are disc jockeys, sports-casters, news-casters, and hucksters, and their style of performing is that of the public speaker or the circus barker.

Television itself has had no significant effect on style or technique in acting because T.V. acting is the same as motion picture acting. Almost all the dramatic programs shown on television are filmed in a studio under exactly the same conditions as any other movie. The few live dramatic shows offer little variation in style or technique, and the daily re-runs of old motion pictures are exactly that: re-runs of old motion pictures. The stars of stage and screen appear frequently on television but they use the same style they have developed for use in talking pictures.

The popular theatre of the nineteenth century—vaudeville, minstrelsy, burlesque, circus, and Tom shows—offered a rich variety of entertainment; it also developed a lively, joyous, direct, performer-to-audience kind of acting which is still seen in revues and night clubs. The popular theatre of the twentieth century—movies, radio, and television—is less varied than its predecessor but it, too, particularly in silent motion pictures, developed a unique style of communication which reached a fine art in the performances of actors like Douglas Fairbanks and Charles Chaplin. The best performers in present day television and cinema still retain many of the skills of the early days, combining them with the subtle vocal skills demanded by the talkies. The popular theatre of this century reaches an enormously larger audience than any form of theatre in previous centuries and, faulty though television, radio, and cinema may be much of the time, they promise to remain the major forms of theatre for many years to come.

ACTING IN THE LIVING THEATRE BETWEEN
TWO WORLD WARS

During the years of the prosperous twenties and the depressed thirties, and despite the overpowering competition of the movies and radio,

American players of the living stage continued to contribute memorable performances.

John Barrymore carried on the traditions of the classic school of acting by playing the roles of Hamlet and Richard III early in his career. His older brother, Lionel, and his sister, Ethel, also performed a variety of serious and romantic parts before they, like John, migrated to Hollywood and became identified with a single type of role. Margaret Anglin, who also performed in the traditions of the classic school, began her career in Bronson Howard's famous melodrama, *Shenandoah;* but she eventually became America's outstanding exponent of the great roles of Greek tragedy—Medea, Antigone, and Electra—which she played with sweep and power and respect for the beauties of Greek verse. Nance O'Neil also is remembered for the controlled emotional intensity she brought to classic roles like Lady Macbeth and to modern parts like Hedda Gabler and Mrs. Phelps in *The Silver Cord.* Alice Brady, another gifted actress of the 1930's, is known to younger theatre fans only as the scatter-brained, garrulous, middle-aged comedienne of many movies whereas, in truth, she was a versatile performer who played both comedy and tragedy effectively and who contributed a superb portrait of the Electra-like Lavinia in Eugene O'Neill's original production of *Mourning Becomes Electra.* Pauline Lord, a contemporary of Miss Brady, contributed several memorable dramatic portraits, foremost among which were her roles in *Anna Christie, They Knew What They Wanted,* and *Ethan Frome.* Equally notable was Laurette Taylor, whose long career stretched from the sensationally successful *Peg O' My Heart* in 1912 to the much lauded portrait of Amanda Wingfield in the 1945 production of *The Glass Menagerie.* Jane Cowl, like Laurette Taylor, began her career by playing the sweet, romantic roles of *Smilin' Through* and *Lilac Time,* but she also succeeded in the classic roles of Juliet, Rosalind, and Cleopatra. Less versatile was the colorful Jeanne Eagels, who is described as being "explosive, mercurial, neurotic, loyal, generous and sweet" [18] and who utilized all these qualities to make a fascinating portrait of her single great role, that of Sadie Thompson in *Rain.* Among the comediennes, Grace George is remembered for the dainty, mirthful charm mixed with wistfulness which she brought to such comedies as *The New York Idea* and *Divorçons,* and Mary Boland is remembered for the saucy, romantic roles of her early career as well as for the robust, garrulous comedy of her later years. These players, and many others, maintained the high standards of American acting in the period between the First and Second World Wars, and prompted Lee Strasberg to write, "After World War I, American actors created outstanding performances that could by all right be called great. . . ." [19]

CONTEMPORARY ACTING

In the American theatre of the 1960's, what is the state of acting on the living stage and who are the notable players of the present day? The diminshed activity of the professional theatre of our time is, inevitably, reflected in the dimished number of eminent performers and in the quality of their performances. There are fewer notable players in America and there are fewer notable performances on our stages. The legitimate theatre, television, and cinema offer some opportunity for gifted actors to appear in challenging roles, but not enough to alter the general impression of decreased quantity and diminished quality. The contributions of the new festival companies, of the civic centers of performing arts, and of the university theatres are too recent to evaluate properly. It is hoped that they represent a new renaissance in the living theatre, but the number of new performers which may be developed, the new styles of acting which may emerge, and the quality of both remain a promise and a hope.

The established corps of contemporary actors represent many of the styles which have flourished in the past history of American acting. The heroic school of Edwin Forrest reappears in the acting of some of the muscular heroes of western drama and in some of the costume epics seen on stage and screen. The personality school has many successful exponents, particularly among actresses. Such eminent and greatly admired performers as Lynn Fontanne, Katharine Hepburn, and Tallulah Bankhead belong in this group because, with rare exceptions, they substitute their own unique individualities for the dramatic character they are playing or they portray those characters which exactly suit their own individualities. Their manner of performing is related to the style of earlier actresses like Maude Adams, Ada Rehan, and Viola Allen, although the contemporary group differs from their predecessors by basing their appeal on more varied attractions than womanly loveliness and feminine virtue. The personality school is also well represented in the cinema and television where practically all roles are cast strictly to fit the personality of the individual player.

Three contemporary actresses who in many respects can claim kinship to the classic school are Judith Anderson, Helen Hayes, and Katharine Cornell. These eminent women have performed roles of high seriousness in a variety of plays both modern and classic. Miss Anderson is noted for her powerful performances in Greek tragedy, Helen Hayes for such parts as Mary of Scotland, Queen Victoria, and Harriet Beecher Stowe, while Katharine Cornell will be remembered for her portrayal of Shaw's St. Joan, Shakespeare's Juliet, and Besier's Elizabeth Barrett of Wimpole Street. No contemporary actress seems to have the range or the power of Charlotte Cushman or Helen Modjeska, but Anderson, Hayes, and Cornell have given to their careers an integrity, a devotion, and a standard which resemble the ideals of the classic school.

It is difficult to find male performers today who have fulfilled the ideals of the classic school. The only versatile tragedians who perform in the contemporary American theatre are English by birth, by training, and, generally, by citizenship. Sir Lawrence Olivier, Sir John Gielgud, Sir Ralph Richardson, as well as Maurice Evans, Michael Redgrave, and Richard Burton all belong to the British tradition. Christopher Plummer is Canadian born and trained. They are all versatile, gifted players, worthy of the standards established by Edwin Booth and E. L. Davenport but, alas, they are not American. Three successful native actors, Alfred Lunt, Orson Welles, and Frederic March, who might be considered exponents of the classic style have rarely or never attempted the great roles of classic tragedy. Orson Welles has acted a few Shakespearean parts successfully, including Macbeth and Othello, but he is largely identified with so-called character roles in which, more often than not, he plays Orson Welles. Alfred Lunt has specialized in comedy during much of his career, including the role of Shakespeare's Petruchio. Even when he could have named his own parts, his serious roles have not been Hamlet or Lear or Macbeth but less challenging parts in modern plays such as Sherwood's *There Shall Be No Night* and Duerrenmatt's *The Visit*. Frederic March, perhaps the most versatile of the three, has portrayed a wide variety of characters with skill and conviction but his ability has never been tested in the greatest roles of the classic school. Other gifted American performers, like Morris Carnovsky and Jason Robards, Jr., have largely devoted themselves to roles in contemporary plays although with the establishment of the Shakespearean festivals in Stratford, Connecticut, and Stratford, Ontario, they have met the challenge of a limited number of Shakespearean characters. Carnovsky gained fame as a member of the Group Theatre in the 1930's. Since then he has successfully played such parts as Shylock and Claudius. Jason Robards, Jr., vividly remembered for his acting in O'Neill's *The Iceman Cometh, Long Day's Journey into Night,* and *Hughie,* has also appeared in Shakespearean roles with the Stratford, Ontario, company and in 1959 he starred in *Macbeth.* It is true, of course, that the plays of the classic repertory are rarely given today in the American commercial theatre (although they are frequently done in England) so that American players have little opportunity to test themselves in the great roles. Whatever the reasons, few contemporary American actors have measured up to the high standards set by the best American tragedians of the 19th century.

One school of the past which has few adherents among contemporary players is the school of emotionalism. The lack of representation is not due so much to a dearth of talent as to a change in playwriting and public taste. No Queen of Spasms has appeared to carry on the tradition of Clara Morris because contemporary plays do not include this type of emotionalistic display, and the public will not tolerate them except when they are deliberately burlesqued. Modern ideals of acting which emphasize truthfulness, restraint, and balance have almost completely eliminated the tears and hysteria of the old "hydrostatic" order.

The style of acting most frequently seen and acclaimed on the contemporary American stage is the school of psychological naturalism, or the Stanislavsky method of acting. The two are identical in aim and similiar in the means of achieving the aim. The school of psychological naturalism, whose chief exponent and teacher was Minnie Maddern Fiske, emphasized psychological truthfulness in the portrayal of a role, concentration on inner feeling with repressed overt responses, cultivation of a simple true-to-contemporary-life manner of moving and speaking (which often led to careless delivery), and fidelity to the over-all design of the play. The close relationship of these ideals to the Stanislavsky method is illustrated by the statements of Lee Strasberg, leading teacher of "Method" acting in the United States. He writes that when an actor takes the stage "His appearance . . . is not the beginning, but is a continuation of the given circumstances that have previously taken place." Moreover, the actor must "create the impression of being private in public" and must train his senses "so that he is able to see, hear, touch, taste, smell, and relate to the many objects which compose his imaginary situation." He must also "delve beneath the lines to find the meaning or sub-text of a play . . . to find the 'kernel' or core of a part. . . ." [20] Thus, the Method actor, as did Mrs. Fiske, seeks the basic motivation of a character and concentrates on inner truthfulness. He, like Mrs. Fiske, is not interested in surface response or external display but, rather, in re-creating the soul of a dramatic character and letting the imaginary character direct his movements and expressions. The Method actor feels perfectly at home following Mrs. Fiske's practice, cited in Chapter IX, of re-creating a character as he or she must have been before the action of the play begins and then acting out imaginary scenes from this pre-play existence.

The Actors Studio of New York, under the artistic direction of Lee Strasberg, and the Neighborhood Playhouse School of the Theatre, directed for many years by Sanford Meisner, have been two of the nation's leading centers for the teaching of Method acting. In addition, ideals similar to those of Stanislavsky and closely related to those of Mrs. Fiske are taught by the American Academy of Dramatic Arts, the oldest professional school of acting in the United States. The late Aristide D'Angelo, for many years the authority on acting at the Academy, said that the ideal of the school "has always been to work from within: to build the idea, the concept, the truth of the character and scene—and let the form of expression follow naturally." Mr. D'Angelo also stated that the "Academy ideal and Stanislavsky's ideal are much the same, but Stanislavsky formalized the method of responding while the Academy has not." [21]

The latter statement names the principal difference between the Stanislavsky school of acting and Mrs. Fiske's school or the Academy style. Stanislavsky organized his principles and evolved a detailed method of teaching them. He wrote several treatises on acting to expound his theories and techniques. He developed exercises and methods for achieving the aims he sought. His exercises and methods changed with the years, and sometimes a later practice seems contradictory to an earlier one, but his aim was always the same, namely, to find a "grammar of acting" or, as Strasberg describes it, "to achieve that level of inspiration, or of living on the stage, which great actors had found accidentally and sporadically. . . . Stanislavsky tried to find means to stimulate and develop the actor's essential requirements: his concentration, his belief, and his imagination. He did not seek to fabricate inspiration, but to create the proper foundation for its appearance." [22]

It is Stanislavsky's clarification and formalization of the means of liberating an actor's creativity which have made his method so sought-after and which have caused many contemporary actors and theatre-goers to forget that similar ideals were held by many great performers in the past and are particularly close both to the aim and the method of Mrs. Fiske's school of psychological naturalism.

Most of the notable young actors in modern America have been trained in the Stanislavsky method or in the style of psychological naturalism or in some related school, and they all represent similar aims and ideals. Their achievements in many cases have been outstanding. Actresses like Kim Stanley, Julie Harris, Uta Hagen, Shirley Booth, and Maureen Stapleton have contributed moving, authentic portraits of the troubled heroines of contemporary drama. Eli Wallach and Marlon Brando have achieved equal success in male roles. It is too early to evaluate their total contribution, and it is too early to chart their further development. Performers of the past have always been judged, eventually, by their success in the great comic or tragic roles of Shakespeare, Sophocles, Schiller, Goethe, Molière, Sheridan, and others. The younger players of today have little opportunity to test their ability in these roles and without the perspective of time it is hard to judge whether parts in contemporary plays offer a comparable challenge.

It is probable that the younger players in the United States are as gifted as any generation of actors in the past. It is also probable that there exists a great reservoir of talent which will be developed only if the living theatre prospers and offers increased opportunities to the coming generation of players and playwrights. Certainly the fabulous history of American acting, which began so many years ago, is not about to end. The ranks of notable players stretching back to Mary Ann Duff and Edwin Forrest will be filled with talented new actors, perhaps inspired and trained in civic or university theatres, and they will add new styles, new insights, and new achievements to the colorful and continuing pageant of American acting.

NOTES

GENERAL INTRODUCTION

1 Lewis C. Strang, *Players and Plays of the Last Quarter Century,* Vol. I (Boston, 1903), p. 156.

2 Katherine Goodale, *Behind the Scenes with Edwin Booth* (Boston & New York, 1931), p. 232.

3 See Lawrence Barrett, *Charlotte Cushman—A Lecture* (New York: The Dunlap Society, 1889), p. 14.

4 William Winter, *The Life and Art of Edwin Booth* (New York and London, 1893), p. 223.

5 Henry Austin Clapp, *Reminiscences of a Dramatic Critic* (Boston & New York, 1902), p. 215.

6 Lily B. Campbell, "The Rise of a Theory of Stage Presentation in England During the Eighteenth Century," *PMLA,* XXXII (1917), p. 164. [I am indebted to Miss Campbell's excellent article for much of my material on English styles of acting in the eighteenth century.]

7 Ibid., p. 165.

8 Ibid., p. 188.

9 Margaret G. Mayorga, *A Short History of the American Drama* (New York, 1934), p. 54.

I. THE HEROIC SCHOOL

1 Lawrence Barrett, *Edwin Forrest* (Boston, 1881), p. 4.

2 James E. Murdoch, *The Stage* (Philadelphia, 1880), p. 281.

3 James Rees, *The Life of Edwin Forrest* (Philadelphia, 1874), p. 55.

4 Barrett, op. cit., p. 46.

5 W. R. Alger, *Life of Edwin Forrest,* Vol. I (Philadelphia, 1877), p. 142.

6 Quoted in several biographies, among them Montrose Moses, *The Fabulous Forrest* (Boston, 1929), p. 74.

7 Richard Moody, *Edwin Forrest* (New York, 1960), p. 399.

8 Alger, op. cit., Vol. I, p. 178.

9 Moody, op. cit., p. 68.

10 Rees, op. cit., p. 226.

11 Gabriel Harrison, *Edwin Forrest, The Actor and the Man* (Brooklyn, 1889), p. 37.

12 Ibid., p. 37.

13 Alger, op. cit., Vol. I, p. 477.

14 Ibid., p. 477.

15 Rees, op. cit., p. 200.

16 Alger, op. cit., Vol. II, p. 649.

17 Barrett, op. cit., p. 125.

18 Moody, op. cit., p. 396.

19 Moses, op. cit., p. 326.

20 Murdoch, op. cit., p. 295.

21 Harrison, op. cit., p. 133.

22 Quoted in Moses, op. cit., pp. 338–339.

23 Moody, op. cit., p. 405.

24 Barrett, op. cit., p. 156.

25 Alger, op. cit., p. 643.

26 Susie C. Clark, *John McCullough* (Boston, 1905), pp. 31–32. See also William Winter, *Other Days* (New York, 1908), p. 212.

27 See Leander Richardson, "John McCullough—of the Palmy Days," *Vanity Fair* (March, 1916).

28 Joseph I. C. Clarke, *My Life and Memories* (New York, 1925), p. 266.

29 Clark, op. cit., p. 33.

30 Clarke, op. cit., p. 266.

31 Winter, *Other Days,* p. 214.

32 *The San Francisco Chronicle,* August 27, 1877.

33 Clarke, op. cit., p. 267.

34 See Percy MacKaye, *Epoch, The Life of Steele MacKaye,* Vol. I (New York, 1927), pp. 270–271.

35 Alfred Ayres, "America's Greater Players No. 4—Murdoch, McCullough and Rush," *The Theatre* (March, 1902), p. 22.

36 When praised for being "second only to Booth," McCullough said with great sincerity, "I will always gladly be second to Edwin." See Winter, op. cit., pp. 205–206.

37 Ibid., p. 204.

38 Ibid., p. 224.

39 Ibid., p. 224.

40 William Winter, *The Wallet of Time,* Vol. I (New York, 1913), pp. 264–268.

41 Ibid., p. 264.

42 Quoted in Clark, op. cit., p. 89.

43 From an unidentified newspaper clipping in the Players Collection, New York Public Library.

44 Walter M. Leman, *Memories of an Old Actor* (San Francisco, 1886), p. 37.

45 Alfred Ayres, *Acting and Actors—Elocution and Elocutionists* (New York, 1899), p. 235.

46 Winter, *Other Days,* p. 44.

47 Robert L. Sherman, *Actors and Authors* (Chicago, 1951), p. 179.

48 Francis C. Wemyss, *Twenty-Six Years of the Life of an Actor and Manager* (New York, 1847), p. 191.

49 Barrett, op. cit., p. 46.

50 Alger, op. cit., p. 643.

II. THE CLASSIC SCHOOL: THE LADIES

1 Lewis C. Strang, *Players and Plays of the Last Quarter Century,* Vol. I (Boston, 1903), p. 129.

2 Joseph N. Ireland, *Mrs. Duff* (Boston, 1882), p. 146.

3 Ibid., pp. 1–2.

4 Ibid., p. 21.

5 William W. Clapp, Jr., *A Record of the Boston Stage* (Boston, 1853), p. 116.

6 John Smith Kendall, "The American Siddons," *The Louisiana Historical Quarterly,* XXVIII (July, 1945), 925.

7 Ibid., p. 55.

8 Horace Greeley, *Recollections of a Busy Life* (New York, 1868), p. 203.

9 Noah M. Ludlow, *Dramatic Life as I Found It* (St. Louis, 1880), pp. 463–464.

10 New York *Mirror,* May 5, 1827, quoted in Joseph N. Ireland, *Records of the New York Stage from 1750 to 1860,* I (New York, 1866), 419.

11 See Ireland, op. cit., p. 42.

12 Strang, op. cit., p. 194.

13 Boston *Herald,* June 18, 1889.

14 Edward Robins, *Twelve Great Actresses* (New York, 1900), p. 359.

15 Lawrence Barrett, *Charlotte Cushman—A Lecture* (New York, 1889), p. 17.

16 See Appendix to Barrett, *Charlotte Cushman,* pp. 37–44.

17 *Spirit of the Times,* New York, November 14, 1874.

18 George Vandenhoff, *Dramatic Reminiscences; or, Actors and Actresses in England and America* (London, 1860), p. 184. The masculine strain in Miss Cushman's nature was sometimes the subject of ridicule by the press. In a jocular mood, *The Spirit of the Times* for August 6, 1870, said: "She discovered the circulation of the blood by squeezing a young man's hand a good many years ago. His name was Harvey—hence the erroneous idea that Harvey made the discovery. Chemically considered, Miss Cushman is a success. She possesses ferruginous properties, which made her an exceedingly difficult woman to borrow money from."

19 *Spirit of the Times,* New York, October 31, 1874.

20 William Winter, *Other Days* (New York, 1908), pp. 152–153.

21 Strang, op. cit., p. 98.

22 Brander Matthews and Laurence Hutton, *Actors and Actresses of Great Britain and the United States—Macready and Forrest and Their Contemporaries* (New York, 1886), pp. 146–147.

23 Alfred Ayres, "America's Greater Players No. 2—Charlotte Cushman," *The Theatre,* II (January, 1902), 19.

24 *The Theatre* (April, 1905).

25 Henry P. Goddard, "Some Actresses I Have Known," *The Theatre Magazine,* VI (August, 1906), 206.

26 See letter in the handwriting of Charlotte Cushman addressed to Mr. J. B. Wright, Esq., and dated from New York, September 30, 1851, in the Robinson Locke collection of dramatic scrapbooks, Volume 139, New York Public Library.

27 Letter reproduced in the Chicago *Record* for January 10, 1909.

28 *Spirit of the Times,* New York, November 14, 1874.

29 James E. Murdoch, *The Stage* (Philadelphia, 1880), p. 240.

30 Winter, op. cit., pp. 158–159.

31 *Spirit of the Times,* New York, November 16, 1860.

32 S. R. Elliott, "A Group of Notable Women No. 2—Glimpses of Charlotte Cushman," *The Delineator,* LIX (February, 1902), 274.

33 Letter reprinted in the *Spirit of the Times,* New York, July 4, 1846.

34 Ibid., pp. 91–92.

35 John B. Clapp and Edwin F. Edgett, *Players of the Present,* Vol. II (New York, 1900), p. 172.

36 Philip Hale, "Mme. Janauschek," in McKay and Wingate, *Famous American Actors of Today,* Vol. I (New York, 1896), p. 22.

37 Walter Prichard Eaton, "Helena Modjeska," *Dictionary of American Biography,* Vol. XIII (New York, 1934), p. 73.

38 William Winter, *The Wallet of Time,* Vol. I (New York, 1913), p. 367.

39 See Helena Modjeska, *Memories and Impressions* (New York, 1910), p. 109.

40 John R. Towse, *Sixty Years of the Theater* (New York, 1916), p. 210.

41 Ibid., p. 211.

42 Hale, op. cit., p. 22.

43 Ibid., p. 211.

44 Otis Skinner, *Footlights and Spotlights* (Indianapolis, 1924), p. 62.

45 Towse, op. cit., p. 212.

46 Skinner, op. cit., p. 63.

47 Ibid., p. 125.

48 Ibid.

49 Modjeska, op. cit., p. 500.

50 Winter, op. cit., p. 360. Winter also notes another aspect of her style worth recording. He says, "Her movements, always graceful, were sometimes electric in their rapidity and long sinuous reach." Ibid., p. 370.

51 John Creahan, *The Life of Laura Keene* (Philadelphia, 1897), p. 122.

52 Eaton, op. cit., p. 73.

53 Skinner, op. cit., pp. 199–200.

54 Lewis C. Strang, *Famous Actresses of the Day in America* (Boston, 1899), p. 309.

55 Ibid., p. 320.

56 Skinner, op. cit., p. 221.

57 Modjeska, op. cit., pp. 129–130.

58 Winter, op. cit., p. 367.

59 Mary Anderson, *A Few Memories* (New York, 1895), pp. 44–45.

60 *The Spirit of the Times,* New York, November 17, 1877.

61 Anderson, op. cit., p. 197.

62 William Winter, *Stage Life of Mary Anderson* (New York, 1886), pp. 29–30.

63 Anderson, op. cit., pp. 85, 97.

64 Towse, op. cit., pp. 216–217.

65 Anderson, op. cit., p. 119.

66 Towse, op. cit., p. 217.

67 Miss Anderson's only reappearances on the stage were for five charity performances given in England during the First World War.

68 Towse, op. cit., p. 215. Henry Austin Clapp, noted as a judicious critic, makes the following comparison between Mary Anderson and Charlotte Cushman: "Miss Anderson, perhaps the most celebrated of our home-born actresses, bore about the same relation to Charlotte Cushman as a march of Sousa to a symphony of Beethoven." See Clapp, *Reminiscences of a Dramatic Critic* (Boston, 1902), p. 83. On the other hand, William Winter, in 1892, reversed his earlier judgment of Miss Anderson and argued that her art was the kind which needed special insight, and when this insight was applied her acting revealed all the elements of greatness. See William Winter, *Shadows of the Stage* (New York, 1892), pp. 97–102.

III. THE CLASSIC SCHOOL: THE GENTLEMEN

1 Lewis C. Strang, *Players and Plays of the Last Quarter Century,* Vol. I (Boston, 1903), p. 129.

2 Katherine Goodale, *Behind the Scenes with Edwin Booth* (Boston, 1931), pp. 59–60.

3 William R. Alger, *Life of Edwin Forrest,* Vol. I (Philadelphia, 1877), p. 142.

4 Stanley Kimmel, *The Mad Booths of Maryland* (Indianapolis, 1940), p. 312.

5 Edwina Booth Grossmann, *Edwin Booth* (New York, 1894), p. 35.

6 Ibid., p. 277.

7 William Winter, *The Life and Art of Edwin Booth* (New York, 1893), p. 3.

8 Ibid., p. 224.

9 John R. Towse, *Sixty Years of the Theater* (New York, 1916), p. 181.

10 Quoted in Strang, op. cit., p. 179. The critics as a whole agreed that Booth excelled in voice and delivery. One dissenting observer was Alfred Ayres who declared that Booth's reading "was exceedingly faulty. Never, probably, has there been another actor, with a great reputation, that misplaced his emphasis as often as did Edwin Booth." (Alfred Ayres in *The Theatre,* New York, Feb. 12, 1902, p. 19.) Ayres ranked Edwin Forrest as the greatest American player and Charlotte Cushman as the second greatest.

11 Kimmel, op cit., p. 309.

12 Strang, op. cit., p. 156.

13 Winter, op. cit., p. 223.

14 Ibid., p. 129.

15 Goodale, *Behind the Scenes with Edwin Booth*, p. 75.

16 Asia Booth Clarke, *The Elder and the Younger Booth* (Boston, 1882), p. 160.

17 Henry Austin Clapp, *Reminiscences of a Dramatic Critic* (Boston and New York, 1902), pp. 134–135.

18 Ibid., p. 135.

19 Grossman, op. cit., p. 263.

20 Ibid., p. 268.

21 Towse, op. cit., p. 190.

22 Goodale, op. cit., p. 84.

23 Walt Whitman was not a Booth enthusiast. He said that Booth "never made me forget everything else and follow him, as the greatest fellows, when they let themselves go, always do." See Gamaliel Bradford, *As God Made Them* (Boston, 1929), p. 178. In this opinion, Whitman differed from the vast majority of the critics. In the final years of Booth's life, he was criticized with increasing frequency for carelessness and coldness. Otis Skinner says that the years "had dug devitalizing claws into his strength, his spirit, and his ambition." See Otis Skinner, *Footlights and Spotlights* (Indianapolis, 1924), p. 171.

24 Winter, op. cit., p. 111.

25 Although Booth played these parts with success for many years, comedy was not his forte. Clapp notes: "Like his father, and all his father's other sons, he had small gift in mirth. It was therefore of interest to note that his Petruchio, Benedict, and Don Caesar de Bazan were almost sufficient, by virtue of his vivacity, fire, and mental alertness, and, in the case of the last two characters, by the elegance and distinction of his manners and speech." See Clapp, op. cit., p. 138.

26 Strang, op. cit., p. 156.

27 William Winter, *Edwin Booth in Twelve Dramatic Characters* (Boston, 1872), p. 50.

28 Skinner, op. cit., p. 171.

29 Ibid., p. 172.

30 Towse, op. cit., p. 194.

31 From J. Bunting's biographical sketch of Murdoch, found in the introduction to James E. Murdoch's *The Stage* (Philadelphia, 1880), p. 17.

32 *Analytic Elocution* (New York, 1884); *A Plea for Spoken Language* (New York, 1883); *The Stage* (Philadelphia, 1880).

33 Murdoch, *The Stage*, p. 27.

34 *Ibid.*, p. 37.

35 Ibid., p. 32.

36 Ibid., p. 252.

37 Ibid., pp. 30–31.

38 Ibid., p. 42.

39 Ibid., p. 74.

40 Ibid., p. 114.

41 At its worst it was mechanical and pedantic. In his zeal for faultless de-

livery, Murdoch was often guilty of being overly precise and refined. Alfred Ayres in *The Theatre* magazine for March, 1902, says: "With the adherents of the Murdoch school voice and tone are not everything, but they come so close to being everything that they destroy any tendency there might otherwise be to be natural."

42 Ayres, in the magazine article quoted in the preceding note.

43 *Spirit of the Times,* New York, Oct. 25, 1845. Quoted in Odell, *Annals of the New York Stage,* Vol. V, p. 169.

44 Skinner, op. cit., p. 121.

45 Thomas C. Trueblood, a student of Murdoch's and one of the pioneer teachers of speech in the Middle West, has written of Murdoch: "He was the greatest reader of his time and had incomparably the finest voice I ever listened to. It was of wide range, powerful, a clear ringing baritone. He was not only a great reader, but an inspiring teacher, for he taught from the scientific standpoint and led one to find the way." See "A Chapter on the Organization of College Courses in Public Speaking," *The Quarterly Journal of Speech Education,* February, 1926, Vol. XII, pp. 2–3.

46 Murdoch, *A Plea for Spoken Language,* p. 77.

47 Murdoch, *Analytic Elocution,* p. 357.

48 Ibid., p. 360.

49 Murdoch, *A Plea for Spoken Language,* pp. 73–74.

50 Ibid., p. 84.

51 Ibid., p. 83.

52 Edwin F. Edgett, *Edward Loomis Davenport* (New York, 1901), p. 105.

53 Strang, op. cit., pp. 129–30.

54 Anna Cora Mowatt, *Autobiography of an Actress* (Boston, 1854), pp. 253–54.

55 Unidentified newspaper clipping in Vol. 146 of the Robinson Locke collection, New York Public Library.

56 Henry Edwards in Matthews and Hutton, *Actors and Actresses of Great Britain and the United States,* Vol. IV (New York, 1886), pp. 128–29.

57 H. D. Stone in Matthews and Hutton, op. cit., p. 136.

58 Clara Morris, *Life on the Stage* (New York, 1901), p. 185.

59 Mrs. John Drew, *Autobiographical Sketch* (London, 1900), p. 113.

60 Morris, op. cit., p. 185.

61 Strang, op. cit., p. 144.

62 Skinner, op. cit., p. 110.

63 Ibid.

64 Ibid., p. 109.

65 See *Le Chat Noir* for July 26, 1889.

66 Alfred Ayres, "America's Greater Players, No. 5," *The Theatre,* April 1902.

67 Ibid.

68 See the correspondence between Booth and Barrett in Otis Skinner's *The Last Tragedian* (New York, 1939), pp. 158–181.

69 Ayres, op. cit.

70 Skinner, *Footlights and Spotlights,* p. 111.

71 Strang, op. cit., p. 153.

72 Barrett resented Booth's superiority. In the bitter letter written to Booth on January 1, 1873, which caused a seven year break in the friendship of the two men, Barrett wrote: "When you offer me your own inferiors as my equals I reply that if *you* really stand at the head of my profession then *you* only are my compeer—I own no rivals save such as *you* allow, and when Time, the great connector of all things gives his judgment, I may not after all be so very far behind your illustrious self, whom I care now as little to see or hear from as I was once anxious and delighted." See Skinner, *The Last Tragedian,* pp. 180–181.

73 Clara Morris, op. cit., p. 221.

74 William M. Laffan in Matthews and Hutton, *Actors and Actresses of Great Britain and the United States,* Vol. V (New York, 1886), p. 42.

75 Mrs. John E. Owens, *Memories of John E. Owens* (Baltimore, 1892), p. 73.

76 William Winter, *Vagrant Memories* (New York, 1915), p. 139.

77 Clara Morris, *Life on the Stage* (New York, 1902), p. 195.

78 Joseph Jefferson, *Autobiography* (London, 1889), p. 323.

79 Winter, op. cit., pp. 142–43.

80 Melbourne MacDowell as quoted by Lewis C. Strang, *Famous Actors of the Day in America,* First Series (Boston, 1900), p. 244.

81 William Winter, *The Life of David Belasco* (New York, 1918), Vol. I, p. 274.

82 Edgar S. Werner, ed., *The Delsarte System of Oratory* (New York, 1893), p. 127.

83 Percy MacKaye, *Epoch, The Life of Steele MacKay,* Vol. I (New York, 1927), p. 271.

84 *Annual Catalogue,* The American Academy of Dramatic Arts, 1939–40, p. 9.

NOTES ON THE SETTING

1 William Winter, *The Wallet of Time,* Vol. I (New York, 1913), p. 23.

IV. THE SCHOOL OF EMOTIONALISM

1 George Henry Lewes, *On Actors and the Art of Acting* (New York, 1878), p. 91.

2 Laurence Hutton, *Curiosities of the American Stage* (New York, 1891), p. 67.

3 From *The Broadway Journal,* July 19, 1845, reproduced in *The Complete Works of Edgar Allen Poe,* Virginia Edition, XII (New York, 1902), p. 187.

4 Ibid., p. 188.

5 Ibid., p. 191.

6 Quoted in Anna Cora Mowatt, *Autobiography of an Actress* (Boston, 1854), p. 300.

7 Ibid., p. 221.

8 Joseph Jefferson, *Autobiography* (New York, 1889), pp. 138–139.

9 Mowatt, op. cit., p. 241.

10 Ibid., p. 242.

11 Ibid., p. 244.

12 Hutton, op. cit., pp. 64–65.

13 Arthur Hobson Quinn, *History of the American Drama from the Beginning to the Civil War,* 2nd ed. (New York, 1943), p. 319.

14 G. C. D. Odell, *Some Theatrical Stock Companies of New York* (An essay issued by The Brander Matthews Dramatic Museum, Columbia University, to accompany its exhibition, "Two Centuries of the New York Theatre," March–October, 1951), p. 9.

15 Catherine M. Reignolds-Winslow, *Yesterday with Actors* (Boston, 1887), p. 67.

16 See John Creahan, *Life of Laura Keene* (Philadelphia, 1897), p. 138.

17 Jefferson, op. cit., p. 206.

18 Odell, op. cit., p. 13.

19 William Winter, *Vagrant Memories* (New York, 1915), p. 56.

20 Jefferson, op. cit., p. 206.

21 Creahan, op. cit., p. 101.

22 Winter, op. cit., p. 57.

23 Ibid., p. 59.

24 According to her daughter. See Creahan, op. cit., p. 15.

25 Helen Ormsbee, *Backstage with Actors* (New York, 1938), p. 150.

26 Reignolds-Winslow, op. cit., p. 110.

27 William Winter, New York *Tribune,* March 12, 1877.

28 Clara Morris, *Life on the Stage* (New York, 1901), pp. 141 and 317.

29 Ibid., p. 257.

30 Ibid., pp. 316–317.

31 According to an anecdote, Sarah Bernhardt once attended a performance of Miss Morris in *Camille.* For a long time the French actress was uninterested, but at a certain point in the play she sat up and exclaimed, "Mon dieu! that woman is not acting, she is suffering." From an unidentified clipping in the Robinson Locke collection of dramatic scrapbooks, Volume 351, New York Public Library.

32 New York *World,* September 25, 1885.

33 Morris, op. cit., p. 69.

34 From an unidentified review in the Robinson Locke collection of dramatic scrapbooks, Volume 351, New York Public Library, concerning the premier of Octave Feuillet's *The Sphinx,* done at the Union Square Theatre, September 21, 1874. This same scene was described in less complimentary fashion by the critic of the New York *Mail* who wrote, on September 22, 1874, as follows: ". . . the last convulsions of death are simulated on the stage. Miss Morris chews soap, turns the whites of her eyes up and the corners of her mouth down, smears white powder and red paint over her cheeks and chin, angles her wrists and stiffens her back. Such is the pleasing spectacle presented to a horrified audience as the final tableau of this moral drama. . . ."

35 Morris, op. cit., p. 340.

36 Brander Matthews and Laurence Hutton, *Actors and Actresses of Great Britain and the United States—The Present Time* (New York, 1886), p. 224.

37 Lewis Strang, *Players and Plays of the Last Quarter Century,* Vol. II (Boston, 1903), p. 237.

38 Vivia Ogden, "Childish Recollections of Clara Morris," *The Theatre,* Vol. II (June, 1902), p. 17.

39 *Spirit of the Times,* New York, November 6, 1880.

40 Ibid., November 25, 1876.

41 Ibid., April 7, 1888.

42 Alan Dale, "Why the Ex-Tragedienne Should Be Muzzled," New York *American,* April 27, 1902.

43 John R. Towse, *Sixty Years of the Theater* (New York, 1916), pp. 150–151.

44 See Morris, op. cit., p. 285.

45 Mary Caroline Crawford, *Romance of the American Theatre* (Boston, 1925), p. 339.

46 William Winter, *Vagrant Memories* (New York, 1915), p. 229.

47 Towse, op. cit., pp. 125–126.

48 Ibid., p. 129.

49 Ibid., p. 130.

50 Ibid., p. 133.

51 Brander Matthews, *These Many Years* (New York, 1917), p. 349.

52 Montrose Moses, *Famous Actor Families in America* (New York, 1906), p. 253.

53 Quoted in an obituary notice appearing in *Newsweek,* Vol. X (November 22, 1937), p. 6.

54 See Franklin E. Fyles, "Mrs. Leslie Carter—A Study," *Leslie's Magazine,* Vol. LIII (April, 1902), p. 658.

55 Lewis Strang, *Famous Actresses of the Day in America,* Second Series (Boston, 1902), p. 201.

56 Fyles, op. cit., p. 658.

57 William Winter, *The Wallet of Time,* Vol. II (New York, 1913), p. 327.

58 Ibid., p. 332.

59 Heywood Broun, "On the New York Stage," *Collier's,* Vol. LXVIII (November 26, 1921), p. 24.

V. THE PERSONALITY SCHOOL

1 Noah M. Ludlow, *Dramatic Life as I Found It* (St. Louis, 1880), p. 375.

2 Brander Matthews and Laurence Hutton, *Actors and Actresses of Great Britain and the United States—Kean and Booth; and Their Contemporaries* (New York, 1886), p. 262.

3 Laurence Hutton, *Curiosities of the American Stage* (New York, 1891), p. 237.

4 Matthews and Hutton, op. cit., p. 263.

5 James E. Murdoch, *The Stage* (Philadelphia, 1880), p. 235.

6 Matthews and Hutton, op. cit., p. 272.

7 Oral S. Coad and Edwin Mims, *The American Stage* (New Haven, 1929), p. 191.

8 Luther L. Holden, "Maggie Mitchell" in McKay and Wingate's *Famous American Actors of Today,* Vol. II (New York, 1896), pp. 319–320.

9 David Gray, "Maude Adams A Public Influence," *Hampton's Magazine,* Vol. XXVI (June, 1911), p. 725.

10 Lewis Strang, *Famous Actresses of the Day* (Boston, 1902), Second Series, p. 55.

11 New York *Tribune,* May 9, 1899.

12 Gray, op. cit., p. 737.

13 Arthur Symons, *Great Acting in English* (London, 1907), p. 13.

14 William Winter, *Vagrant Memories* (New York, 1915), p. 469.

15 Symons, op. cit., p. 7. Symons also declared that Marlowe and Sothern alone in the English speaking world were giving great performances of Shakespeare's plays.

16 Winter, op. cit., p. 473.

17 Gray, op. cit., pp. 725–726.

18 Miss Rehan's family name was Crehan, but on the occasion of her debut at the Arch Street Theatre she was erroneously billed as Rehan, a name which Mrs. Drew persuaded her to keep because her debut had been so successful.

19 William Winter, *Ada Rehan* (New York, 1891–1898), p. 36.

20 Ibid., p. 45.

21 Ibid., p. 102.

22 Ibid., p. 133.

23 Ibid., p. 153.

24 Walter Prichard Eaton, "Ada Rehan," *Dictionary of American Biography,* Vol. XV (New York, 1935), p. 472.

25 Otis Skinner, *Footlights and Spotlights* (Indianapolis, 1924), p. 138.

26 George Bernard Shaw, *Dramatic Opinions and Essays,* Vol. I (New York, 1906), p. 174.

27 John R. Towse, *Sixty Years of the Theater* (New York, 1916), pp. 356–357.

28 Shaw, op. cit., pp. 173–174.

29 Bernard Shaw, *To a Young Actress* (New York, 1960), p. 16.

30 Winter, *Ada Rehan,* p. 141.

31 Otis Skinner, op. cit., p. 270.

VI. THE COMIC STAGE

1 New York *Mirror,* June 20, 1829, quoted in Brander Matthews and Laurence Hutton, *Actors and Actresses of Great Britain and the United States— Kean and Booth; and Their Contemporaries* (New York, 1886), p. 153.

2 G. C. D. Odell, *Some Theatrical Stock Companies of New York* (An essay issued by The Brander Matthews Dramatic Museum, Columbia University,

to accompany its exhibition, "Two Centuries of the New York Theatre," March–October, 1951), p. 8.

3 Henry Dickinson Stone, *Personal Recollections of the Drama or Theatrical Reminiscences* (Albany, New York, 1873), p. 13.

4 Laurence Hutton, *Plays and Players* (New York, 1875), p. 236.

5 Joseph Jefferson, *Autobiography* (New York, 1889), pp. 100–101.

6 Odell, op. cit., p. 6.

7 John R. Towse, *Sixty Years of the Theater* (New York, 1916), pp. 99–100.

8 William Winter, *The Wallet of Time,* I (New York, 1913), p. 158.

9 Brander Matthews, *These Many Years* (New York, 1917), p. 349.

10 Winter, op. cit., p. 157.

11 Catherine M. Reignolds-Winslow, *Yesterday with Actors* (Boston, 1887), pp. 127–128.

12 Mary Shaw, "The Boston Museum and Daly's Theatre," *The Saturday Evening Post* (May 20, 1911).

13 Henry Clay Barnabee, *Reminiscences* (Boston, 1913), pp. 178–179.

14 Lewis Strang, *Players and Plays of the Last Quarter Century,* I (Boston, 1903), 281.

15 Jefferson, op. cit., p. 403.

16 Strang, op. cit., p. 267.

17 William Winter, *Other Days* (New York, 1908), p. 44.

18 Noah M. Ludlow, *Dramatic Life as I Found It* (St. Louis, 1880), p. 427.

19 Francis C. Wemyss, *Twenty-Six Years of the Life of an Actor and Manager* (New York, 1847), p. 271.

20 Towse, op. cit., p. 124.

21 Winter, *Other Days,* p. 125.

22 Ibid., p. 129.

23 Arthur H. Quinn, *A History of the American Drama from the Beginning to the Civil War, Second Edition* (New York, 1951), p. 384.

24 Winter, *Other Days,* p. 145.

25 Vance Thompson, "Dion Boucicault," in McKay and Wingate's *Famous American Actors of Today* (New York, 1896), p. 84.

26 Towse, op. cit., p. 229.

27 Henry Austin Clapp, *Reminiscences of a Dramatic Critic* (Boston and New York), p. 64.

28 Strang, op. cit., p. 269.

29 Jefferson, op. cit., p. 223.

30 Clara Morris, *Life on the Stage* (New York, 1901), p. 198.

31 Strang, op. cit., p. 268. For those who are interested in the story of Jefferson's career and in a discussion of his artistic principles and practices, his famous *Autobiography* is still absorbing reading.

32 Clapp, op. cit., pp. 64–65.

33 Lawrence Barrett, *Edwin Forrest* (Boston, 1881), p. 46.

34 Phineas T. Barnum, *Life of P. T. Barnum* (Buffalo, 1888), p. 37.

35 Townsend Walsh, *The Career of Dion Boucicault* (New York, 1915), pp. 50–51.

36 Foster R. Dulles, *America Learns to Play* (New York, 1940), p. 112.

37 Ibid., p. 119.

38 Carl Wittke, *Tambo and Bones* (Durham, North Carolina, 1930), p. 20.

39 Marjorie Barstow Greenbie, *American Saga* (New York, 1939), pp. 278–279.

40 Dulles, op. cit., p. 116.

41 Arthur Hobson Quinn, *A History of the American Drama from the Civil War to the Present Day* (New York, 1927), p. 84.

42 E. J. Kahn, Jr., *The Merry Partners, The Age and Stage of Harrigan and Hart* (New York, 1955), p. 14.

43 Ibid., p. 9.

44 Ibid., p. 10.

45 Ibid., p. 38.

46 Montrose J. Moses, *Representative American Dramas, National and Local* (Boston, 1926), p. 4.

47 Caroline Caffin, *Vaudeville* (New York, 1914), p. 10.

48 Ibid., p. 19.

49 Wittke, op. cit., pp. 159–160.

50 "The Talk of the Town," *The New Yorker,* Vol. XLI (April 17, 1965), p. 39.

51 Walter Prichard Eaton, *The Actor's Heritage* (Boston, 1924), p. 214.

52 Constance Rourke, *Troupers of the Gold Coast or the Rise of Lotta Crabtree* (New York, 1928), pp. 155–156.

53 John R. Towse, *Sixty Years of the Theater* (New York, 1916), p. 89.

54 Rourke, op. cit., p. 154.

55 Deshler Welch, "Lotta Crabtree," in McKay and Wingate's *Famous American Actors of Today* (New York, 1896), p. 326.

56 Helena Modjeska, *Memories and Impressions* (New York, 1910), pp. 374–375.

57 Otis Skinner, *Footlights and Spotlights* (Indianapolis, 1924), p. 65.

VII. COMEDIANS OF THE TRANSITION

1 William Winter, *The Life of David Belasco,* Vol. II (New York, 1918), p. 428.

2 Lewis Strang, *Famous Actors of the Day in America,* First Series (Boston, 1900), p. 59.

3 William Winter, *The Wallet of Time,* Vol. II (New York, 1913), p. 536.

4 Daniel Blum, *Great Stars of the American Stage* (New York, 1952), Profile 22.

5 Lewis Strang, *Famous Actresses of the Day in America* (Boston, 1899), p. 174.

6 Francis Wilson, *Life of Himself* (Boston, 1924), p. 370.

7 Lewis Strang, *Famous Actors of the Day in America,* Second Series (Boston, 1902), p. 77.

8 Strang, *Famous Actors,* First Series, pp. 297–98.

9 A. D. Storms, *The Players Blue Book* (Worcester, Mass.), p. 30.

10 Strang, *Famous Actors,* Second Series, p. 185.

VIII. HEIRS OF THE CLASSIC AND HEROIC SCHOOLS

1 Montrose J. Moses, "Belasco: Stage Realist," *The Independent* (May 29, 1916), p. 336.

2 David Belasco, *The Theatre Through Its Stage Door* (New York, 1919), p. 229.

3 Ibid., p. 61.

4 David Belasco, "What I Am Trying to Do," *The World's Work* (July, 1912), p. 299.

5 John R. Towse, *Sixty Years of the Theater* (New York, 1916), p. 318.

6 Walter Prichard Eaton in *Dictionary of American Biography,* Vol. 12, p. 260.

7 Towse, op. cit., p. 319.

8 Ibid.

9 William Winter, *The Life and Art of Richard Mansfield,* Vol. II (New York, 1910), p. 145.

10 Towse, op. cit., p. 339.

11 Towse's phrases. See his *Sixty Years of the Theater,* p. 333.

12 Eaton, op. cit., pp. 260–261.

13 Towse, op. cit., p. 334.

14 Winter, op. cit., p. 251.

15 Lewis C. Strang, *Famous Actors of the Day in America,* Second Series (Boston, 1902), p. 12.

16 Walter Prichard Eaton in *Dictionary of American Biography,* Vol. 17, p. 402.

17 William Winter, *Vagrant Memories* (New York, 1915), pp. 433–434.

18 Arthur Symons, *Great Acting in English* (London, 1907), p. 6.

19 Ibid., p. 6.

20 Ibid., p. 8.

21 Winter, *Vagrant Memories,* p. 438.

22 Ibid., pp. 445–446.

23 Otis Skinner, *Footlights and Spotlights* (Indianapolis, 1924), p. 42.

24 Lewis C. Strang, *Famous Actors of the Day in America,* First Series (Boston, 1900), p. 276.

25 Skinner, op. cit., p. 80.

26 Amy Leslie, *Some Players* (New York, 1906), p. 26.

27 Strang, *Famous Actors,* First Series, p. 261.

28 Eaton, op. cit., p. 402.

29 Otis Skinner, "Kindling the Divine Spark," *Theatre Arts Monthly* (Sept., 1938), p. 670.

30 Strang, *Famous Actors,* First Series, p. 260.

31 John Mason Brown, *Upstage* (New York, 1930), pp. 100–102.

32 Skinner, *Footlights and Spotlights,* pp. 353–354.

33 Strang, *Famous Actors,* First Series, p. 95.

34 Daniel Blum, *Great Stars of the American Stage* (New York, 1952), Profile 8.

35 Strang, *Famous Actors,* First Series, pp. 110–111.

36 Strang, *Famous Actors,* Second Series, pp. 64–65.

37 Blum, op. cit., Profile 10.

38 Ibid.

39 William H. Gillette, *The Illusion of the First Time in Acting* (New York, 1915), p. 46.

40 Ibid., p. 43.

IX. MRS. MINNIE MADDERN FISKE

1 See clipping in the Robinson Locke collection of dramatic scrapbooks, Volume 202, New York Public Library.

2 Lewis Strang, *Players and Plays of the Last Quarter Century,* Vol. II (Boston, 1903), pp. 297–298.

3 New York *News,* March 23, 1896.

4 Strang, op. cit., p. 300.

5 Alexander Woollcott, *Mrs. Fiske, Her Views on Actors, Acting and the Problems of Production* (New York, 1917), p. 79.

6 Beatrice Sturges, "Mrs. Fiske: Actress Manager," *Public Opinion,* XXXVIII (May 20, 1905), p. 777.

7 Woollcott, op. cit., p. 76.

8 From an unidentified clipping in the Robinson Locke collection of dramatic scrapbooks, Volume 203, New York Public Library.

9 Lewis Strang, *Famous Actresses of the Day in America* (Boston, 1899), p. 67.

10 Milwaukee *Sentinel,* October 7, 1906.

11 Woollcott, op. cit., p. 228.

12 Archie Binns, *Mrs. Fiske and the American Theatre* (New York, 1955), p. 204.

13 George Arliss, *Up the Years from Bloomsbury* (New York, 1927), p. 215.

14 Pittsburg *Gazette,* November 17, 1903.

15 New York *Mirror,* June 4, 1898.

16 Woollcott, op. cit., p. 82.

17 Ibid., pp. 84–85.

18 Ibid., p. 95.

19 From an unidentified clipping in the Robinson Locke collection of dramatic scrapbooks, Volume 203, New York Public Library.

20 Arliss, op. cit., p. 215.

21 From an interview reported in the Brooklyn *Eagle* for August 13, 1899.

22 Binns, op. cit., p. 139.

23 Minnie Maddern Fiske, "Ethics of the Drama," an address delivered to the Harvard Ethical Society, printed in the Boston *Transcript,* December 13, 1905.

24 John R. Towse, *Sixty Years of the Theater* (New York, 1916), p. 413.

25 Walter Prichard Eaton, "Mrs. Fiske and Her Influence on the American Stage," *Century Magazine,* LXXXI (April, 1911), p. 867.

26 Woollcott, op. cit., p. 160.

27 Fiske, "Ethics of the Drama," Boston *Transcript,* December 13, 1905.

28 Arliss, op. cit., p. 215.

29 Amy Leslie in the New York *Mirror,* November 17, 1906.

30 Toledo *Blade,* November 2, 1898.

31 Sturges, op. cit., p. 778.

32 Binns, op. cit., p. 175.

33 Woollcott, op. cit., p. 117.

34 Fiske, "Ethics of the Drama," Boston *Transcript,* December 13, 1905.

35 Binns, op. cit., p. 251.

NOTES ON A NEW SETTING

1 Sheldon Cheney, *The Theatre* (Tudor Edition, New York, 1949), p. 428.

2 Daniel Frohman, "Do Motion Pictures Mean the Death of the Drama," *The Theatre,* Vol. XXII (December, 1915), p. 310.

3 Henry Hewes, "The American Theatre '64, Its Problems and Promise," *The Saturday Review,* Vol. XLVII (February 22, 1964), p. 29.

4 "Regional Theatre," *Life,* Vol. 56 (February 28, 1964), p. 9.

X. THE ACTOR IN THE NEW THEATRE

1 Mortimer J. Adler, *Art and Prudence* (New York and Toronto, 1937), p. 485.

2 Iris Barry, *Let's Go To The Movies* (New York, 1936), p. 17.

3 Elinor Hughes, *Famous Stars of Filmdom (Women)* (Boston, 1931), p. 270.

4 Ibid., p. 273.

5 Alistair Cooke, *Douglas Fairbanks—The Making of a Screen Character* (The Museum of Modern Art, New York, 1940), p. 13.

6 Arthur Knight, "Douglas Fairbanks," *Dictionary of American Biography,* Vol. XXII (New York, 1958), p. 172.

7 Cooke, op. cit., p. 31.

8 Ibid., pp. 29–30.

9 Knight, op. cit., p. 173.

10 Cooke, op. cit., pp. 24–25.

11 Charles Chaplin, *My Autobiography* (New York, 1964), p. 199.

12 Inez and Helen Klumph, *Screen Acting* (New York, 1922), p. 103.

13 Chaplin, op. cit., p. 21.

14 Ibid., p. 144.

15 Robert Payne, *The Great Charlie* (London, 1952), p. 33.

16 Ibid., p. 278.

17 Lee Strasberg, "Acting," *The Encyclopaedia Britannica,* Vol. I (Chicago, 1960), p. 132.

18 Daniel Blum, *Great Stars of the American Stage* (New York, 1952), Profile 80.

19 Strasberg, op. cit., p. 132.

20 Ibid., p. 131.

21 Statements from a private conversation held with Mr. D'Angelo at the Academy in New York in September, 1939.

22 Strasberg, op. cit., p. 131.

INDEX